Assessment
in Political Science

Michelle D. Deardorff
Kerstin Hamann
John Ishiyama

editors

AMERICAN POLITICAL SCIENCE ASSOCIATION
STATE OF THE PROFESSION SERIES

ISBN 1-878147-52-8

TABLE OF CONTENTS

List of Tables and Figures...v

List of Appendices...vi

Preface..vii

Foreword
Theda Skocpol.. xi

PART I: AN INTRODUCTION TO ASSESSMENT

1. Introduction
   Michelle D. Deardorff, Kerstin Hamann, John Ishiyama 3

2. Assessing for Understanding: Toward a Theory of Assessment
   as Learning
   Christopher J. Voparil...17

3. An Overview of the Assessment Movement
   E. Fletcher McClellan 39

PART II: DEPARTMENTAL AND PROGRAM ASSESSMENT

4. Comparing Learning Assessment Plans in Political Science
   John Ishiyama 61

5. Making Assessment Matter: Structuring Assessment,
   Transforming Departments
   Michelle D. Deardorff, Paul J. Folger..................................... 77

6. Who Will Be the Assessment Champion? And Other Conditions
   for a Culture of Assessment
   Jeffrey S. Hill, Charles R. Pastors.. 97

7. Program Evaluation and Assessment: Integrating Methods,
   Processes, and Culture 117
   Candace C. Young

8. Political Science and General Education Assessment
   Scott Erb 141

PART III: EXAMPLES OF CLASSROOM ASSESSMENT

9. Assessment *of* Learning and *for* Learning: Testing the Effectiveness and Accuracy of the Standard Scoring Instruments
   Mariya Y. Omelicheva 163

10. Classroom Assessment of Learning Communities for Political Scientists
    Juan Carlos Huerta 181

11. Assessment in the Online Environment
    Philip H. Pollock, Kerstin Hamann, Bruce M. Wilson 197

12. The Critical Portfolio: Facilitating the Reflective Political Science Student in the Experiential Environment
    Veronica Donahue, John Ishiyama 217

Editors and Contributors 235

TABLES, FIGURES AND APPENDICES

TABLES

Table 4-1 List of Schools Included in the Study 64

Table 4-2 Learning Outcomes 66

Table 4-3 Most Frequently Mentioned Assessment Techniques............. 67

Table 7-1 Overview of Assessment Methods............................122

Table 7-2 Examples of Direct/Indirect and External/
Internal Measures...128

Table 8-1 Summary of General Education Goals.....................148

Table 8-2 Comparison of Average ACP Scores........................152

Table 8-3 ACP Score vs. Grade by Course 153

Table 8-4 Semester Progress: Short Paper...............................154

Table 8-5 ACP Score by Rubric Components...........................154

Table 9-1 Itemized Differences in Student Performance.........172

Table 11-1 Traditional Lecture and Reduced Seat-Time Compared:
Pre–Post Changes in Political Knowledge, Attentiveness,
Efficacy, and Trust 203

Table 11-2 Mean Percentage of Independent and Dependent
Statements, by Gender and Gender Composition 207

Table 11-3 Average Course Grade, by GPA and Reading Behavior........208

FIGURES

Figure 4-1 Number of External Assessment Techniques 69

Figure 4-2 External Assessment Techniques Score By Selectivity
of Institution 69

Figure 4-3 External Assessment Techniques Score By Private
or Public Institution...70

Figure 4-4 External Assessment Techniques Score By
Student Faculty Ratio..70

Figure 4-5 External Assessment Techniques Score By Highest
Degree Offered By Department 71

Figure 4-6 External Assessment Techniques Score By Size of Student Population 72

Figure 8-1 Example of Assignment Documentation 149

Figure 8-2 Explanation of Fit to General Education Goals 149

Figure 9-1 Sample Evaluation Form for Assessing a Written Assignment 165

Figure 9-2 Scale for Evaluating an Analysis of International News 166

Figure 9-3 A Rubric Fragment 167

Figure 12-1 Contents of the Critical Portfolio 223

Figure 12-2 Example Rubric 230

Figure 12-3 Examples of Rating Scales 230

APPENDICES

Appendix 10-1 Learning Community Resources 192

Appendix 10-2 Portfolio Two Focus 192

Appendix 11-1 Simple Rubric for Writing Assignments 211

Appendix 11-2 Coding Protocol for Online Discussions 212

PREFACE

This volume has been "a long time coming." It represents the culmination of several years of effort, collaboration, and reflection and, we hope, helps fill a need in our discipline—a resource that can assist our colleagues in meeting the challenge of assessing student learning in political science. The book is intended to be a resource to help political science faculty think about assessment as a departmental undertaking as well as enable them to plan and implement programmatic and classroom assessment. While books and materials on assessment in general are readily available, this volume applies these concepts and ideas specifically to political science programs and classrooms.

The book itself is the product of the intersection of three developments. First, all three editors have engaged in assessment for quite some time and in various ways, and have witnessed firsthand, if done well and carefully, the benefits of assessment in developing political science programs. Second, during conversations we have had about the necessity and challenges of assessment, the scarcity of discipline-specific resources became apparent to us. Simultaneously, we noted a significant rise in interest in assessment among our colleagues across the country—each of us was regularly contacted by others in the discipline who were charged with designing and implementing an assessment program in their departments and did not know where to start or where to find useful guidelines, examples, and resources to help them in their endeavors. Again, the lack of easily accessed resources and means to share experiences and examples was evident. We became increasingly aware of the frustrations of those launching into assessment faced with the dearth of models of successful assessment plans in political science, and of the paucity of outlets to share and reflect on assessment experiences. And third, the APSA Teaching and Learning Conference (TLC) played a pivotal role as a catalyst in our efforts to put this volume together. The conference provides a forum for those engaged and interested in assessment to share ideas, relate experiences, discuss issues and problems related to assessment, and to reflect on the meaning of assessment in the discipline. As all three of us have acted as leaders for the assessment tracks in several of the conferences, we became conscious of the many outstanding efforts that have already been made in assessment in political science, but that are not widely known to those not participating in the conference. The presentations at the TLC on assessment methods, approaches, and findings made us keenly aware of issues and trends in assessment in the discipline. The workshops on assessment organized by the Political Science Education section at recent APSA annual meetings, as well as several conference panels on the topic, provided further opportunities to discuss issues related to assessment in political science. Also, the section's peer-reviewed journal, *The Journal of Political Science Education*, as well as *PS: Political Science & Politics*, had published many thoughtful, well-researched articles on programmatic and learning assessment.

Combined, these developments demonstrated to us that while resources on assessment in the discipline have been growing and evolving, they are not readily accessible to those interested in or charged with assessment. It was, in fact, at one of the TLC conferences that the idea for this volume was born in an attempt to publish some of the existing resources and make them conveniently available to all political scientists. Not surprisingly, most of the contributors to this volume have previously presented their ideas and experiences with assessment at the TLC. This volume allows us to make assessment resources available beyond the confines of the conference. We hope it will be of use to those involved in assessment in political science. We are sure that the chapters in this volume constitute just the beginning of the debate as assessment rapidly takes hold in all types of institutions of higher learning across the country. To assist our discipline in this endeavor, a supplemental website hosts additional resources and assessment plans and will be regularly updated to provide further guidelines and examples. The website is available at www.apsanet.org/~assessment.

This volume would not have been possible without the help and contributions of many, and we would like to express our deepest gratitude to all of them. This includes all the presenters and discussants in the assessment tracks of the Teaching and Learning Conference since its inception in 2004; they provided the incentive to produce this volume and have certainly influenced our thinking on all aspects of assessment. Many thanks for the spirited discussions over the years! We would also like to thank all those involved with the publication of this volume at APSA—in particular, Michael Brintnall, who has been instrumental in establishing the TLC and has been supportive of our efforts from the beginning, and Polly Karpowicz, who has overseen the editorial process related to this volume, as well as Kim Mealy. Jasmine Jones, a graduate student at Jackson State University, has provided invaluable help in compiling the materials available on the accompanying website, and Kerri Milita, a graduate student at the University of Central Florida, provided outstanding support in checking references for much of the volume. We deeply appreciate and thank both of them for their efforts. Our gratitude also goes to our departments, past and current, that provided support as well as an arena to gather and test out our ideas on assessment. Furthermore, we would like to thank the reviewers of this volume—Vicky Golich, Karen Kedrowski, Brian Klunk, Kenneth Campbell, Marisa Kelly, and Sheilah Mann—whose insightful comments and suggestions made this a better book. Most of all, we are indebted to all those who began thinking about and implementing assessment in political science classrooms and programs for years and who have generously shared their insights. Without these pioneering attempts, this volume would not have been possible. And finally, we would like to express our deepest gratitude and appreciation to our families, who have patiently endured many discussions about assessment over the years, particularly during the time this volume was taking shape.

Michelle D. Deardorff

Kerstin Hamann

John Ishiyama

THEDA SKOCPOL, VICTOR S. THOMAS PROFESSOR OF GOVERNMENT AND
SOCIOLOGY AND FORMER DEAN OF THE GRADUATE SCHOOL OF ARTS AND
SCIENCES, HARVARD UNIVERSITY

FOREWORD

"It's about the pursuit of excellence in teaching." This was how I put the challenge faced by the Task Force on Teaching and Career Development at Harvard University, a group of faculty members who made recommendations in early 2007 designed to encourage pedagogical improvement at Harvard and other research universities. I say the same about this important collection of essays published by the American Political Science Association—a collection that highlights the special challenges and opportunities for assessing and improving teaching and student learning about the dynamics of politics in the United States and across the globe.

Assessment is about intelligent efforts to improve instructional quality. It provides tools and information that enable teachers to discern whether they are achieving their personal goals and the goals of their institutions. To foster a commitment to steady improvement in teaching and student learning, we don't need artificial external interventions or rules. We need mechanisms that work from within—that respect academic freedom and mesh with the individual, departmental, and institutional cultures where learning occurs. The approaches to assessment proposed in this collection point us in those directions, encouraging vigorous efforts to sharpen our purpose as teachers and gauge our achievements. The proposals sketched here encourage normal adjustments through peer review and respect the autonomy of the scholar-teacher.

Higher education finds itself anchored in sacred traditions yet buffeted and attracted by shifts in knowledge and modes of communication, by increased diversity in the communities we serve, and by calls to address new real-world problems requiring interdisciplinary approaches. Our teaching and our institutions are anchored in precious traditions, with values and integrity worth preserving. But in the effort to preserve worthy values, scholar-teachers in colleges and universities have sometimes failed to make or master valuable improvements. Just as we encourage our students to adopt the flexibility of mind, the analytical resources, and the gauging of plans and performance essential to mastery in a rapidly changing world, so too do we need to equip ourselves as faculty to adopt useful innovations and assess our own effectiveness as teachers.

Higher education flourishes through relationships between teachers and students. We professors tend to excel at developing what we wish to bring to these transactions: writing syllabi, outlining lectures, and crafting assignments. But we have been less effective than we should be at experimenting and assessing, at judging how well we achieve our educational goals, and at making adjustments and improvements along the way.

This collection points us in the right direction. The challenge of assessing quality and excellence in our teaching binds together academics from all sorts and sizes of institutions. We can all learn from each other in this process. These essays are a collective nudge, showing what others are doing with success and suggesting to each of us that "yes we can" do it, too.

The volume contains lessons for individual professors, departments, and institutions:

For the individual professor, these essays offer both models and encouragement. They show that assessment done right can improve teaching—and at the same time make it more rewarding and enjoyable.

For departments, there is a bigger challenge: to launch and sustain a continuous conversation about teaching and learning in political science and sister disciplines. What are we trying to do—for majors, for minors, for students in general? How would we know if we are succeeding, not just course by course, but over several years, and for students who will not become specialists as well as for those who want to continue in our discipline? This is a challenge for departments in all institutions, not just in those labeled "teaching institutions." Our major research institutions, public and private, carry on a vital role in teaching, too. At such institutions, peer critique of new scholarship is axiomatic, and there are equally inviting opportunities to marshal collegial assessments to foster improved teaching and learning for both graduate and undergraduate students.

As for institutions, we know from recent discussions at Harvard that genuine commitment to the principles of pedagogical assessment requires reexamination of cultural values and practices of reward and recognition. Leadership must come from administrators and tenured professors, if we truly mean to foster steady pedagogical improvement and reward those who practice intelligent assessment and experiment with better ways to do classroom instruction and student advising.

But individual scholars and teachers need not wait for their department or institution to act. Faculty can make a difference, one by one, in the classroom and in the department. The essays brought together here offer insight, support, and ideas. I encourage you to explore these offerings to improve the quality of your own teaching and become a voice for change in your institution and the discipline—just as the authors of these essays have done.

I

AN INTRODUCTION TO
ASSESSMENT

MICHELLE D. DEARDORFF, JACKSON STATE UNIVERSITY
KERSTIN HAMANN, UNIVERSITY OF CENTRAL FLORIDA
JOHN ISHIYAMA, UNIVERSITY OF NORTH TEXAS

INTRODUCTION

Assessment is becoming increasingly important in the academic world. Recent news articles report on discussions about nationally normed college tests, accreditation agencies require documentation on what and how students learn, state legislatures are looking for evidence that taxpayers' money is well spent, and, with increased tuition costs, parents and students want universities to provide evidence of effective teaching. As a consequence, universities are requiring departments to assess their programs, their classes, and their students' learning. In some departments, faculty members or chairs assume responsibility to investigate the culture of learning in their program and, accordingly, to engage in assessment efforts. In sum, assessment is here, and it seems to be here to stay. Yet, there is very little literature available on the different aspects of assessment specifically in political science that can be used as a guide for departments or professors engaging in assessment exercises. Because assessment choices will vary widely based on institutional type and departmental character, it is clearly necessary to provide multiple models that are adaptable.

While assessment can take various forms and can serve multiple purposes, the primary concern of assessment is student learning. This is true whether assessment is driven by faculty members attempting to understand and improve student learning or by accreditation agencies demanding documentation of student learning. In many cases, faculty members or departments realized that students, even those with high GPAs, were not learning the skills and content that the political science faculty believed were important—e.g., students were graduating without the requisite skills and knowledge that would make them marketable for a variety of careers. Many professors have already engaged in assessing student learning in their own classes either through formative assessment (assessment "in progress") or summative assessment (of final student work). Determining what students learn in the classroom is, obviously, the first step toward designing new assignments or teaching techniques that attempt to improve student learning. Only when we find out exactly what students do or do not learn in a class can we work on improving our teaching, and students' learning, in our classrooms.

However, assessment also occurs in departments and programs that are interested in what students have learned throughout the various stages of their college careers and certainly by the time they complete their degrees and graduate. Departments may have an inherent interest in this question when they are contemplating curriculum revisions or hiring preferences. More often, however, departments respond to calls for assessment from university administrators and accreditation agencies. While departmental assessment can involve insights gained from classroom assessment, it is also a more encompassing task. Generally speaking, in academic departments, assessment often involves the following basic components: (1) the development of an explicit mission or purpose statement by the department or program; (2) the development of a set of broadly stated goals and more specifically stated and measurable outcome objectives for student learning; (3) the systematic collection of information that demonstrates to what degree these objectives are being accomplished; and (4) departmental or programmatic efforts to identify and implement necessary program changes to enhance student learning. As Weiss points out, "assessment seeks to create a systematic and continuous process of improvement in academic departments so that they are better able to achieve their goals and objectives" (2002, 392). That is, there is little point in engaging in assessment efforts if the lessons learned are not used to improve student learning, or to "close the feedback loop."

Thus, assessment is really concerned with the empirical demonstration to ourselves and to others that our students are actually learning what we would like them to learn and, if not, to discuss and implement what can be done to improve student learning. As naturally skeptical empirical political scientists, we are usually unconvinced when someone says that something works (e.g., a particular pedagogical technique) just because the faculty member *thinks* it works. This hardly constitutes the

However, beyond issues of academic freedom, other legitimate concerns regarding assessment can be voiced. For instance, assessment is labor intensive, and may appear to be an activity that is poorly rewarded, if recognized at all. Why, then, would it be in the professional interest of faculty members to become involved in assessment? It is correct that assessment requires time and energy. Many faculty members are already stretched thin with their scholarly requirements and commitments, service involvement, heavy teaching loads, and—at times—large classes and, consequently, substantial amounts of grading. Spending additional time on assessing learner outcomes might be a burden particularly for untenured faculty members in research-intensive departments and institutions. Other serious concerns regard the use of assessment data by department chairs and university administrators, for example. But if we take seriously the notion that student learning is at the core of what we do in our classrooms, then it is in our interest to gauge whether our students are actually learning. As political scientists, we assess our research findings and implications both publicly and privately; we can model the same qualities of intellectual rigor in our teaching. As we demonstrate to our students the methods of evaluating their learning and the success of our programs, we are also teaching them how to evaluate their own learning. The skills that we teach in our courses in political science are uniquely suited to engaging students in the assessment process.

THE SCHOLARSHIP OF ASSESSMENT

To broaden our perspective on assessment, we might add that assessment also offers potential professional payoff in the form of publications that might compensate at least partially for the cost (especially of time) to faculty members invested in assessment. As exemplified in several chapters of this volume, assessment has the potential of feeding directly into the growing movement of the Scholarship of Teaching and Learning (SoTL), which is gaining importance in academia as SoTL is promoted by the Carnegie Foundation, among others (Boyer 1990; Glassick, et al. 1997). Assessment results, when written up and published in appropriate venues, contribute to the growing body of SoTL, and professors across the country are beginning to earn credit toward promotion and tenure for publishing in the field of the Scholarship of Teaching and Learning.

Thus, the book is also of great interest to those faculty in the discipline who are looking for roadmaps and examples of how to conduct SoTL, and several chapters in the volume are examples of just that. The publication outlets for work that address the "scholarship of assessment/teaching and learning" include the APSA's *PS: Political Science & Politics* and the APSA Political Science Education section's peer-reviewed *The Journal of Political Science Education*, which started publication in 2005. Additional publication outlets exist in general higher education journals, and a book series published by Jossey-Bass on Assessment in the Disciplines (including political science) edited by Trudy Banta (2007). Further, an increasing number of conferences in the discipline offer the opportunity to present papers on assessment, including APSA's Teaching and Learning Conference, but also the panels organized by the teaching and learning sections of APSA, MPSA, and SPSA, among others. Thus, faculty members engaging in assessment have an opportunity to benefit from this extra work professionally and to raise their scholarly profile through the dissemination of their work at professional conferences and in peer-reviewed journals. The publications and conferences also offer an opportunity to engage in a productive discourse on assessment within political science and to share the findings of assessment processes in public forums, paralleling the norms and procedures of the substantive fields in the discipline.

ASSESSMENT RESOURCES IN POLITICAL SCIENCE

Higher education offers plenty of advice on and resource for assessment, including a widening literature on classroom and programmatic assessment (e.g., Angelo and Cross 1993; Suskie 2004; Palomba 1999; and Allen 2004, among many others), and conferences specifically focused on assessment, such as the annual Assessment Institute at Indiana University–Purdue University in Indianapolis.[1] In contrast, as a discipline, political science has developed few resources to provide guidance for assessment (e.g., examples of assessment plans on the APSA website). Nonetheless, a growing number of faculty members have been building assessment plans for several years within their institutions. Some of this work is available in published form (see Breuning et al. 2001; Deardorff 2005; Deardorff and Folger 2005; Hill 2005; Ishiyama and Breuning 2008; Ishiyama and Hartlaub 2003; Suskie 2007). Second, the APSA Teaching and Learning

Conference (TLC) has annually hosted at least one (and as many as three) tracks/working groups on assessment, with well over 100 individuals participating in the presentations and discussions of assessment plans and experiences (see the 2008, 2007, 2006, 2005, and 2004 July issues of *PS: Political Science & Politics* for track summaries). In 2008, the TLC program committee encouraged issues of assessment to be integrated throughout all of the tracks, regardless of topic. The working groups at the TLC on assessment have provided an opportunity for faculty members to assemble and share the assessment techniques their departments and programs have employed, voice their concerns, and create a community of experts that can be called upon for service on committees and task forces, as external reviewers for accreditation purposes, and as a pool of consultants to help design assessment programs that meet the requirements of higher education accreditation organizations.

Other grassroots efforts to facilitate assessment have included occasional short courses on assessment sponsored by the Political Science Education section at APSA's Annual Meeting. The TLC has also offered workshops on assessment in addition to the working groups/tracks, and APSA organized a Chairs' Workshop on Assessment at the 2006 Annual Meeting (for presenter reports, see Campbell 2007; Deardorff 2007; Hamann 2007; Suskie 2007). Thus, this book is a timely addition to existing efforts to assist faculty and departments in managing this relatively new task that is increasingly added to their traditional mix of professional responsibilities.

In sum, while individual faculty members and political science departments have clearly been involved in all aspects of assessment—from classroom assessment to program assessment (undergraduate and graduate), and from community colleges to Ph.D. granting departments—of yet been no publication has systematically collected and disseminated the insights of these efforts. This book is intended to meet the rising demand for information on assessment in political science.

THE CONTRIBUTION OF THIS VOLUME

Most of the chapters contained in this book grew out of the APSA Teaching and Learning Conferences, where many of the contributors to this volume presented research on various aspects of assessment. The book contains a collection of chapters designed to assist political science faculty and departments in their assessment efforts. Authors of these chapters have gained their assessment experience from departments located in community colleges, small private universities, large public institutions, historically Black- and Hispanic-serving universities, master's level programs, and Ph.D.-granting and R1 institutions. Their observations and recommendations stem from these varied backgrounds. This volume provides examples and perspectives on assessment designed to help guide professors and departments through the maze of assessment tools. By referring to real-world examples that have been tested and applied in political science, as opposed to a theoretical debate over the merits of assessment, the purpose of this book is to be a handbook-type resource. It is our hope that these examples will prove useful to anyone involved in assessment within the discipline of political science. While some of the chapters are based on campus-specific experiences, the authors are careful to demonstrate how these strategies can be adjusted to different environments.

Throughout this volume, we reference two levels of assessment. *Classroom assessment* denotes activities at the classroom or course level aimed at helping the professor improve the performance of specific individuals or a particular course of instruction. Three main types of classroom assessment can be distinguished: (1) assessment of individual student learning (for example, peer or instructor feedback on the draft of a paper or student performance in a senior capstone seminar); (2) assessment of individual teaching performance (such as using pre-test/post-test data in a particular course to measure the success of a specific teaching technique, or the use of a teaching portfolio to demonstrate teaching adjustments and improvement over time—see Hutchings 1996); and (3) assessment of the effect of a course of instruction on specific knowledge, attitudes, and/or skills of students (for example, measuring the impact of a research methods course on critical or analytical thinking). The examples of classroom assessment provided in this volume are not restricted to the type of institutions where they were developed, but can be used in classes in any type of institution, regardless of the highest degree offered. The second type of assessment is *program assessment*, which refers to "any effort to gather, analyze, and interpret evidence which describes institutional, departmental, and divisional or agency effectiveness" (Upcraft and Schuh 1996). This can involve collecting information about individual student performance, but the results are aggregated to provide information about the effect of a program or curriculum on student learning.[2]

The book is consequently organized into three sections. The first part, which this chapter begins, is a basic "Introduction to Assessment." Christopher Voparil provides the initial substantive chapter, in which he explores the theoretical significance of assessment in education. He argues for the need to assess for understanding and consequently integrate assessment into the process of learning. If we decontextualize the assessment process, it becomes another insignificant exercise disconnected from the interests of the discipline of political science. Fletcher McClellan concludes this section with a historical review of the assessment movement and its significance both in higher education and within the discipline of political science. Examining assessment as a public policy movement, this chapter explicates its expansion and anticipates its trajectory.

The second part of the book examines "Departmental and Program Assessment." The chapters in this section provide various models, assert specific case studies, and provide data on the status of assessment plans across the discipline. The authors of these chapters reflect a variety of different institutions and departmental missions. In Chapter 4, John Ishiyama provides the reader with a broad survey of the most frequently used assessment activities cited by political science programs throughout the country and explores whether these choices are related to institutional or departmental characteristics. This chapter will enable faculty to help determine which approaches to assessment are most typically used in departments similar to their own. In Chapter 5, Michelle D. Deardorff and Paul Folger help departments new to assessment consider the relevant factors to determine what model of assessment would work best in their particular department—the "mission-based" approach or the "grassroots-based" approach. They argue that if departments are able to identify which structure is most appropriate for their own culture and circumstances, assessment may be more fertile, and possibly culturally transformative, for the department. In Chapter 6, Jeffrey S. Hill and Charles R. Pastors aim to assist chairs and departmental assessment directors with developing the five conditions they believe are necessary to create a culture of trust essential for assessment to succeed. More particularly, they argue that within the department there is the need for an assessment champion, who might not be the departmental chair. Candace Young, in Chapter 7, describes methods, processes, and cultural dimensions associated with effective assessment for political science departments. She not only identifies a variety of assessment methods, but also discusses the conditions within departments that can enhance success. Scott Erb, in Chapter 8, concludes this section of the book by describing the initial stages of an assessment program designed to measure how well political science courses meet the university's stated general education goals, and to provide preliminary evidence on student performance in general education skills that overlap with disciplinary goals: writing, public presentation, technology, and research.

The final section of the book, "Examples of Classroom Assessment," examines how departments and faculty can best assess student performance in the classroom, or the utility of specific pedagogical strategies or learning experiences. The authors provide examples of several elements often present in undergraduate programs, including internships, online classes, and learning communities, that can be applied in any type of institution that offers these types of courses or modes of instruction. In Chapter 9, Mariya Omelicheva evaluates three popular assessment techniques for the measurement of student learning: evaluation forms, scales, and rubrics, all of which can be used for a variety of class settings. She explores the ways in which rubrics allow students to assess and improve their own learning in the political science curriculum and increase the validity of assessment. In Chapter 10, Juan Carlos Huerta details the process by which political science departments can assess learning communities in their classrooms and programs and outlines the resulting benefits. His exploration of the assessment of such programming will be of special value for departments implementing learning communities for the first time. Philip Pollock, Kerstin Hamann, and Bruce Wilson in Chapter 11 expand our understanding of the classroom community in the online environment and address the specific questions and issues that arise when assessing the effectiveness of online courses. Their chapter explores in particular the ways in which student learning behavior is linked to learner outcomes. In the final chapter of this section, Veronica Donahue and John Ishiyama discuss means of assessing that stalwart element of the political science curriculum—the internship. They describe and advocate the technique of using an internship portfolio as a means of evaluating experiential learning programs.

We hope that this book will provide resources for faculty members and departments beginning systematic assessment and will offer encouragement and ideas for departments involved in the ongoing process of assessment. We work in a discipline that does not have established national standards or accreditation requirements; this freedom is both a strength of our discipline and can have an isolating effect on faculty when they attempt to engage in assessment on their own. Departmentally, we must establish our own learning goals and objectives that we will collectively attempt to achieve. To encourage departments in this endeavor, we have also provided a webpage that has collected best practices, models, surveys, matrices, and other tools for departments to adopt for their own purposes, available at www.apsanet.org/~assessment. These references represent the work conducted at most types of institutions—reflecting the scope of the discipline in our work to teach and educate from the undergraduate level to the doctoral level.

NOTES

1. Information about the conference is available online at http://planning.iupui.edu/conferences/national/nationalconf.html.
2. Thank you to Fletcher McClellan for his thoughtful definition and explication of these terms.

REFERENCES

Allen, Mary J. 2004. *Assessing Programs in Higher Education*. Bolton, MA: Anker.

Angelo, Thomas A., and K. Patricia Cross. 1993. *Classroom Assessment Techniques*. San Francisco: Jossey-Bass.

Banta, Trudy W. 2007. *Assessing Student Learning in the Disciplines: Assessment Update Collections*. San Francisco: Jossey-Bass.

Bollag, Burton. 2006. "Controversial Proposal on Accreditation Fails to Make Panel's Final Report." *Chronicle of Higher Education*, September 1. http://chronicle.com/weekly/v53/i02/02a04201.htm.

Boyer, Ernest L. 1990. *Scholarship Reconsidered: Priorities of the Professoriate.* San Francisco: Jossey-Bass.

Breuning, Marijke, Paul. E. Parker, and John Ishiyama. 2001. "The Last Laugh: Skill Building through a Liberal Arts Political Science Curriculum." *PS: Political Science & Politics* 34 (September): 657–61.

Campbell, Kenneth J. 2007. "Assessment Advice for Beginners." *PS: Political Science & Politics* 40 (January): 99.

Deardorff, Michelle D. 2005. "Assessment Through the Grassroots: Assessing the Department via Student Peer Evaluation." *Journal of Political Science Education* 1 (1): 109-27.

———. "Methods of Effectively Leveraging Departmental Assessment Programs." *PS: Political Science & Politics* 40 (January): 100–01.

Deardorff, Michelle D., and Paul Folger. 2005. "Assessment that Matters: Integrating the 'Chore' of Department-Based Assessment with Real Improvements in Political Science Education." *Journal of Political Science Education* 1 (3): 277–87.

Fischer, Karin. 2006. "Lengthy Fights Are Expected Over Measures on Accountability: Higher-education Leaders Are Divided over Proposal for Student-tracking System." *Chronicle of Higher Education*, September 1. http://chronicle.com/weekly/v53/i02/02a04202.htm.

Glassick, Charles E., Mary Taylor Huber, and Gene I. Maeroff. 1997. *Scholarship Assessed: Evaluation of the Professoriate.* San Francisco: Jossey-Bass.

Hamann, Kerstin. 2007. "Presentation for Chairs' Workshop on Assessment." *PS: Political Science & Politics* 40 (January): 101–02.

Hill, Jeffrey. 2005. "Developing a Culture of Assessment: Insights from Theory and Experience." *Journal of Political Science Education* 1 (1): 29–37.

Hutchings, Pat. 1996. *Making Teaching Community Property: A Menu for Peer Collaboration and Peer Review.* Sterling, VA: Stylus Publishing.

Ishiyama, John, and Marijke Breuning. 2008. "Assessing Assessment: Examining the Assessment Plans at 50 Political Science Departments." *PS: Political Science & Politics* 41 (January): 167–70.

Ishiyama, John, and Stephen Hartlaub. 2003. "Sequential or Flexible? The Impact of Differently Structured Political Science Majors on the Development of Student Reasoning." *PS: Political Science & Politics* 36 (January): 83–86.

Middle States Commission on Higher Education. 2005. "Assessing Student Learning and Institutional Effectiveness: Understanding Middle States Expectations." Philadelphia, PA: Middle States Commission on Higher Education.

Palomba, Catherine. 1999. *Assessment Essentials: Planning, Implementing, and Improving Assessment in Higher Education.* San Francisco: Jossey-Bass.

Spellings, Margaret. 2006. *A Test of Leadership: Charting the Future of U.S. Higher Education.* A Report of the Commission Appointed by Secretary of Education Margaret Spellings. Washington, D.C.: U.S. Department of Education.

Suskie, Linda. 2004. *Assessing Student Learning: A Common Sense Guide*. Bolton, MA: Anker.

———. 2007. "Some Thoughts and Suggestions on Assessing Student Learning." *PS: Political Science & Politics* 40 (January): 102.

Upcraft, M. Lee, and John H. Schuh. 1996. *Assessment in Student Affairs: A Guide for Practitioners*. San Francisco: Jossey-Bass.

Weiss, Gregory L. 2002. "The Current Status of Assessment in Sociology Departments." *Teaching Sociology* 30 (January): 391–402.

CHRISTOPHER J. VOPARIL, UNION INSTITUTE & UNIVERSITY

ASSESSING FOR UNDERSTANDING: TOWARD A THEORY OF ASSESSMENT AS LEARNING

2

The reality of assessment for institutions of higher education in this country has the characteristics of a Tocquevillean providential fact. Assessment is, or will soon be, both "universal" and "enduring." Yet while the growing pressures of the assessment movement may seem unyielding, it would be a mistake to think that assessment "escapes human power." Altering its course, however, will require greater theoretical guidance than currently exists. By and large, the literature on assessment is dominated by case studies, "how to" discussions, and a practical orientation that seldom ground the tools and instruments of assessment in a larger theoretical framework (Yorke 2003).[1] Absent a coherent theory or vision that links assessment to the goals of the educational process, we run the risk that our use of assessment will impair rather than improve student learning.

This chapter attempts to address the vacuum surrounding the role and theory of formative assessment—assessment that takes place in the classroom—by offering the pedagogical theory and vision necessary to inform and advance our thinking about assessment as learning. Drawing on the educational philosophy of John Dewey and Michael Oakeshott, along with recent work by Howard Gardner, I argue that just as we teach for understanding, we need to engage in assessment for understanding, integrating assessment into the process of learning itself. The central claim of this chapter is that the challenges of 21st-century higher education require a fundamental shift away from a primary concern with the outcomes or end products of education toward the specifics of the learning process.

In order for faculty to take an active role in this realignment and recast assessment to improve student learning, an understanding of learning theory is crucial.[2] Five particular insights from the literature on learning are essential: a Deweyan conception of learning as "growth;" the importance of context in the learning process; the idea that learning is grounded in the subjectivity of the learner, which I examine via Oakeshott's idea of "liberal learning;" the profound importance of unlearning, established by Gardner and others; and the value of cultivating habits of self-assessment in students. Although the last few years have seen marked improvement, as a discipline political science has been relatively slow to embrace assessment.[3] For the most part, the attention assessment receives has been and continues to be dominated by departmental approaches to *summative* assessment, designed to demonstrate to external stakeholders what students have already learned, rather than *formative* assessment, directly aimed at providing feedback that will benefit students who are in the process of learning—a distinction that will be discussed further below.[4] Although the argument is more theoretical than practical, this chapter aims to move us toward a view of assessment grounded in learning theory that can inform a faculty-driven reorientation of assessment toward the path to genuine understanding and lifelong learning.

From Summative to Formative Assessment

The current discourse on assessment, both at the national and institutional levels, revolves primarily around the issue of *summative* assessment, or assessment *of* learning, to use Lorna Earl's useful tripartite typology: assessment *of, for,* and *as* learning (2003). Its purpose is to summarize, measure, and judge the degree and quality of student learning so that it can be reported. As Earl notes, this form of assessment is usually done at the end of *something*—be it a unit, a course, a year, or a degree—and is typically reported symbolically, as a number or letter grade. The most common form of assessment, the results of summative assessment, can be reported internally, to the students, program directors, and provosts; or, externally, to parents, accrediting bodies, and state and federal agencies. These measures indicate how well or poorly students are performing, and are comparative in nature. Because ease of reporting is part of the *raison d'etre* of these results, however, "the test content is generally too limited and the scoring too simplistic to represent the broad range of skills and knowledge that has been covered" (Earl 2003, 23).

Less common, assessment *for* learning, is *formative* rather than *summative*, designed to further the process of learning itself, as opposed to merely measuring the outcome. Formative assessment is typically classroom assessment, which may take the form of observation of students, worksheets, student–teacher conferences, and even in-class discussion. Yorke (2003) describes it as "assessment that helps students to appreciate the standards that are expected from them" (480). Reporting as such is less the purpose than to provide instructors with information about the progress of individual students and to provide feedback to students themselves, with the ultimate aim of enhancing their learning. As one commentator observed, this type of formative assessment "can become so commonplace that it gets ignored and becomes underconceptualized" (Boud 2000, 155).[5]

The third type, assessment *as* learning, is the focus of this chapter. Also a mode of formative assessment, the notion of assessment *as* learning emphasizes the role of the student as the crucial link between assessment and the learning process. As Earl explains it, assessment *as* learning makes students themselves assessors, so that they "personally monitor what they are learning and use the feedback from this monitoring to make adjustments, adaptations, and even major changes in what they understand" (2003, 25). Comparative, norm-referenced standards are even less important here, as the relevant reference points are the students' own previous work and the goals or outcomes of continued learning. An individualized or personal measure, assessment *as* learning is meant to foster self-assessment, as a critical habit or practice necessary for facilitating the process of learning itself (see Boud 1995).

The focus of this chapter then is on the formative assessment that occurs in the classroom and that fosters continued learning as it happens, rather than to certify learning that has already taken place. My assumption, following Daniel Boud, is that formative assessment in the classroom must influence a student's own self-assessment for it to have lasting value. Nothing in this chapter is incompatible with the forms of summative assessment discussed above that do serve a purpose and in any case are here to stay. However, it is also worth taking seriously Boud's point that, in the larger view, "existing assessment practices are perhaps the greatest influence inhibiting moves towards a learning society" (2000, 155-7). If the oft-cited Deweyan idea of lifelong learning means anything, it must involve cultivating habits that are carried outside the classroom and beyond the university. And the best way to do this is through an approach to assessment *as* learning that stimulates and teaches student self-assessment, which I will turn to below. In the end, the extent to which assessment inhibits rather than promotes student learning is something that falls within the human power of teachers to influence.

Dewey and the Context of Learning

In Dewey's vernacular, education is "the enterprise of supplying the conditions which insure growth" ([1916] 1944, 51).[6] Elevating in this way something as vague and unspecific as creating a certain set of conditions to education's highest end may grate on the ears of those accustomed to talk of the ultimate goal as test scores or the acquisition of knowledge or the demonstration of particular abilities or skills. Yet this fundamental shift away from a primary concern with the outcomes or end products of education toward the characteristics of the learning process itself marks a key focus of Deweyan pedagogy. Indeed, Dewey's appreciation of the importance of context ran deep. All human action, thought, and imaginative endeavor, from the most rudimentary sense perceptions to the most elaborate theoretical constructs, must be seen as a response to the changing conditions of its environment. As he claimed in *Human Nature and Conduct*, "all knowing, judgment, belief represent an acquired result of the workings of natural impulses in connection with the environment" (1922, 187).

The process of learning is no exception. For Dewey, learning is a name for our adjustments to moments of conflict or discontinuity between the human organism and its environment. This fundamental corrective behavior or "activity" inheres in life itself: "In order that life may persist, this activity has to be both continuous and adapted to the environment" ([1920] 1982, 125-8). The thrust of Dewey's educational theory, baldly put, is to make classroom learning an extension of this natural human activity or "motion" rather than an impediment to it. By virtue of the human organism's natural participation in this constant exchange with its environment, which always includes physical reactions as well as mental acts, Dewey believed students or "learners," a category which includes children and adults, possessed an array of "natural powers" or "natural capital" always operative in the form of reflection or thinking. This includes curiosity, suggestion (ideas or beliefs stimulated by experience), and intellectual organization. For Dewey, these natural powers of individuals are "urgent for development, needing to be acted out in order to secure their own efficiency and discipline." Though they may require a certain guidance and the inculcation of traits of "seriousness, absorption, and definiteness of purpose" to receive their highest expression, these powers are poised to unfold naturally, while engaging the full emotional and intellectual range of the self–that is, an ineluctable part of "a normal development of a life process" (1922, 185).[7]

The task for educators is to create classroom conditions that build on these natural powers and development rather than thwart them in favor of activities more easily regulated and assessed but always less engaging to students. When it comes to classroom assessment, the fundamental challenge resides in designing forms of assessment that promote rather than impede the natural human activity of learning, while contributing to the overall end of ensuring growth. Projects, active learning assignments, and peer-to-peer learning that both communicate to teachers where students are at in the learning process, and spur new learning stimulated by immersion in problem-saturated contexts, are the goal. So if learning is a response to changing conditions, the issue is embedding forms of assessment—understood as direct feedback on student learning—within the learning processes of the classroom context. Here, the key point is that the feedback given students is linked to opportunities for improvement, so that the feedback is utilized to yield enhanced work (Boud 2000, 158).

Although far from today's classrooms, the best historical example of a contextualized approach that embeds assessment—understood as immediate, individualized feedback on learning—is in the institution of the apprenticeship. Interestingly, not only Dewey but Howard Gardner, the developer of the "multiple intelligences" concept, have written with admiration about the learning model of the apprenticeship.[8] Indeed, Gardner identifies two dominant modes of learning or the "training" of human intelligence in human history: the traditional apprenticeship, which emphasized observation, demonstration, teaching by example, and learning by doing; and the formal scholastic setting more familiar today, which stresses the importance of memorizing and understanding material from lectures and textbooks that is to be marshaled for homework, exams, and success in later life. The key distinction Gardner wishes to illustrate by way of this contrast is the difference between teaching and learning that occurs in context, in the flow of an engagement with a project of some kind, and decontextualized instruction that takes place in a sterile classroom setting isolated from the stream of ordinary experience (1993a, 162).

Clearly, the *bete noir* of education from Gardner's point of view, given what we know about the diverse manners in which individuals learn, is what he has termed "the uniform view of schooling"—namely, the belief that, as much as possible, students not only should study the same material, but that this material should be conveyed and assessed in the same manner via standardized assessments administered at regularized intervals. Part and parcel of this approach is a heavy reliance on what Gardner calls the "text-test" model. Unlike the apprenticeship model, where both instruction and assessment occur in the context of "performances" of understanding, putting what is learned into practice, here the scene of assessment is de-contextualized, removing the demonstration of what has been learned from its natural embeddedness in the context of performative activity. Severed from the process of learning itself, what can be demonstrated in these formal testing situations is limited to literal repetitions of the material of instruction, as opposed to the kind of demonstration of understanding that could only be displayed in the course of putting that material to use. Inevitably, the "testing tail wags the curricular dog," as Gardner put it, and the matter to be taught is reduced to what can be most readily regurgitated and most efficiently scored on the decontextualized exams. Depth of instruction is sacrificed to greater "coverage." Learning is reduced to mere absorption and rote repetition; teaching becomes simply the transmission of information. Although less quantifiable, projects and performances of understanding nonetheless serve the purposes of external accountability or summative assessment (1993a, 70; 161-5).

Oakeshott's Third Way: Exercising versus Assessing

While the two approaches Gardner juxtaposes—the apprenticeship model versus the formal testing model—do offer a valuable contrast that is very instructive for his purposes, as well as for contrasting current realities with how they could be otherwise, neither seems a model that can be directly emulated by universities of the 21ˢᵗ century. I would suggest a third possibility, one inherent in what philosopher Michael Oakeshott captured by his phrase "liberal learning." Intimating a sort of middle ground between Gardner's two poles, Oakeshott argued that what we know cannot be separated from the use we make of it. Neither the "knowing how" imparted in the apprenticeship model or the "knowing what" that is instructed in the classroom should be taught in isolation from one another. As a result, knowledge must be understood as something other than the mere transmission of information without regard for its use. Here the thrust is clearly toward getting outside the classroom and traditional lecture formats (Oakeshott 2001, 45; 53).[9]

Despite harboring something of a romanticized ideal of the university, Oakeshott's conception of learning was eminently practical: "acquiring something you can use because you understand it."[10] The simplicity of this concept allows Oakeshott to escape the "famous dilemma," as he calls it, which seems to underlie Gardner's two models: the dilemma of conceptualizing learning as the acquisition of knowledge or as the development of the personality of the learner. To put it another way, it is the dilemma of choosing between standardized and individualized approaches to teaching and assessment. At the most fundamental level, for Oakeshott learning is a defining characteristic of the human condition; we become human only through learning. As a result, knowledge ceases to be something external to the individual and cannot possess value independently of her self-understanding. Ultimately, everything we know is in terms of what it means to us (2001, 6-8; 40).[11] This subjective character of learning is what renders the practice of self-assessment so important, as we shall see below.

There are two key points here. The first is that while both information and judgment must be learned, they cannot be taught or learned separately. However, the catch is that information and judgment, which Oakeshott also refers to as "being able to think," cannot be taught—or assessed—in the same manner: "Since learning to think is not acquiring additional information, it cannot be pursued in the same way as we add to our stock of information." Unlike information, judgment cannot be imparted directly; on the contrary, it must be taught indirectly or "obliquely" in the course of the instruction of information, rather than apart from it (2001, 57). Because judgment obtains in the areas left undefined by rules, thinking cannot be separated from the personal exploration Oakeshott elsewhere embraces as essential to the pursuit of learning. That is the second point.

The upshot of this for our discussion is the central role accorded assessment, broadly understood. One of the main tasks of the teacher, Oakeshott believed, is to "exercise" the students in the information that has been instructed. While formal examinations may qualify as this sort of "exercise," to the extent they rely upon mere memorization they may very well fail the key requirement in Oakeshott's conception, which is that the students be exercised in such a way that "what has been acquired may be recognized in forms other than those in which it was first acquired, and may be recollected on all the occasions when it is relevant" (2001, 56).[12] Calling to mind Gardner's idea of teaching for understanding, Oakeshott held that the importance of information is not merely "the accuracy with which it is learned." Knowledge or understanding involves "the readiness with which it can be recollected and used" (2001, 56). This orientation, like the one Gardner has been propounding for two decades, points unequivocally toward forms of assessment that occur in context, and which are grounded in the subjectivity and experience of the learner.

ASSESSMENT AND UNLEARNING: THE EDUCATION OF HABIT AND SELF-ASSESSMENT

In one of his many formulations, Dewey described education as "a continuous reconstruction or reorganization of experience"—or, better, "a process of renewal of the meanings of experience" ([1916] 1944, 321-2).[13] The language of "renewal" and "reconstruction" are not overstatements or hollow rhetoric. For Dewey, learning always involves more than mere absorption; in the absence of the renewal or reconstruction of personal experience that accompanies "growth," it is not clear that learning occurs at all: "a child's character, knowledge, and skill are not reconstructed by sitting in a room where events happen. Events must *happen* to *him*, in a way to bring a full and interested response" (Suzzallo 1979, 470).

Contemporary theorists of learning have deepened this point further. The "text-test model," as Gardner calls the absorption approach, is limited by its failure to stimulate reconstruction of experience, or, in Seymour Sarason's phrase, to help students "unlearn" (2004, 152). Gardner too has been particularly insightful on the issue of the "constraints" operative in the mind that inhibit understanding. Recent research has suggested that structures of assumptions or theories about how the world works are already entrenched in the mind by the end of childhood. Contrary to accepted wisdom, these early frames of mind prove extraordinarily difficult to alter, even with considerable amounts of schooling (Gardner 1983, xviii; 1999, 120).

Striking examples of the power of such constraints can be found even at elite universities, like MIT and Johns Hopkins. In one study, when asked to apply theoretical concepts to relatively simple phenomena, "A" physics students provided incredibly unlearned responses. Gardner observed not only that the students failed to give correct answers, but that the answers given mirrored those of people who had never studied physics, including younger children. "Despite years of schooling," he concluded, rote learning of external curricula had ensured "the minds of these college students remain fundamentally unschooled" (1999, 120; 1993b). In Deweyan terms, their accumulated experiences failed to be reconstructed or renewed in any way.

The existing "natural lines of force" within these students' intelligences, as Gardner described them, reminiscent of Dewey's notion of "active powers," rendered their ability to learn new, more complex theories surprisingly difficult. In short, they were never able to *unlearn* them. Here Sarason is especially clear:

> The road of learning has its ups and downs and their major source is a way of thinking and acting that in some way prevents you from a different way that you (or someone else) want or need to acquire. The source may be personal, cognitive, emotional, motivation, or all of these, and if that source is not identified, the individual has a hard time of it (2004, 152).

So what would it mean to take the need to unlearn into account in our approach to assessment? The place where regular, embedded forms of assessment become relevant is in fostering habits that promote this crucial process of "unlearning." Specifically, unlearning invites an emphasis on formative self-assessment, understood in the context of what Dewey described as the "reconstruction" of experience.

The concept of self-assessment involves recognizing the role of the student as an assessor of her own work. The aim, as Earl argues, is to establish the student rather than the professor as the "key assessor" so that self-monitoring and self-correction or adjustment become natural, in the sense of a habituated process of learning.[14] Her point is that "learning is also dependent upon self-monitoring and awareness" (2003, 100). As we know, at the most basic level, assessment is about standards or benchmarks, and measuring student performance relative to desired outcomes and criteria. There is no better way to foster learning than by involving students in the evaluative process endemic to assessment. In other words, if students are given clear examples of what quality work looks like, understand the steps required to get there, have knowledge of the standards by which we are judging their work, and of course multiple opportunities for practice, they can become the best evaluators of their own work—not simply to pronounce a final judgment on it, but to foster a continual process of self-evaluation and improvement that, in the end, will improve learning outcomes, rather than simply measure them.

The problem is that statements of learning outcomes and standards commonly encountered on syllabi are often "generally insufficient to convey the richness of the meaning that is wrapped up within them" (Yorke 2003, 480). Here the ubiquitous "Bloom's taxonomy" is especially guilty. As Yorke argues, fostering student self-assessment in the classroom is a way to "maximize the intersubjectivity of understanding" between the teacher and students about the demands of the course that provides the requisite exemplification and discussion for students to fully understand the criteria and standards involved (480). As Earl puts it, if we want students to become critical thinkers, we can't create contexts where students must "wait for someone to tell them the right answer" (2003, 102).

In *Human Nature and Conduct* (1922), Dewey offered the example of a stalled traveler to illustrate the role of habits and context in learning that also underscores how self-assessment and self-adjustment are crucial for the development of genuine critical thinking. Viewed from without, a traveler is marching forward, striding confidently with little attention to his path or destination. Suddenly, his progress is disturbed, his forward motion quelled. An obstacle has been encountered that needs to be surmounted before his movement can continue. The traveler is momentarily confused, at a loss for how to proceed. The emotions are engaged: shock, confusion, perturbation, uncertainty. He does not know what hit him, or where he was going. But a new impulse is spurred, which becomes the starting point of an investigation. Dewey continued:

> Habits, which were interfered with, begin to get a new direction as they cluster about the impulse to look and see. The blocked habits of locomotion give him a sense of where he *was* going, of what he had set out to do, and of the ground already traversed. As he looks, he sees definite things which are not just things at large but which are related to his course of action. The momentum of the activity entered upon persists as a sense of direction, of aim, it is an anticipatory project. In short, he recollects, observes, and plans (1922, 181-2).

From here, the fruits of observation and recollection are projected and generalized into principles. Rooted in the context of his environment, the traveler seeks the unity or synthesis necessary to return him to a consistent, productive relation to his surroundings. Knowledge results as old habits are adapted to the new impulse. The confused situation is "cleared up," which for Dewey is "the essential function of intelligence" (1922, 183; 180).

This process is precisely what students should be taught to "monitor" through the practice of self-assessment.[15] But how does one implement this in the classroom? The most basic form of self-assessment and easiest to employ is the student journal–or any kind of regular, brief, reflective assignment that allows students to reflect on their own learning. Margaret Mott (2008) has described a wonderfully creative and deeply engaging way to incorporate personal reflections through assignments that promote linking individual experiences to theoretical concepts and claims from political theory texts. In tandem with readings from thinkers who offer models of "reflective subjectivity," like Montaigne, Foucault, and Audre Lorde, she uses an assignment that involves expressing the voice of one's "internal critic" on the top half of the page and then attempting to defend oneself against this critic on the bottom half. Promoting implicit self-assessment, Mott insists that, with all personal writing, "the writer must be both producer and first judge" (2008, 210). Student journal assignments need not be this specific or theoretical. Fishman and McCarthy's "Class Reflection Log," which involves brief questions distributed at the end of class to be addressed by the next class, fosters habits of self-assessment with questions like: "Reflecting on today's class [...] did you learn anything as you listened to your classmates' remarks? Which classmate's comments had the most weight for you and why?"

These brief reflections can pertain to particular assignments: "Compare the letter exchange and the study questions. Which helped you learn more about the assigned texts?" Or, be more general: "What have you learned in the class so far, and how have you learned it?" They can even go beyond the particular class: "Compare two classes [you are taking this semester] in terms of how you figured out how to do well. Please be specific about the things which have helped you figure it out in each class." Toward the end of the course, students were asked, "How has this class affected your self-confidence as a learner?" And, "Has this class caused you to alter or see in new ways any of your views?" (Fishman and McCarthy 1998, 227-30).[16]

Framing what we have called "unlearning" in a slightly different way that makes it of particular relevance to political science, Sato et. al. (2005) hold that "changing your mind is the best kind of learning," and describe the use of "learning journals" where students reflected in each class not only on what they were learning but on how their minds were changing (179). Given the myths and simplistic shorthands about political life that virtually any course in political science seeks to challenge and in a Socratic spirit get students to rethink, regular use of this sort of self-assessment focused on the changing of minds seems not only appropriate but essential.[17] Not only does this practice benefit students, in terms of the development of critical habits, the information gleaned from student journals can inform teaching, allowing instructors to make adjustments based on what students are understanding or not understanding (Sato et al. 2005, 180). That students in political science may be able to meet desired learning outcomes without having changed their minds in any fundamental way would seem sufficient cause to question any approach to assessment that does not include self-assessment.

One of the virtues of an emphasis on self-assessment is that it teaches students that they share a responsibility in their own learning. Not only is this important in itself, as a means to creating independent, lifelong learners; giving students greater control over their own achievements has a positive effect on motivation and self-esteem.[18] Here Gardner, as well as the advocates of self-assessment, agree that regular, multiple, and challenging opportunities to practice and develop these skills and habits are essential. As Boud holds, suggesting a link between formative and summative assessment, "the challenge is to find a balance between providing a wide range of new learning opportunities for students and enabling them to complete the feedback loop enough times for them to gain the confidence that their achievements are secure and can really demonstrate the desired outcomes" (2001, 158).[19] Moreover, through the use of electronic or "e-portfolios," these forms of self-assessment, along with more traditional papers and projects, can be compiled across a student's university career to create a summative measure that documents learning outcomes (Gibson and Barrett 2003; Ittelson 2001).

TOWARD ASSESSING FOR UNDERSTANDING

The overarching claim of this chapter has been that it is possible to understand and recast assessment in a way that coheres with the pedagogical orientation Gardner has called "teaching for understanding." Not unlike Oakeshott, in Gardner's view, an individual understands "whenever he or she is able to apply knowledge, concepts, or skills acquired in some kind of an educational setting to a new instance or situation, where that knowledge is in fact relevant" (1993a, 188). Even highly touted improvements on standardized tests around the country may only rarely be linked to actual gains in understanding (Knight 2002).

To grasp fully what it would mean to assess for understanding, we must think through the practical implications of the five insights outlined at the outset. Although there may well be more, in the space that remains I will briefly touch on four: the resulting changes with regard to learning styles, curriculum, tests, and assignments, and grading. Given the current state of our knowledge of human learning and intelligence, Gardner outlines three general criteria that any new form of assessment should meet. First, it must be "intelligence-fair." Given the existence of multiple, independent dimensions of intelligence, assessment of the effectiveness of an intelligence must proceed directly; that is, musical intelligence, for example, must be assessed through musical means—a performance, presumably—and not "screened" through the lens of logic and language.[20] Second, it must be "developmentally appropriate" for the individual's developmental level in the given domain of knowledge to be assessed. Lastly, assessment must be linked to recommendations, which in turn should be linked to opportunities for improvement. In other words, assessment should involve the kind of feedback from which students can benefit—in a word, from which they can *learn*—such that their future growth and education path can proceed more wisely (Gardner 1993a, 72).

Underscoring a point many teachers have long perceived, Gardner emphasizes that "short-answer, multiple choice tests stifle students' and teachers' initiative." Forms of assessment that fit this model are not learning experiences and rarely offer students useful feedback. On the whole, the direction of Gardner's work pushes teachers to develop "more probing, open-ended forms of assessment," as opposed to "one-shot" exercises (1993a, 82). Similarly, Torrance and Pryor distinguish between "convergent" and "divergent" assessment (cited in Yorke 2003, 480). While convergent assessments gauge student performance on pre-specified objectives, divergent assessments evaluate student learning in more open-ended tasks. In their view, both formative and summative assessments need to be slanted toward divergent forms.

Gardner's approach involves more than performance and doing. Discussion and analysis play an integral role, and instruction seeks to foster ways of thinking rather than mere information. Here curriculum and assessment must intimately intertwine, uniting learning and assessment through the medium of the project. More specifically, Gardner discusses the use of "domain projects." A domain project is a set of exercises that simultaneously serve as a part of the teaching and a form of assessment, and which feature perceptual, productive, and reflective elements (1993a, 144-9).[21]

Another form of assessment in line with Gardner's approach is the portfolio or "processfolio," to use his preferred nomenclature. Unlike a traditional portfolio, which showcases finished products, a processfolio contains both drafts and completed works, emphasizing the notion of a creative process. Here, again, both learning and assessment occur in context. "Rather than being imposed 'externally' at odd times during the year," Gardner explains, "assessment ought to become part of the natural learning environment." Although not nearly as amenable to efficient, clear-cut assessment, these open-ended projects do provide formal evaluation. Most importantly, they afford individual creativity ample room to operate and develop, avoiding not only the unnatural constraints inherent in formal testing, but the "intrinsic dullness of the materials" as well. Because rooted in the personal experience of the learner, they are both motivational *and* educative (Gardner 1993a, 174; 178).[22]

In this way, Gardner underscores the importance of approaching assessment as a "performance of understanding." Unlike more commonly encountered examinations, such performances beget deep student engagement. Students inevitably "take regular and increasingly major responsibility for reflecting on the nature of their performances and on the means for improving them." Because these types of projects and performances are not quick, in-and-out transactions, they unavoidably are more time consuming. This fact, in addition to the overall implications of Gardnerian (and Deweyan) pedagogy, counsels a "radical foreshortening" of the curriculum, as Gardner puts it. Having to scurry throughout the term at a breakneck pace to "cover" large swaths of history or curriculum marks the ruin of many a course. Instead, Gardner advocates a much narrower—but more profound—focus on several "rich or generative concepts" that can serve as an occasion for reflection and extended contextualized learning and assessment.

For instance, even in an introductory course in political theory, one might focus on four or five representative works from different historical periods—e.g., Plato's *Republic*, Augustine's *City of God*, Machiavelli's *The Prince*, and Locke's *Second Treatise*—that can be pursued in greater depth, rather than cramming a broad but more superficial survey of many more works into one course. The idea of focusing on several "case studies," so to speak—that can be approached in a deeper way from multiple angles and richer forms of assessment—could be applied to a course on liberation struggles or comparative government or American political development. An excessive quantity of things to be learned often constrains instructors to more quantifiable but less engaging forms of assessment. As Gardner put it, "so long as one tries to cover a huge amount of material in school, an education nuanced in the light of multiple intelligences becomes virtually impossible" (1993a, 191; 202-3).

The last issue worth touching on in our discussion of formative assessment is grading. For starters, the commonplace notion inherited from an inordinate stress on summative assessment that grading itself is sufficient as feedback on student learning must be displaced. There is evidence to suggest that grades can act as an impediment to student learning. Feedback, in the form of specific comments that, importantly, "allow students to see the gap between their actual production and some reference point that makes sense to them," plus grades, may lead to lesser learning than feedback without grades (Earl 2003, 105; Boud

2000, 157).[23] In addition to formal feedback on particular assignments, informal opportunities to provide feedback, including teacher–student conferences, are also integral. One of the most difficult shifts when it comes to grading, especially for divergent forms of assessment, may be what Sato, Coffey, and Moorthy (2005) describe as the change from assessing based on the accuracy of the response to the criteria of completion and progress. As they report, "students provided fuller responses and [...] took more risks when they were not trying to figure out the 'right' response that [the instructor] wanted" (179). Peer assessment also has a role to play. But it is important that such exercises are well-designed and appropriately performed. Students must know that mistakes are a normal part of learning.[24]

CONCLUSION

Assessment is here to stay. The question is no longer whether assessment will become a part of the pedagogical practices of all faculty; it is whether the forms of assessment faculty employ will be an enhancement or a hindrance to student learning. The theoretical orientation of this chapter is meant to offer the kind of framework and knowledge of learning theory that can inform faculty efforts to think creatively about forms of assessment that fulfill not only the needs of their universities and their departments, but their students as well. In the absence of clear continuities between assessment and classroom experience, the forms of assessment we employ may prove to be "mis-educative" rather than truly educative.[25]

NOTES

1. Noteworthy exceptions include Earl (2003) and Boud (2000).
2. On this point, see Bain (2004) and Earl (2003), who hold, "knowing about learning for teachers is like knowing about anatomy for doctors" (114).
3. A special APSA panel on assessment for department chairs in 2001 found that political science "has not been in the forefront in interpreting assessment objectives and designing procedures... In most departments, assessment is regarded as a lot of work unlikely to be worth doing... The majority of participants' remarks challenged assessment mandates, their costs and their usefulness in informing program development and reform" (quoted in Smoller 2004, 875).
4. For example, see Kelly and Klunk (2003); Campbell (2007); Deardorff (2007); Hamann (2007); Suskie (2007). The exception here in recent years has been the ideas generated via the APSA's annual Teaching and Learning Conference, which continues to be the discipline's greatest engine for new ideas in the areas of pedagogy and assessment. However, even here the commitment to assessment as a vehicle for improving student learning amounts to little more than lip service, in that it is not linked to a more developed theoretical vision outlining how to get there. See Axel et al (2006).
5. Boud continues, on the same page, "Ironically, we have given insufficient attention to those aspects of assessment that contribute most to students' ability to learn for themselves and thus contribute to a learning society."
6. A few more recent voices, like that of Seymour Sarason (2004), have seconded this insight and noted that the highest priority of educators is attending to the context of learning.
7. Apart from Dewey, seminal works on moral and intellectual development include Kohlberg (1964), Perry (1968), and Chickering (1969). See also Magolda (2001).
8. Interestingly, the demise of the institution of the apprenticeship marks a recurring lament in Dewey's educational writings. In the apprenticeship, learning takes place in a context that unites thinking and doing, theory and practice, rather than attempting to teach swimming while outside the pool, as Dewey once characterized purely intellectualized learning. The apprenticeship also fostered certain habits of discipline, responsibility, and obligation to produce something in the world. Dewey called it "character-building" (1964, 297–98).
9. On experiential learning suggested in this last point, see Roberts (2005).
10. Oakeshott famously defended the institution of the university as "a place of learning" set apart from "the muddle, the crudity, the sentimentality, the intellectual poverty and the emotional morass of ordinary life." Above all, it affords "liberation from the here and now of current engagements"—in a word, an "interval," defined neither by utility for later life nor by a specific set of values, in which the individual is invited to further understand herself and her world:

"an endless unrehearsed intellectual adventure in which, in imagination, we enter into a variety of modes of understanding the world and ourselves and are not disconcerted by the differences or dismayed by the inconclusiveness of it all" (2001, 18; 30; see also 105-17).

11. See also (2001, 113–17).

12. Here I am reminded of the complaint students often make about what they regard as unfair or "tricky" exams that contain "surprises" or unfamiliar contexts. The problem lies less in the tricky questions than in the fact that little in the preparation leading up to the exam involved the application of concepts or imparting the ability to think.

13. As we have seen, learning is a process. As Sarason put it, nicely capturing the inseparability of the group and individual dynamics, it is a process that "occurs in an interpersonal and group context, and it is always composed of an interaction of factors to which we append labels such as motivation, cognition, emotion or affect, or attitude" (2004, vii).

14. Interestingly, Dewey believed that even what we refer to as consciousness was a function of habits. For instance, he explained that a baby can "know little" and an adult "know much" when confronted by the same thing, "not because the latter has a 'mind' which the former has not, but because one has already formed habits which the other has still to acquire." The philosopher, the scientist, the physician, and the politician "know with their habits not with their 'consciousness'" (1922, 178).

15. Stephen Fishman nicely describes the emotional dimension always present in such moments: "[Learning] happens when desire is frustrated, attention is aroused, and we investigate our surroundings with purpose, learning new ways to achieve our sought-after ends" (Fishman and McCarthy 1998, 19).

16. Fishman and McCarthy include all 22 Class Reflection Log queries in the appendix of their book (1998, 227–30). Fishman even had students reflect on his own in-class exams by having them write responses to things like: "What sort of questions did you expect; that is, did the exam questions surprise you in any way?" "Do you feel you learned anything by getting ready for the exam?" "How do you feel about your grade?" On other days, students reflected upon: "What responses from the teacher to your recitations in class or to your writing do you particularly remember?" "What were their effects on you?"—all offering invaluable feedback to him as well (229).

17. For a rich discussion of the linkage between these critical habits of mind and citizenship more generally, see Villa (2001).

18. As Boud puts it, "Assessment practices must contribute towards the building of students' confidence in their ability to learn, not undermine it" (2000, 157).

19. Boud continues, "Unless students are able to use feedback to produce improved work, through for example redoing the same assignment, neither they nor those giving feedback will know that it has been effective" (2000, 158).

20. For more on multiple intelligences in the context of political science, see Gershkoff (2005).

21. One such project is called the "biography of a work." Here students observe sets of sketches that preceded the composition of two significant works of art. In one instance, Andrew Wyeth's *Brown Swiss* and Picasso's *Guernica* were used. Following the examples of these two artists, students are asked to create a work that expresses something about them. After a second session on the metaphorical use of objects in art, students return to their sketches, adding another dimension. In a third session, students examine their successive drafts and set about composing their final work. A key element of the domain project is the use of self-assessment procedures during the project to afford students the opportunity and invitation for learning and growth. Gardner's examples are not drawn from political science, but with a bit of creativity instructors could surely apply his concepts and approach. One of the initiatives of Gardner and his colleagues at Harvard's Project Zero is a program called Arts PROPEL, whose approach (and acronym) emphasizes production, perception, reflection, and learning. See Gardner (1993a, Chapter 9).

22. Gardner reproduces the guidelines for the processsfolio assessment system (1993a, 150–1). He also reports progress being made in a collaboration between Project Zero and the Educational Testing Service (ETS), responsible for the SAT and other standardized tests toward the development of procedures for evaluation projects and portfolios (1993a, 185).

23. See also Black and William (1998).

24. Boud stresses, "Having peers rate each other on relatively uninformative scales to produce marks which are used primarily for classificatory purposes tends to disrupt learning altogether" (2000, 157). In this context, Earl gives the example of the "fishbowl" exercise. A few students discuss or debate a problem or issue and their analysis of it, while the rest of the class sits in a circle around them, making notes, thinking about rival hypotheses, other resources that may be useful, etc. This feedback from the class is then offered to the fishbowl participants as the starting point for their next discussion (2003, 106).

25. Dewey asserted, "Any experience is mis-educative that has the effect of arresting or distorting the growth of further experience" ([1938] 1997, 25).

REFERENCES

Axel, Donna, Gordon Babst, Elizabeth Bennion, John Berg, Amy Brandon, Mitchell Brown, and Lisa A. Cave, et al. 2006. "2006 APSA Teaching and Learning Conference Track Summaries." *PS: Political Science & Politics* 39 (July): 533–44.

Bain, Ken. 2004. *What the Best College Teachers Do.* Cambridge, MA: Harvard University Press.

Black, P., and D. Wiliam. 1998. "Assessment and Classroom Learning." *Assessment in Education* 5 (1): 7–74.

Boud, David. 1995. *Enhancing Learning through Self Assessment.* London: Kogan Page.

———. 2000. "Sustainable Assessment: Rethinking Assessment for the Learning Society." *Studies in Continuing Education* 22 (2): 151–67.

Campbell, Kenneth J. 2007. "Assessment Advice for Beginners." *PS: Political Science & Politics* 40 (January): 99.

Chickering, Arthur W. 1969. *Education and Identity.* San Francisco: Jossey-Bass.

Deardorff, Michelle D. 2007. "Methods of Effectively Leveraging Departmental Assessment Programs." *PS: Political Science & Politics* 40 (January): 100–01.

Dewey, John. 1922. *Human Nature and Conduct: An Introduction to Social Psychology.* New York: The Modern Library.

———. [1916] 1944. *Democracy and Education.* New York: The Free Press.

———. 1964. "The School and Society." In *John Dewey on Education: Selected Writings,* ed. Reginald D. Archambault. New York: The Modern Library, 295–310.

———. [1920] 1982. "Reconstruction in Philosophy." In *The Middle Works of John Dewey, 1899–1924* (Vol. 12), ed. Jo Ann Boydston. Carbondale, IL: Southern Illinois University Press, 77–201.

———. [1938] 1997. *Experience and Education.* New York: Touchstone.

Earl, Lorna. 2004. *Assessment as Learning: Using Classroom Assessment to Maximize Student Learning.* Thousand Oaks, CA: Corwin Press.

Fishman, Stephen M., and Lucille McCarthy. 1998. *John Dewey and the Challenge of Classroom Practice.* New York: Teachers College Press.

Gardner, Howard. 1983. *Frames of Mind: The Theory of Multiple Intelligences.* New York: Basic Books.

———. 1993a. *Multiple Intelligences: The Theory in Practice.* New York: Basic Books.

———. 1993b. *The Unschooled Mind: How Children Think and How Schools Should Teach.* New York: Basic Books.

———. 1999. *The Disciplined Mind: What All Students Should Understand.* New York: Simon & Schuster.

Gershkoff, Amy. 2005. "Multiple Methods, More Success: How to Help Students of All Learning Styles Succeed in Quantitative Political Analysis Courses." *PS: Political Science & Politics* 38 (April): 299–304.

Gibson, David, and Helen Barrett. 2003. "Directions in Electronic Portfolio Development." *Contemporary Issues in Technology and Teacher Education* 2 (4): www.citejournal.org/vol2/iss4/general/article3.cfm.

Hamann, Kerstin. 2007. "Presentation for Chairs' Workshop on Assessment, APSA 2006." *PS: Political Science & Politics* 40 (January): 101–02.

Ittelson, John C. 2001. "Building an E-dentity for Each Student." *Educause Quarterly* 24 (1): 43–45.

Kelly, Marisa, and Brian E. Klunk. 2003. "Learning Assessment in Political Science Departments: Survey Results." *PS: Political Science & Politics* 36 (July): 451–55.

Knight, Peter T. 2002. "Summative Assessment in Higher Education: Practices in Disarray." *Studies in Higher Education* 27 (3): 275–86.

Kohlberg, Lawrence. 1964. "Development of Moral Character and Moral Ideology." In *Review of Child Development Research*, Vol. 1, ed. Martin L. Hoffman and Lois W. Hoffman. New York: Russell Sage Foundation, 383–432.

Magolda, Marcia B. Baxter. 2001. *Making Their Own Way: Narratives for Transforming Higher Education to Promote Self-Development.* Sterling, VA: Stylus.

Mott, Margaret. 2008. "Passing Our Lives through the Fire of Thought: The Personal Essay in the Political Theory Classroom." *PS: Political Science & Politics* 41 (January): 207–11.

Oakeshott, Michael. 2001. "Learning and Teaching." In *The Voice of Liberal Learning*, ed. Timothy Fuller. Indianapolis: Liberty Fund, 35–61.

Perry, William G., Jr. 1968. *Forms of Intellectual and Ethical Development in the College Years.* Cambridge: Bureau of Study Counsel at Harvard University.

Roberts, Jay W. 2005. "Disney, Dewey, and the Death of Experience in Education." *Education and Culture* 21 (2): 12–30.

Sarason, Seymour. 2004. *And What Do You Mean by Learning?* Portsmouth, NH: Heinemann.

Sato, Mistilina, Janet Coffey, and Savitha Moorthy. 2005. "Two Teachers Making Assessment for Learning Their Own." *The Curriculum Journal* 16 (2): 171–91.

Smoller, Fred. 2004. "Assessment is Not a Four-Letter Word." *PS: Political Science & Politics* 37 (October): 871–74.

Suskie, Linda. 2007. "Some Thoughts and Suggestions on Assessing Student Learning." *PS: Political Science & Politics* 40 (January): 102.

Suzzallo, Henry. 1979. "Editor's Introduction to *Efforts in Education*." In *The Middle Works of John Dewey, 1899–24*, vol. 7, ed. Jo Ann Boydston. Carbondale: Southern Illinois University Press, 469–71.

Tocqueville, Alexis de. 2000. *Democracy in America.* Trans. Harvey C. Mansfield and Delba Winthrop. Chicago: University of Chicago Press.

Villa, Dana. 2001. *Socratic Citizenship.* Princeton: Princeton University Press.

Yorke, Mantz. 2003. "Formative Assessment in Higher Education: Moves Towards Theory and the Enhancement of Pedagogic Practice." *Higher Education* 45 (June): 477–501.

E. Fletcher McClellan, Elizabethtown College

An Overview of the Assessment Movement

The modern assessment movement in higher education emerged in the 1980s from two concerns, expressed by separate groups, about the effectiveness of education policies and practices in the United States. Coming from stakeholders outside the academic community was the idea that educational institutions, starting with K-12 but extending to colleges and universities, should be held accountable to public policymakers for their success in producing students who were prepared to meet the demands of the global economy. The second concern, which emerged from within the academy, was the need to make teaching the highest priority of the professoriate and to find ways to strengthen the undergraduate curriculum and improve the quality of instruction. Both constituencies saw outcomes assessment as an important means to address their respective issues (Ewell 2002).

As a result, assessment efforts in American colleges and universities have taken place in an uncertain, often tense atmosphere. By opening educational processes to outside scrutiny, assessment on many campuses became associated with interference from politicians and accreditors. Faculty members were suspicious of how college administrators, situated between both the accountability and improvement camps, might use assessment results.

This chapter examines the development of the assessment movement in higher education nationally and in the political science discipline. The first section applies John Kingdon's version of the "garbage can" model of agenda-setting in public policy (Kingdon 2003) to the question of how assessment became a preferred solution in efforts to reform higher education.

Though many people in higher education believe that assessment was an externally driven phenomenon, this analysis shares the view of the political scientist and assessment chronicler Peter Ewell (2002) that the movement was a convergence of simultaneous, separate streams of activity.

The second part of the chapter focuses on assessment activities in political science. The argument is that, as a discipline, political science was slow to recognize the importance and staying power of the assessment movement, so much so that the profession was accused of being "ignorant" (Julian, Chamberlain, and Seay 1991). This began to change with the APSA task force report on reforming the political science major (Wahlke 1991), which recommended that the discipline pay greater attention to how individual students and departmental programs are evaluated. At annual meetings in the 1990s, APSA committees and staff sponsored panels on teaching and learning issues and specific programs on assessment for department chairs. By 2000, one-half of political science departments were involved in some kind of assessment activity and faculty scholarship in teaching and learning increased significantly. In the current decade, APSA intensified its efforts to provide leadership and support. The APSA Conference on Teaching and Learning, held annually since 2004, has become an important forum for discussion and scholarship of assessment in the discipline.

OUTCOMES ASSESSMENT AS A CASE STUDY IN AGENDA-SETTING

ANATOMY OF A MOVEMENT I: ASSESSMENT IN THE PROBLEM STREAM

A major change in U.S. education policy took place in the late 1970s and early 1980s. The primary goal of federal policy during the Great Society years, extending into the early 1970s, was increasing educational opportunity through such programs as the Elementary and Secondary Education Act of 1965, the Higher Education Act of 1965, and affirmative action. By the end of President Reagan's first term, however, the thrust of education policy had shifted toward how efficiently and effectively education dollars were spent. That is, the attention of policymakers at the federal and state levels turned from increasing educational "inputs" to scrutinizing educational "outputs" (Ewell 1997).

How was education policy redefined? According to Kingdon's discussion of the "problem stream," problems come to the attention of people in and around government in several ways. Crises and disasters may suddenly bring issues to the forefront, as the 9/11 attacks demonstrated. More routinely, secular or significant changes in key statistical indicators, such as a rise in gas prices, may raise public awareness. Special studies, commissioned by the government or the private sector, may highlight such indicators (Kingdon 2003, 91).

In the case of education, the report of the National Commission on Excellence in Education, established by U.S. Secretary of Education Terrel Bell, titled *A Nation at Risk* (1983), used dramatic language to emphasize deteriorating performance on SAT tests over a generation, growing numbers of functionally illiterate teenagers and adults, and low rankings of American students in international comparisons of student achievement. Stating that a "rising tide of mediocrity" threatened the educational foundations of society, the commission added:

> If an unfriendly foreign power had attempted to impose on America the mediocre educational performance that exists today, we might well have viewed it as an act of war.... We have, in effect, been committing an act of unthinking, unilateral educational disarmament (National Commission on Excellence in Education 1983, 5).

Set against a backdrop of three recessions in the past decade, as well as reports of the rising economic power of Japan and Western Europe, *A Nation at Risk* helped citizens connect declining educational performance to anxieties about economic competitiveness. These concerns were felt most strongly at the state level, where governors and legislatures have direct responsibility for education. Recognizing that investments in education were a key to economic and workforce development, states increased funding for teacher salaries, basic skills courses, and lengthening the school year. However, greater accountability was demanded, not just from elementary and secondary schools (a major issue during this period was merit pay for teachers) but also from higher education (Ewell 1997).

Noting that the rising cost of going to college far exceeded inflation rates, the report, *A Time for Results*, a culmination of a year-long study by the National Governors Association (NGA) in 1986, asked for evidence of what the public was getting for its money. Among the report's findings:

> Many colleges and universities do not have a systematic way to demonstrate whether student learning is taking place. Rather, learning—and especially developing abilities to utilize knowledge—is assumed to take place as long as students take courses, accumulate hours and progress "satisfactorily" toward a degree (National Governors Association 1986).

Governor John Ashcroft of Missouri, who chaired the governors' task force on college quality, stated the case for accountability directly:

> The public has a right to know what it is getting for its expenditure of tax resources; the public has a right to know and understand the quality of undergraduate education that young people receive from public colleges and universities (National Governors Association 1986, Preface).

Reflecting Ashcroft's views, *A Time for Results* recommended that colleges and universities define their missions, goals, and objectives, and that the regional accrediting associations require assessment of progress in student learning. To demonstrate that assessment could bring positive consequences, the NGA report stipulated that colleges with documented success should be rewarded for their efforts. In Tennessee, for example, a $50 million performance fund was established to boost appropriations for state institutions that showed improvement in graduation rates, job placement, and student, alumni, and employer satisfaction (Banta 1986). On the other hand, several states served notice to state universities that failure to develop assessment programs would result in automatic cuts of annual appropriations (Ewell 1997).

Taken together, *A Nation at Risk* and *A Time for Results* raised questions of accountability, cost, and quality in higher education. The impact of both reports was magnified by their appeal to national prestige at a time of economic uncertainty. Sponsored by the nation's chief political executives who had the authority to turn recommendations into reality, the reports played a significant role in redefining the education "problem."

ANATOMY OF A MOVEMENT II:
ASSESSMENT IN THE POLICY STREAM

For politicians, the problem with higher education was lack of accountability. For those inside higher education, the problem was a lack of attention to teaching and undergraduate student learning. Well before the Reagan administration came to power, reformers in the professoriate were working on ways to improve undergraduate education. As a means to promote evidence-based reflection and improvement of academic programs and classroom teaching, assessment became a valuable approach for reformers as well as for those concerned about accountability. How assessment became a preferred answer to the problems facing higher education requires a discussion of what normally goes on in the "policy stream."

In the policy stream, proposals for government action in response to a perceived problem are developed and refined (Kingdon 2003, 4). Specialists in the bureaucracy, legislative staff units, think tanks, and academia are the main participants, floating ideas in the "policy primeval soup" (Kingdon 2003, 116–17). Much of this activity takes place independently of the problem and political streams, so that many solutions are looking for a problem to latch onto.

In the case of assessment, academics worked closely with government agencies, advocacy groups in higher education, and private foundations to advance ideas about improving the teaching and learning process. Going back to the 1930s and 1940s, educational researchers have examined the effects of the college experience on student learning. Studies in the late 1970s, such as Alexander Astin's *Four Critical Years* (1977), specifically used the language of outputs and outcomes to ascertain what students get out of college, and what environmental, instructional, and behavioral factors have the greatest impact. Astin argued that colleges should be evaluated according to their results—i.e., how much they contribute to student learning—not their resources or reputation.

The findings of research on student learning provided new insights that stimulated reform efforts within the scholarly community. Organized by the U.S. Department of Education's National Institute of Education (NIE) shortly after the release of *A Nation at Risk*, the Study Group on the Conditions of Excellence in American Higher Education issued *Involvement in Learning* (1984). The NIE group, which included Astin, found that colleges can maximize learning by setting high expectations, promoting student involvement in the classroom and co-curriculum, and providing students with prompt and useful feedback on their performance. Colleges should conduct assessment of student achievement not just to improve individual student learning, the report added, but also to improve the educational process.

Numerous reports from national higher education organizations followed, several of which touted assessment as a key element of reform (Association of American Colleges 1985; Boyer 1987). In the midst of these studies, the first national conference on assessment was organized in 1985 by the NIE and the American Association for Higher Education. A second AAHE meeting was held two years later, leading to the establishment of an annual AAHE Assessment Forum that for the next 15 years was the premier gathering in the field for colleges and universities under new state or accreditation mandates wanting to learn how to do assessment.

In addition to practical discussions at AAHE, a scholarship of assessment emerged. Among the early landmarks was Patricia Cross and Thomas Angelo's manual, *Classroom Assessment Techniques*, which described ways for faculty to learn from student performance in courses (Cross and Angelo 1988). Organized in the late 1980s, the Harvard Assessment Seminars interviewed hundreds of undergraduates on what aspects of college life contributed most to their learning (Light 1990). The newsletter *Assessment Update* was launched for scholars and practitioners in 1989 under the editorship of Trudy Banta, and continues today.

FROM STREAMS TO MAINSTREAM: ASSESSMENT BECOMES INSTITUTIONALIZED

Ideas in the problem stream may continue to float, die out, change into new forms, or survive to capture the attention of government officials. Those that reach the latter stage are able to meet several tests in the policy process: technical feasibility, value acceptability, economic feasibility, and public acceptance (Kingdon 2003, 131–39).

Applying Kingdon's criteria for success in the policy stream, outcomes assessment emerged as a viable alternative for several reasons. First, it satisfied the test of technical feasibility. In the 1970s and 1980s, several colleges and more than a few states had experimented with different kinds of assessment models, with some approaches receiving considerable praise. Moreover, there was an emerging research agenda that was action-focused, developing ready-made prescriptions for improving teaching and learning in college.

Second, to the extent that assessment was a means by which education policies could be judged as cost-effective, assessment was consistent with the value consensus of the 1980s, which stressed efficiency more than equity, and with the actions of the Reagan administration, which cut federal spending for education in absolute dollars during the president's first term. Assessment was a policy that could be implemented without a substantial increase of public expenditures, thus meeting economic criteria.

Finally, since assessment itself is a process for evaluating curricula rather than a prescription for a particular kind of academic program, state universities and private colleges could sidestep political controversies associated with the "culture war" such as whether colleges should re-emphasize the Western canon in general education (Bennett 1984; Bloom 1987). It is true that assessment brings its own set of political issues, but as it is implemented at the campus level, the politics of assessment are localized.

Even if an idea satisfies the criteria, that does not guarantee its adoption into public policy. Conditions in the "political stream" must also be favorable. Swings in the national mood, the balance of organized groups, and changes in the composition of government may block or facilitate the progress of a proposal (Kingdon 2003, 145–64). With regard to assessment, the political currents were favorable. Though the Reagan administration sought to reduce federal education spending, the fact that it advocated education reform helped to mitigate partisanship (Bell 1988). Since assessment was viewed as a remedy for a variety of problems with education in the U.S., including cost, quality, and accountability, leaders in both political parties across the federal executive branch, Congress, and the states supported the idea.

For a lucky few ideas, conditions in all three streams may converge to create the feeling of "an idea whose time has come." If, as in the case for assessment, there is widespread agreement that there is a public problem that needs government attention, a policy alternative that could meet the need, and political support for government action, policy can result. There is still the chance that an idea could fall by the wayside if key actors do not take advantage of the "window of opportunity." As Kingdon notes, it requires a keen sense of timing for policy entrepreneurs or advocates for the proposal to help officials and the public make the connection and drive the idea to the top of the policy agenda (Kingdon 2003, 165-95).

By the end of the 1980s, both accountability and improvement advocates pushed assessment to the forefront of higher education reform. Governors such as Lamar Alexander in Tennessee, Tom Kean in New Jersey, and John Ashcroft in Missouri (Republicans, notably) took the role as advocates for education reform and implemented innovative assessment programs in their respective states. Leaders in higher education such as Ernest Boyer included assessment in their prescriptions for improving undergraduate education. Within the Reagan administration were officials such as Secretary of Education Terrel Bell and his successor, William Bennett.

Five years after the release of *A Time for Results*, forty states mandated some form of assessment for their respective university systems. The Southern Association of Colleges and Schools (SACS) and the North Central Association of Colleges and Schools became the first regional accreditation organizations to require member institutions to adopt assessment plans and, following an executive order by Secretary Bennett in 1988, the remaining accreditors followed suit. By 1993, 98% of colleges and universities claimed to have developed or were in the process of developing assessment plans (Ewell 2002, 13).

THE ASSESSMENT MOVEMENT AND POLITICAL SCIENCE

A FOLLOWER, NOT A LEADER:
POLITICAL SCIENTISTS AND ASSESSMENT IN THE 1980S

With the exception of a few departments at institutions that were ahead of the assessment trend (Thompson 1991; Magruder and Young 1996; O'Brien et al. 1996), political science faculty showed little interest in outcomes assessment when the movement began. A national survey of political science departments, conducted by Julian, Chamberlain, and Seay (1991), revealed that less than one-sixth of responding programs had stated policies mandating collection of certain kinds of outcomes data. Nearly all of those departments with mandated assessment programs were accredited by SACS or North Central, which were leaders in the assessment movement, as noted above.

Though over one-half of all respondents in the Julian et al. survey replied that they had plans to increase their assessment efforts in the near future, the results were disappointing to the authors. Noting the negative comments from several respondents, who questioned the need for gathering outcomes data and the uses to which external actors may put assessment results, they observed little awareness within the discipline of the power of the assessment wave:

> While it is understandable that a professor may care little for the idea of measuring outcomes, it is much more difficult to understand how political scientists could be ignorant of such a massive educational and political movement (Julian, Chamberlain, and Seay 1991, 208).

TOWARD ASSESSMENT IN POLITICAL SCIENCE: THE WAHLKE REPORT

Around the time of the 1991 assessment survey of political science departments, however, the results of a national project to reform undergraduate majors were released. Following up on its 1985 report, *Integrity in the College Classroom*, AAC enlisted twelve learned societies, including the American Political Science Association, to examine the state of their respective undergraduate majors among member institutions and formulate recommendations that would lead to greater structure and coherence in major programs (Zemsky 1989; Association of American Colleges 1991).

Appointed by Lucian Pye, then President of APSA, the Task Force on the Political Science Major, chaired by former APSA President John Wahlke, discovered that few departments organized major programs that exposed students to core subject matter of the discipline, provided sequential learning, or promoted integration of students' knowledge. Published by AAC and reprinted in *PS: Political Science & Politics* as a "Report to the Profession" in 1991, the "Wahlke Report" called for a model political science curriculum that would:

1. introduce students to a common set of core topics;
2. develop intellectual skills (analysis, writing, research, oral presentation);

3. provide opportunities to experience at least one real-life political situation off-campus (internships, Washington and state capital seminars, political participation, study abroad); and

4. provide sequential learning that culminates in a *senior capstone experience* that "requires and assists students to survey their whole learning experience, to recognize the interconnections among its pieces, and to comprehend the limitations of our collective knowledge as well as the gaps in our individual knowledge"— e.g., senior seminar, research paper, series of colloquia, senior thesis, comprehensive examinations (Wahlke 1991, 55).

Without using the word "assessment" (the section of the report was titled "Evaluation"), the Wahlke Report made specific comments about the lack of attention to outcomes assessment in the discipline. With regard to individual student performance, the study remarked, "Evaluation of students' overall performance is the most neglected element of the major program...often amount[ing] to little more than a summation of discrete performances in the courses taken..." Departments were urged to:

1. define the goals and standards students are expected to reach, emphasizing not merely quantity of information retained but the coherence and interconnectedness of their knowledge and their analytic ability in dealing with new problems and situations;

2. devise or acquire examination and testing instruments appropriate to measuring progress against those benchmarks; and

3. analyze the evaluation process (and results) regularly and update it frequently (Wahlke 1991, 56).

Moving beyond assessment of student learning to program assessment, the Wahlke Report stated, "Evaluation of the effectiveness of the political science program itself is an equally important, even more rarely addressed, problem." Traditional measures of program effectiveness, such as productivity of faculty members, comparing GPA in the major to that of other majors, and performance in standardized exams were "totally unjustified," the task force asserted. "We urge the APSA," advised the report,

"... to develop and seek support for a study of ways to make reliable and valid evaluations of program performance" (Wahlke 1991, 56).

THE IMPACT OF THE WAHLKE REPORT ON ASSESSMENT IN POLITICAL SCIENCE

Though the Wahlke Report is better known for its recommendations to reform the undergraduate major (Ishiyama, Bruening, and Lopez 2006), it has also been viewed as a strong statement on the need for outcomes assessment in political science at both the classroom and program levels (Bennett 1991). Another way to interpret the report is as a transitional document that called for accountability but did not fully embrace the practice of assessment. Not only did the report avoid the "a-word" in favor of "evaluation," it did not explicitly mention how the results of evaluation can be used to improve individual student or program performance. By aggregating the results of student performances in the senior capstone seminar, for example, political science programs and faculty could measure how well they are promoting student learning. To use language from the assessment literature, the report appeared to be more concerned with whether students and programs have met learning goals (summative evaluation) than with providing feedback for improvement (formative evaluation).

Whether or not the Wahlke Report was a call to political scientists to join the assessment movement, it does not appear that the report had much direct effect on political science programs. Surveying departments nationwide, Kelly and Klunk (2003) showed that only 40% of departments reported that they required a senior capstone course in the major. This finding was similar to what Ishiyama (2005) discovered more recently in a review of Midwestern colleges and universities. Finding that less than 20% of political science programs in the Midwest contained the minimum required courses recommended by the Wahlke Report (common introductory course, research methods course, and a capstone), Ishiyama concluded that the report had little impact on undergraduate, liberal arts institutions.

A GLASS HALF-FULL (OR EMPTY): PROMOTING PROGRAM ASSESSMENT IN THE 1990S

Discussion of program assessment in the aftermath of the Wahlke Report was included in the APSA Roundtable for Department Chairpersons at the 1993 annual meeting. The subject did not appear again on the agenda of the annual conference for department chairs until 1996. APSA department chair sessions devoted to program assessment continued for the next two years. The 1998 and 1999 sessions also focused on the role of assessment in evaluating faculty performance. Evidence of the lack of attention to assessment from political science faculty came in a 1994 survey of how teaching was evaluated in political science departments. Most respondents used student evaluations, peer classroom visits, and faculty self-assessments for evidence of successful teaching. Less than 10%, however, used outcomes data, in terms of measurement of how many students achieve a specified level of competency or skill (Fox and Keeter 1996).

Increased attention to program assessment at APSA annual meetings was no doubt related to outcomes assessment mandates from the states or regional accreditation associations. By 2000, over one-half of undergraduate-only political science departments and 45% of departments offering graduate programs were involved at some stage of developing learning assessment programs (Kelly and Klunk 2003). Kelly and Klunk observed that some programs appeared to be developing and using assessment instruments, such as capstone courses and surveys, before adopting learning objectives for students, perhaps indicating that many departments were "muddling through" the assessment process.

Regardless of the route taken, assessment had some impact on political science programs. Around one-fifth of programs responding to the Kelly and Klunk survey reported making major changes to the curriculum as a result of assessment, one-third added courses to the major, and one-sixth revised their capstone course to address deficiencies in analytical techniques or research methods. Conversely, 37% of departments reported making no changes to their program, either because it was too early in the assessment process, the process confirmed no need to make changes, or no assessment was taking place.

CATCHING A WAVE:
PROMOTING CLASSROOM ASSESSMENT IN THE 1990s

While work on assessment of political science programs proceeded gradually in the 1990s, scholarship in classroom assessment—embedded in discussion of the scholarship of teaching and learning (SoTL)—increased dramatically. Whereas the 1991 APSA annual meeting featured no panels on teaching political science or assessment, the 1994 program included five panels in a new division on teaching and learning in political science. Joining the dialogue in 1997 was a new organized section within APSA on undergraduate education. The two divisions combined for 10 panels at the 1997 annual meeting, then averaged 17 panels between 1998 and 2001.

This surge of interest in teaching and learning at APSA annual meetings was confirmed by a survey of articles, papers, and short courses by political scientists in a sample of conferences and publications from 1990 to 2001. Kehl (2002) calculated a six-fold annual increase in SoTL in the 1998–2001 period over that recorded in 1990–97. The greatest increases were in the areas of civic education, use of technology, and—most connected to classroom assessment—curriculum development and innovative teaching practices.

THE MOVEMENT FULLY JOINED: POLITICAL SCIENCE AND ASSESSMENT IN THE 21ST CENTURY

In recent years, assessment activities in political science at both the classroom and program levels have expanded. The annual APSA Teaching and Learning Conference (TLC), inaugurated in 2004, has become the major venue for discussion of assessment at the classroom and program levels. A search of Political Research Online for papers on teaching and learning from 2004 to June 2008 that include variations on the word "assessment" revealed that 45 of 83 presentations were delivered at the APSA TLC among the international, national, and regional political science conferences covered by the service. The 2006 TLC alone included three tracks on assessment involving 75 participants from a diverse array of institutions, the largest area of interest by far. Focusing not just on how-to issues but also research in assessment, TLC assessment papers are now available to members of the profession online and each year's track summaries are published in *PS: Political Science & Politics* (Axel et al. 2006).

What explains the rapid growth of assessment interest and scholarship in political science? One reason is that more departments are undergoing institutional requirements to conduct program assessment and, as a result, are looking for suitable models and resources. In addition to attending assessment meetings organized by APSA, regional accrediting associations and national organizations, such as the American Association of Colleges and Universities, departments and faculty can consult a broad literature in the general field of student learning and assessment. Some of the more influential works advocate teaching scholarship and its assessment (Wingspread Group 1993; Glassick, Huber, and Maeroff 1997) and provide greater evidence on what college students learn and how (Pascarella and Terenzini 1991; 2005). Those interested principally in assessment have a wider array of conceptual papers (Astin 1991; Anderson et al. 1997) and practical manuals for conducting classroom and program assessment (Angelo and Cross 1993; Banta et al. 1996; Walvoord and Anderson 1998; Palomba and Banta 2002) with which to work.

Second, foundations and government agencies, including Carnegie, Lilly, Pew, Mellon, and the Fund for the Improvement of Post-Secondary Education, have increased support for SoTL proposals from institutions and individuals (Hutchings and Shulman 1999). Teaching and learning centers were established at educational institutions large and small, and the number of outlets for SoTL publication multiplied.

Third and most importantly to members of the political science profession, APSA and interested groups of political scientists are providing greater opportunities for members to engage in the scholarship of teaching and learning. The APSA Conference on Teaching and Learning is the most significant initiative, but it is not the only one.

Within APSA, the Political Science Education (PSE) section has provided leadership to assessment efforts. Together with the division on Teaching and Learning in Political Science, PSE offered an average of 14 panels on issues in teaching scholarship at annual meetings between 2002 and 2007. At these meetings, the section sponsored short courses and panels on program and classroom assessment. In 2005, PSE launched the *Journal of Political Science Education*, thus providing a new outlet for assessment scholarship (Deardorff and Folger 2005).

Of course, APSA continued to sponsor programs for department chairs (Campbell et al. 2007) and the general membership. One symposium worthy of note was a roundtable on SoTL at the 2001 annual meeting, featuring Pat Hutchings from the Carnegie Foundation for the Advancement of Teaching (Clarke et al. 2002). *PS: Political Science & Politics* still published articles on program assessment (Deardorff and Posler 2005) and classroom learning. The APSA website provided departments with links to resources on learning outcomes and a sample of assessment models from a variety of institutions.

Not to be ignored, the International Studies Association (ISA) and regional and state political science associations have promoted discussions of assessment at their annual meetings. The review of assessment presentations from Political Research Online since 2004 showed that papers on classroom or program assessment were delivered at ISA, the Midwest Political Science Association, and the Western Political Science Association in most years.

It should be noted that the accelerated assessment activity in political science is part of a larger trend nationally to ground assessment in disciplinary communities. As Ewell (2006) explained, the increased focus on disciplines made greater sense to assessment advocates, since assessment approaches, such as definitions of critical thinking and how to assess it, differ from field to field. Furthermore, faculty members tend to listen more carefully to disciplinary colleagues than they might to administrators charged with implementing assessment programs.

While the discipline of political science has intensified its efforts to promote assessment, there is still a long way to go. Compared to other disciplines, particularly the natural sciences, mathematics, and the professions, political science was slow to embrace SoTL (Witman and Richlin 2007), in which discussion of assessment issues is usually located. Some of the reasons, such as the lack of incentives for conducting teaching scholarship in the profession and the long-time domination of large research universities in the APSA leadership, are not unlike conditions in other social sciences and the arts and humanities. Other explanations are more unique to political science, including a disciplinary culture that is ambivalent at best about efforts at civic education and the absence of an organizational framework for political scientists interested in teaching and learning to share concerns (Ishiyama, Breuning, and Lopez 2006).

Though some obstacles to promoting assessment have been removed, important issues remain. One is the ongoing concern within the profession about assessment as an accountability mechanism. At the very least, assessment could limit the autonomy of political scientists to determine what students should learn and how to promote desired learning, a development familiar to observers of standards-based assessment in history (Weiner and Benzinger 2005). An overarching concern of assessment track participants at successive APSA TLC meetings was that "if political science does not govern its own discipline with respect to assessment, someone else would" (Axel et al. 2006).[1]

In addition to anxiety about external actors using assessment in ways unfavorable to the discipline, many in political science are concerned about the profession's commitment to assessment as a tool for improvement. Assessment track participants at the 2006 TLC stated that despite the APSA's recent efforts to promote assessment, it was not doing enough. APSA should "become more engaged in the national discussion on assessment, help develop testing instruments that are germane to the discipline [a recommendation reminiscent of the Wahlke Report]…, and take a leadership role in coordinating resources and training for assessment in the profession" (Axel et al. 2006).

A major challenge that political science faces in future assessment efforts is for the profession to come to agreement on what the goals of political science education should be. Forty years before the Wahlke Report, the last major APSA study on the political science curriculum recommended that the goal of political science education should be producing a "good democratic citizen" (Dimock et al. 1951; Fesler et al. 1951). Wahlke did not endorse civic education as an aim for political study, but instead argued that the goal of a political science major should be to turn "politically interested and concerned students, whatever their career plans or their other interests, into politically literate college graduates." That is, the major should "maximize students' capacity to analyze and interpret the significance and dynamics of political events and governmental processes" (Wahlke 1991, 49–50).

Given the limited impact of the Wahlke Report, however, some members of the political science profession have argued for a reexamination of the report and a new debate on the goals of political science education (Ishiyama 2005). If the assessment movement can promote that kind of discussion on individual campuses and at a meaningful cross-institutional level, the opportunity exists for political scientists to make a unique contribution to the scholarship and practice of assessment specifically and to the undergraduate curriculum in general.

NOTE

1. Reinforcing this fear were the 2006 recommendations of the commission appointed by U.S. secretary of education Margaret Spellings, which called upon colleges to measure student achievement on a value-added basis, taking into account students' academic baseline, and report the results "publicly in aggregate form to provide consumers and policy makers an accessible, understandable way to measure the relative effectiveness of different colleges and universities" (The Secretary of Education's Commission 2006, 4). In early 2007, Secretary Spellings attempted through the federal rulemaking process to require the regional accrediting associations to set minimum levels of acceptable performance by institutions on measures of how much their students learn. Higher education organizations opposed the effort, saying that using federal regulation to implement the Spelling recommendations bypasses Congress and could politicize the accreditation process.

REFERENCES

Anderson, Caitlin, Barbara L. Cambridge, and Lion F. Gardiner, eds. 1997. "Principles of Good Practice for Assessing Student Learning." In *Learning Through Assessment: A Resource Guide for Higher Education*. Washington, D.C.: American Association for Higher Education.

Angelo, Thomas A., and K. Patricia Cross. 1993. *Classroom Assessment Techniques: A Handbook for College Teachers*. 2nd ed. San Francisco: Jossey-Bass.

Association of American Colleges. 1985. *Integrity in the College Curriculum: A Report to the Academic Community*. Washington, D.C.: Association of American Colleges.

———. 1991. *The Challenge of Connecting Learning*. Washington: Association of American Colleges.

Astin, Alexander W. 1977. *Four Critical Years*. San Francisco: Jossey-Bass.

———. 1991. *Assessment for Excellence: The Philosophy and Practice of Assessment and Evaluation in Higher Education*. New York: American Council on Education.

Axel, Donna, Gordon Babst, Elizabeth Bennion, John Berg, Amy Brandon, Mitchell Brown, Lisa A. Cave, et al. 2006. "APSA Teaching and Learning Conference Track Summaries." *PS: Political Science & Politics* 39 (July): 533–44.

Banta, Trudy W., ed. 1986. *Performance Funding in Higher Education: A Critical Analysis of Tennessee's Experience*. Boulder, CO: National Center for Higher Education Management Systems.

Banta, Trudy W., Jon P. Lund, Karen E. Black, and Frances W. Oblander, eds. 1996. *Assessment in Practice: Putting Principles to Work on College Campuses*. San Francisco: Jossey-Bass.

Banta, Trudy W., and Associates, eds. 2002. *Building a Scholarship of Assessment*. San Francisco: Jossey-Bass.

Bell, Terrel H. 1988. *The Thirteenth Man: A Reagan Cabinet Memoir*. New York: Free Press.

Bennett, Douglas C. 1991. "Political Science within the Liberal Arts: Towards Renewal of Our Commitment." *PS: Political Science & Politics* 24 (June): 201–04.

Bennett, William J. 1984. *To Reclaim a Legacy: A Report on the Humanities in Higher Education*. Washington, D.C.: National Endowment for the Humanities.

Bloom, Allan. 1987. *The Closing of the American Mind*. New York: Simon and Schuster.

Boyer, Ernest L. 1987. *College: The Undergraduate Experience in America*. New York: Harper & Row.

Campbell, Kenneth J., Michelle D. Deardorff, Kerstin Hamann, and Linda Suskie. 2007. "2006 Workshop for Department Chairs — Planning for Assessment and Accountability Issues." *PS: Political Science & Politics* 40 (January): 99–103.

Clarke, Susan E., Pat Hutchings, Scott Keeter, Grant Reeher, Yvette Alex-Assensoh, and Frank Boyd. 2002. "Transcript: Roundtable on the Scholarship of Teaching and Learning in Political Science." *PS: Political Science & Politics* 35 (June): 223–28.

Cross, K. Patricia, and Thomas A. Angelo. 1988. *Classroom Assessment Techniques: A Handbook for Faculty*. Ann Arbor: National Center for Research to Improve Post-Secondary Teaching and Learning, University of Michigan.

Deardorff, Michelle D., and Paul J. Folger. 2005. "Assessment that Matters: Integrating the 'Chore' of Department-Based Assessment with Real Improvements in Political Science Education." *Journal of Political Science Education* 1 (3): 277–87.

Deardorff, Michelle D., and Brian D. Posler. 2005. "The Mission-Driven Department: Benefits of Departmental Assessment." *PS: Political Science & Politics* 38 (April): 273–76.

Dimock, Marshall E., Howard M. Dorr, Claud E. Hawley, E. Allen Helms, Andrew E. Nuqist, Ruth G. Weintraub, and Howard White. 1951. *Goals for Political Science: Report of the Committee for the Advancement of Teaching*, American Political Science Association. New York: William Sloane Associates, Inc.

Ewell, Peter T. 1997. "Accountability and Assessment in a Second Decade: New Looks or Same Old Story?" In *Assessing Impact: Evidence and Action*, ed. Peter T. Ewell. Washington, D.C.: American Association for Higher Education, 7-22.

———. 2002. "An Emerging Scholarship: A Brief History of Assessment." In *Building a Scholarship of Assessment*, eds. Trudy W. Banta and Associates. San Francisco: Jossey-Bass, 3–25.

———. 2006. "Assessing Assessment: The SAUM Evaluator's Perspective." In *Supporting Assessment in Undergraduate Mathematics*, eds. Lynn Arthur Steen, Bonnie Gold, Laurie Hopkins, Dick Jardine, and William A. Marion. Washington, D.C.: Mathematical Association of America, 19-26.

Fesler, James, Louis Hartz, John H. Hallowell, Victor G. Rosenblum, Walter H.C. Laves, W.A. Robson, and Lindsay Rogers. 1951. "Goals for Political Science: A Discussion." *American Political Science Review* 45 (December): 996–1024.

Fox, J. Clifford, and Scott Keeter. 1996. "Improving Teaching and Its Evaluation: A Survey of Political Science Departments." *PS: Political Science & Politics* 29 (June): 174–80.

Glassick, Charles E., Mary Taylor Huber, and Gene I. Maeroff. 1997. *Scholarship Assessed: Evaluation of the Professoriate.* San Francisco: Jossey-Bass.

Hutchings, Pat, and Lee S. Shulman. 1999. "The Scholarship of Teaching: New Elaborations, New Developments." *Change* 31 (5): 5, 10–15.

Ishiyama, John. 2005. "Examining the Impact of the Wahlke Report: Surveying the Structure of the Political Science Curricula at Liberal Arts Colleges and Universities in the Midwest." *PS: Political Science & Politics* 35 (March): 71–74.

Ishiyama, John, Marijke Breuning, and Linda Lopez. 2006. "A Century of Continuity and (Little) Change in the Undergraduate Political Science Curriculum." *American Political Science Review* 100 (November): 659–65.

Julian, Frank H., Don H. Chamberlain, and Robert A. Seay. 1991. "A National Status Report on Outcomes Assessment by Departments of Political Science." *PS: Political Science & Politics* 24 (June): 205–08.

Kehl, Jenny. 2002. "Indicators of the Increase of Political Science Scholarship on Teaching and Learning in Political Science." *PS: Political Science & Politics* 35 (June): 229–32.

Kelly, Marisa, and Brian E. Klunk. 2003. "Learning Assessment in Political Science Departments: Survey Results." *PS: Political Science & Politics* 36 (July): 457–60.

Kingdon, John W. 2003. *Agendas, Alternatives and Public Policies.* 2nd ed. New York: Longman.

Light, Richard J. 1990. *The Harvard Assessment Seminars: Exploration with Students and Faculty about Teaching, Learning and Student Life.* Cambridge, MA: Harvard University Graduate School of Education.

Magruder, W. Jack, and Candace Cartwright Young. 1996. "Value-Added Talent Development in General Education." In *Assessment in Practice: Putting Principles to Work on College Campuses,* ed. Trudy W. Banta, Jon P. Lund, Karen E. Black and Frances W. Oblander. San Francisco: Jossey-Bass, 169–77.

National Commission on Excellence in Education. 1983. *A Nation at Risk: The Imperative for Educational Reform.* Washington, D.C.: U.S. Government Printing Office.

National Governors Association. 1986. *Time for Results: The Governors' 1991 Report on Education.* Washington, D.C.: National Governors Association.

O'Brien, Jean, Stephanie Bressler, John Ennis, and Mark Michael. 1996. "The Sophomore-Junior Diagnostic Project." In *Assessment in Practice: Putting Principles to Work on College Campuses,* ed. Trudy Banta, Jon Lund, Karen Black, and Frances Oblander. San Francisco: Jossey-Bass, 89–99.

Palomba, Catherine A., and Trudy W. Banta. 1999. *Assessment Essentials: Planning, Implementing, and Improving Assessment in Higher Education.* San Francisco: Jossey-Bass.

Pascarella, Ernest, and Patrick T. Terenzini. 1991. *How College Affects Students: Findings and Insights from Twenty Years of Research.* San Francisco: Jossey-Bass.

———. 2005. *How College Affects Students: Vol. 2. A Third Decade of Research.* San Francisco: Jossey-Bass.

Study Group on the Conditions of Excellence in American Higher Education. 1984. *Involvement in Learning: Realizing the Potential of American Higher Education.* Washington, D.C.: National Institute of Education.

The Secretary of Education's Commission of the Future of Higher Education. 2006. *A Test of Leadership: Charting the Future of U.S. Higher Education.* Washington, D.C.: Department of Education.

Thompson, Joan Hulse. 1991. "Outcomes Assessment: One Department's Experience with Portfolios and Outside Evaluators." *PS: Political Science & Politics* 24 (December): 715–19.

Wahlke, John C. 1991. "Liberal Learning and the Political Science Major: A Report to the Profession." *PS: Political Science & Politics* 24 (March): 48–60.

Walvoord, Barbara, and Virginia Johnson Anderson. 1998. *Effective Grading: A Tool for Learning and Assessment.* San Francisco: Jossey-Bass.

Weiner, Richard, and Karl Benzinger. 2005. "Assessment Governance: Standards, Rubrics and Self-Regulation." Presented at the Second Annual Conference on Teaching and Learning of the American Political Science Association, Washington, D.C.

Wingspread Group on Higher Education. 1993. *An American Imperative: Higher Expectations for Higher Education.* Racine, WI: Johnson Foundation.

Witman, Paul D., and Laurie Richlin. 2007. "The Status of the Scholarship of Teaching and Learning in the Disciplines." *International Journal for the Scholarship of Teaching and Learning* 1 (1): 1–17.

Zemsky, Robert. 1989. *Structure and Coherence: Measuring the Undergraduate Curriculum.* Washington, D.C.: Association of American Colleges.

II

DEPARTMENTAL AND PROGRAM ASSESSMENT

JOHN ISHIYAMA, UNIVERSITY OF NORTH TEXAS

COMPARING LEARNING ASSESSMENT PLANS IN POLITICAL SCIENCE[1]

The issue of student learning assessment is extremely important for our discipline. Not only is it important to address because of external pressures colleges and universities are facing from accrediting agencies and state legislatures, but also because of the growing interest in assessment in political science itself (exemplified in part by the presence of three "tracks" with nearly 50 participants in the 2007 APSA Teaching and Learning Conference). Nonetheless, there are very few resources and models available for political scientists interested in developing a departmental assessment program. Further, most existing studies of assessment in political science tend to be single case studies, reflecting individual departmental experiences.

Unlike individual case studies, this study conducts a broadly comparative analysis of assessment programs. Although this chapter does not claim to be a complete survey of the existing programs, it seeks to partially fill the gap in the literature by providing information on assessment plans across the nation. It should also be emphasized that there is no single "cookie-cutter approach" to developing an assessment program and that the various departments should use a variety of techniques that fit their needs. However, this chapter surveys some of the more commonly used techniques in political science, and notes commonly used techniques that are often found in various political science programs.

To begin, it is necessary to provide some general sense of what is meant by "assessment." Basically, assessment is "an ongoing process of understanding and improving student learning" (Angelo 1995). This involves, among other things, making expectations explicit and public;

setting appropriate criteria and high standards for learning; systematically gathering and interpreting evidence; measuring outcomes by expectation; and using results to explain and improve performance. Further assessment works best when the programs it seeks to improve have clear, explicitly stated purposes (AAHE 1991).

Although there are a number of different assessment techniques, generally, as Wright (2005) suggests, one can distinguish between assessment techniques that require considerable additional effort to implement and those that require fewer institutional or departmental resources. For example, techniques such as review of existing coursework for signs of student learning, examination of student grades/performance, examination of existing course syllabi, or student course evaluation require relatively little additional changes to existing departmental offerings and little in the way of adopting techniques beyond what faculty do as part of their day-to-day activities. However, although easy to use, several of these techniques assess what is taught rather than what students are learning (such as syllabi analyses or evaluations of transcripts for courses taken). On the other hand, other techniques, outside of the normal classroom operations, such as comprehensive examinations, exit interviews, alumni surveys, portfolio analyses, capstone experiences, or graduating-student surveys/questionnaires, go well beyond the regular operations of faculty members.

Recently, there have been a number of articles that have described assessment efforts in a number of individual political science programs (see Hill 2005; Deardorff 2005; Deardorff and Folger 2005). In addition, the American Political Science Association (APSA) has developed a website that focuses on sharing examples of several individual assessment programs in political science (see www.apsanet.org/section_562.cfm). However, despite the recent attention in the APSA to assessment, with few exceptions, little has been done that has surveyed the kinds of assessment techniques being used by political departments, nor have any studies examined the institutional/departmental variables that are associated with variations in assessment plans.

There have been two recent exceptions, both of which sought to comparatively investigate political science assessment plans. The first, by Kelly and Klunk (2003), examined 213 responses to a questionnaire they distributed that asked department chairs to self-report learning objectives and assessment techniques employed by their respective programs. The study also asked questions about resources available, and whether departments believed that assessment had helped to change the political science curriculum. This study was the first real comparative study of assessment plans in political science and it has contributed greatly to our general understanding of trends in departments across the country. However, Kelly and Klunk did not systematically examine differences across different types of institutions and departments (such as differences between private and public institutions, large and small departments in terms of number of faculty, etc.), particularly in terms of whether such differences correlated with the assessment techniques employed. Second, as is the problem with all self-reported survey studies, what department chairs may say they do in response to an anonymous survey may be very different from what is actually officially reported or actually practiced.

A second study, by Ishiyama and Breuning (2008), content analyzed the assessment plans for 50 political science programs across the country. The data was updated for this chapter (to include 70 data points). The data was compiled via an Internet search of various assessment plans posted publicly by political science departments. Since many students narrow down their choice of colleges by examining their websites as a prelude (or sometimes alternative) to a campus visit, websites are becoming an important tool for universities to advertise and explain their majors. It is also an important way to make public to students, parents, administrators at other institutions, and others the way in which political science programs measure the impact they have on students. Although it is certainly true that many departments may not post their assessment plans online, there are enough that do to illustrate the wide variety of techniques that are employed (which, as mentioned above, is likely to be useful for departments considering developing their own assessment plans). Further, while deriving data from university websites may have its limitations, it also provides important insights into each university's offerings as well as an efficient way to gather comparative data.

This study expands upon the earlier Ishiyama and Breuning (2008) study and examined the explicit assessment plans at seventy political science programs that appeared on university and college web pages and, unlike Kelly and Klunk (2003), examined whether different assessment plans were related to such institutional/departmental characteristics such as the extent to which the institution is selective in admissions, the student/faculty ratio, and the highest degree offered in political science by the department. Table 4-1 reports the schools included in this study.

Table 4-1. List of Schools Included in the Study

School	State	School	State
Alabama A&M University	Alabama	Southeastern Louisiana State University	Louisiana
Arizona State University	Arizona	Southern Utah University	Utah
Arkansas Technical University	Arkansas	Southwest Baptist University	Missouri
Baylor University	Texas	St. Ambrose University	Iowa
Bowling Green State University	Ohio	SUNY – Fredonia	New York
Cal State – Sacramento	California	Tennessee Technical University	Tennessee
Cal State – San Bernardino	California	Truman State University	Missouri
Caldwell College	New Jersey	University of Alaska – Anchorage	Alaska
Calvin College	Michigan	University of Arkansas – Little Rock	Arkansas
Carthage College	Wisconsin	University of Michigan – Flint	Michigan
College of New Jersey	New Jersey	Union College	Kentucky
College of St. Benedict/ St. Johns University	Minnesota	University of Maine – Farmington	Maine
Eastern Illinois University	Illinois	University of Alaska – Fairbanks	Alaska
Fort Lewis College	Colorado	University of Central Arkansas	Arkansas
Georgia Southwestern University	Georgia	University of Central Florida	Florida
		University of Colorado	Colorado
Georgia State University	Georgia	University of Georgia	Georgia
Indiana University South Bend	Indiana	University of Illinois	Illinois
Indiana University East	Indiana	University of Montana	Montana
Indiana University / Purdue University – Indianapolis	Indiana	University of Nebraska – Kearney	Nebraska
Kansas State University	Kansas	University of Nebraska	Nebraska
Kent State University	Ohio	University of South Florida	Florida
Longwood University	Virginia	University of Southern Mississippi	Mississippi
Louisiana Technical University	Louisiana	University of Wisconsin – Madison	Wisconsin
Minnesota State University – Mankato	Minnesota	University of Wisconsin – River Falls	Wisconsin
Montana State University	Montana	University of Wisconsin – Whitewater	Wisconsin
North Carolina State University	North Carolina	University of Nevada – Las Vegas	Nevada
Northern Illinois University	Illinois	University of South Florida – St. Petersburg	Florida
Northern Arizona University	Arizona		
Oakland University	Michigan	Utah State University	Utah
Ohio University	Ohio	Virginia Technical University	Virginia
Oklahoma State University	Oklahoma	Weber State University	Utah
Old Dominion University	Virginia	Western Carolina University	North Carolina
Providence College	Rhode Island	Western Michigan University	Michigan
Southeast Missouri State University	Missouri	Westmont College	California
Seton Hall University	New Jersey	Wright State University	Ohio

Seventy political science departmental assessment plans were identified from an Internet search (we used every program that appeared using the keyword searches for "assessment program," "assessment plan," and "political science"). The programs were coded not only for the assessment techniques but also for institutional characteristics. These characteristics included: the extent to which schools were selective (based upon data from *U.S. News & World Report*, 2006), the student/faculty ratio, and the highest degree offered by the program. Of the 70 schools, 1 was least selective, 9 were less selective, 42 were selective, and 18 were more selective. Thirty-four schools had a student/faculty ratio at 17 and below (with a low of 12), and 37 had a student/faculty ratio above 17 (with a high of 28). Fifty-nine of the schools were public institutions and eleven were private colleges or universities. Twelve political science departments offered a Ph.D., 24 offered a master's level degree (including MA and MPA degrees), and 34 offered only bachelor's degrees.

SOME COMPARATIVE DATA ON LEARNING OUTCOMES AND ASSESSMENT TECHNIQUES

In the following section, I provide the results of both the Kelly and Klunk (2003) study and the updated data set from Ishiyama and Breuning (2008). Table 4-2 reports the learning outcomes that were most frequently mentioned by political science departments in both studies. As indicated in *both* studies, the top four most commonly mentioned learning outcomes were: critical thinking, knowledge of the subfields in political science, written communication, and knowledge of theories (all theories, not just political thought) in political science. In the Ishiyama and Breuning study (but not in the Kelly and Klunk study, which did not ask these questions), knowledge of political institutions and processes in the United States (63.8%) and methodology/research skills (62.3%)[1] were also frequently mentioned as goals. On the other hand, citizenship skills (24.6%), career (23.2%), and ethics/values (11.6%) were far less frequently mentioned as goals. Interestingly, there was some disparity in the responses regarding oral communication skills and cultural diversity as goals when comparing the results from the Kelly and Klunk study and the Ishiyama and Breuning study. In the Ishiyama and Breuning study, oral communication and presentation skills were mentioned far more frequently as goals (53.6%) than reported in the Kelly and Klunk study (which reported only 30% of programs mentioning this goal). Further cultivating a sense of cultural diversity was mentioned as an important goal in the written plans of only 17.4% of political science programs—yet, in the Kelly and Klunk study, 26.5% of survey respondents mentioned this as an important goal. Perhaps the disparities are due to what departments officially report that they do (in their written plans) and what they actually practice, or perhaps what they want others to believe they do in response to a survey question. Whatever the case, the differences in these two areas are rather intriguing.

Table 4-2. Learning Outcomes

Learning Outcome	% reported in this study*	% reported in Kelly and Klunk (2003)
Knowledge of Theories	65.2	54.0
Knowledge of Political Institutions and Processes	63.8	Not asked in study
Knowledge of Fields in Political Science	66.7	46.0
Critical Thinking	68.1	55.7
Methods/Research Skills	62.3	Not asked in study
Written Communication Skills	66.7	57.1
Oral Communication/Presentation Skills	53.6	30.7
Citizenship	24.6	Not asked in Study
Career Goals	23.2	Not Asked in Study
Cultural Diversity	17.4	26.5
Ethics/Values	11.6	Not Asked in Study

Table 4-3 reports the most frequently mentioned assessment techniques employed using data from both the Ishiyama and Breuning (2008) study and the Kelly and Klunk (2003) study. As indicated in the table, there were a wide variety of different techniques employed. In both the Kelly and Klunk study and the Ishiyama and Breuning study, senior seminar/capstone courses, senior theses, senior exit interviews, and student portfolio analyses were mentioned in both studies at comparable rates. The Ishiyama and Breuning study included several other assessment techniques not included in the Kelly and Klunk piece. These included the use of a comprehensive exam (either standardized or department designed),[2] analysis of student grades or performance as assessment, random reading of student papers, student course evaluations, alumni surveys/interviews, and syllabi analyses as assessment techniques. Three techniques appeared in the Kelly and Klunk study that did not appear in the Ishiyama and Breuning study: a pre-test/post-test technique, post-test only, and "faculty observations."

Table 4-3. Most Frequently Mentioned Assessment Techniques		
Assessment Technique	% reported in this study	% reported in Kelly and Klunk (2003)
Graduating Student Survey/Questionnaire	50.0	22.2
Analysis of Student Grades/Performance	45.7	Not asked in study
Senior Seminar/Capstone	35.7	39.6
Comprehensive Exam	34.3	Not asked in study
Senior Thesis	32.9	20.3
Senior Exit Interview	24.3	24.1
Portfolio	22.9	17.9
Random Reading of Student Papers	17.1	Not asked in Study
Student Course Evaluations	17.1	Not asked in study
Alumni Survey/Interviews	21.4	Not asked in study
Syllabi Analysis	7.1	Not asked in study
Pre-test/Post-test	Not in study	9.9
Post-test only	Not in study	14.2
Faculty Observations	Not in study	25.0

There appear to be some disparities when comparing the results from the two studies. In the Ishiyama and Breuning (2008) study, the most frequently employed technique was some form of graduating student questionnaire (50.0% of programs used this), whereas only 22.2% of the sample in the Kelly and Klunk study reported using this technique. This disparity may be due to the way in which the two samples were constructed and the fact that the data were collected at different times and in different ways. The Kelly and Klunk study included respondents who reported using no assessment techniques at all (but who had developed learning outcomes and were planning on instituting some form of assessment plan), whereas the Ishiyama and Breuning study included *only* programs that had already developed an assessment program. Thus, one should not make too much of the disparities across columns in Table 4-3. Nonetheless, the most frequently mentioned assessment techniques in both studies are the use of the capstone course, a senior thesis, a senior exit interview, a graduating student survey, and analysis of the student portfolio. Thus, it appears that these are commonly used assessment techniques that have been employed by political science programs across the country.

COMPARING ASSESSMENT TECHNIQUES ACROSS DIFFERENT TYPES OF DEPARTMENTS/INSTITUTIONS

In the literature on assessment (see Wright 2005), there is a distinction made between assessment based on activities that faculty already engage in or that are "internal" to the classroom (such as analysis of grades, reviewing existing coursework for signs of student learning, examinations of existing course syllabi, or student course evaluations) and assessment activities that are "external" to normal classroom operations, such as comprehensive examinations, exit interviews, alumni surveys, portfolio analyses, capstone experiences, or graduating-student surveys/questionnaires. The distinction between internal and external forms is that internal approaches can be accomplished without any additional work by faculty members beyond the day-to-day operation of a class, whereas external approaches require effort (often collaborative between faculty members in a department) outside of classroom activities. Generally, the former can be accomplished without much in the way of additional resources or faculty effort, whereas the latter techniques represent, to some degree, a commitment to assessment that goes well beyond the regular operations of faculty members. Thus, by implication, the use of external techniques represents a more rigorous indicator of the level of commitment to assessment by a political science program.

In this section, I use an updated data set from Ishiyama and Breuning (2008) to investigate differences in assessment techniques employed across 70 undergraduate political science programs to see if the techniques used varied according to departmental and institutional characteristics (since the Kelly and Klunk study did not analyze differences across varied departments and institutions). Figure 4-1 illustrates the distribution of external assessment techniques used, by frequency of schools. As indicated, 9 programs employed none of the external assessment techniques (i.e., they only employed internal techniques), 16 employed at least one, 22 at least two, and 8 at least 3. Only fifteen programs used 4 or more of the external techniques (with 3 political science programs using all 6).

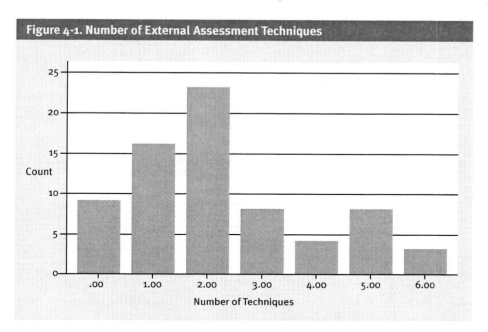

Figure 4-1. Number of External Assessment Techniques

Figure 4-2 compares schools that were more selective to all other schools to examine whether the level of selectivity is related to whether the political science program used external assessment techniques. To ascertain this, we compiled a simple additive index combining the number of external assessment techniques used. The resulting score created values ranging from 0–6.

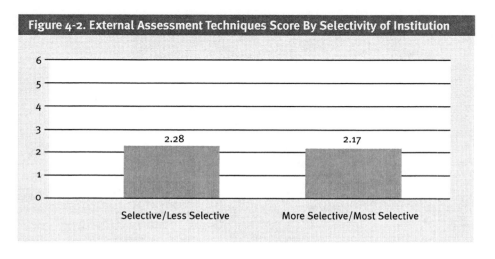

Figure 4-2. External Assessment Techniques Score By Selectivity of Institution

As indicated in Figure 4-2, above, more selective institutions tend to use fewer external assessment techniques on average than less selective institutions. However, a difference of means test indicated that this difference was not statistically significant (t = .26; p = .80). Thus, nothing definitive can be claimed as to whether less selective schools are more likely to employ external assessment techniques than are more selective schools.

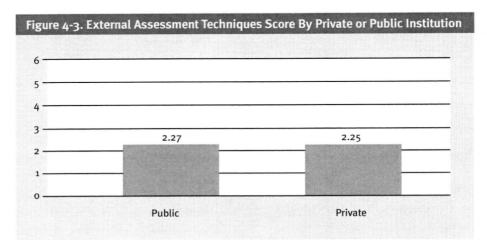

Figure 4-3. External Assessment Techniques Score By Private or Public Institution

Further, Figure 4-3 reports the results for private and public institutions. As indicated, there appears to be no statistically significant difference between public and private institutions (t = .04; p = .97).

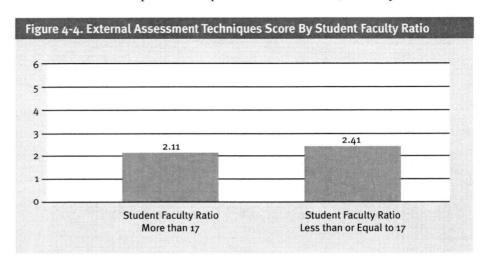

Figure 4-4. External Assessment Techniques Score By Student Faculty Ratio

Figure 4 compares schools in terms of the reported student/faculty ratio at the institution. Although an imperfect measure of the size of the political science undergraduate program (a more direct measure would be the political science student/political science faculty ratio, which was largely unavailable), the measure nonetheless represents an adequate surrogate—it is reasonable to assume that the general student/faculty ratio reflects the student/faculty ratio in political science.

This measure is bifurcated into two categories—schools with student/faculty ratios of more than 17 and student/faculty ratios less than or equal to 17. As mentioned above, this bifurcated the sample into two equal parts (of 25 schools for each category). As indicated, schools with smaller student/faculty ratios were more likely to use external assessment techniques than schools that had a larger student/faculty ratio. However, this difference was not statistically significant ($t = -.77$; $p = .44$)—therefore, nothing conclusive can be said about the relationship between the institutional student/faculty ratio and the propensity of a political science department to employ external assessment techniques.

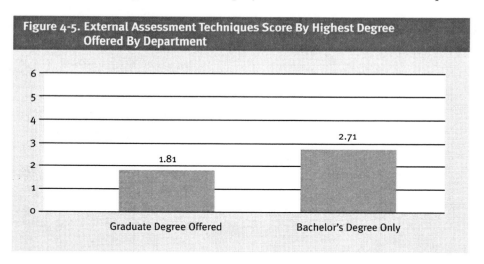

Figure 4-5. External Assessment Techniques Score By Highest Degree Offered By Department

Finally, Figures 4-5 and 4-6 compare the average External Assessment Techniques Scores for political science programs that offer a graduate-level degree with programs that only offer a bachelor's-level degree in political science, and includes consideration of the size of the institution in terms of student population. One might expect that since pressure to adopt assessment programs by state legislatures and accrediting agencies has been directed primarily at undergraduate programs, political science departments that offer only undergraduate degrees would be more likely to adopt external assessment techniques. Further, since bachelor's-only departments are likely to be located at smaller schools, and since external assessment techniques would require less effort with smaller numbers of students, it is more likely that such techniques would be adopted at bachelor's-only departments. Indeed, as Figure 4-5 indicates, bachelor's-degree-only political science departments are, on average, significantly more likely to employ techniques such as exit interviews, comprehensive examinations, and alumni surveys than departments offering graduate degrees (t = -2.39; p = .02). Figure 4-6 further reinforces the observation that smaller institutions are more likely to adopt external assessment techniques than are larger institutions (t = -2.98; p = .004).

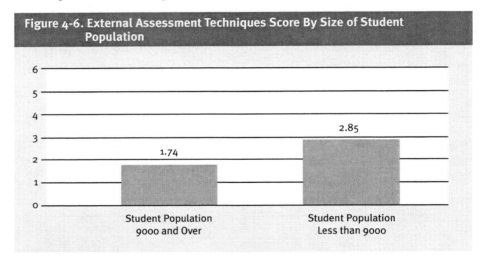

Figure 4-6. External Assessment Techniques Score By Size of Student Population

CONCLUSION

The above chapter provided a brief overview of the existing data on assessment practices of political science departments across the country. As indicated above, there are a wide variety of learning outcomes expressed and assessment techniques employed. Clearly, there is not a single model to conduct student learning assessment. However, there are some discernable patterns that can be identified, which is all the more remarkable given that there has been little discipline-wide guidance as to how to construct an assessment program. It is very interesting that, independently, so many political science departments have hit upon similar learning outcomes and similar kinds of assessment techniques.

Most of the learning outcomes expressed deal directly with the content of the political science discipline and the promotion of critical thinking, writing, and oral communication skills as opposed to the promotion of citizenship and ethics/values. Although many assessment techniques are employed, internal techniques (such as analysis of grades, reviewing existing coursework for signs of student learning, examinations of existing course syllabi, or student course evaluations) are more likely to be used than are external assessment activities (such as comprehensive examinations, exit interviews, alumni surveys, portfolio analyses, capstone experiences, or graduating-student surveys/questionnaires). This may be largely due to the relative ease with which these internal techniques can be implemented when compared to external techniques. However, several of these techniques assess what is taught (such as syllabi analyses or evaluations of transcripts for courses taken) but not what students learn—and this does not necessarily comport with the intent of learning assessment.

In terms of the relationship between institutional and departmental characteristics and assessment techniques, although the use of external assessment activities does not vary by the level of institutional selectivity (considering whether they were public or private institutions, or considering the institution's student/faculty ratio), it does appear to vary according to whether a department offers a graduate degree, and the size of the institution. Primarily undergraduate departments and smaller institutions are more likely to employ external assessment techniques than larger graduate-degree granting departments. This might indicate that the external techniques are more easily implemented at smaller institutions that have smaller class sizes and fewer majors than the larger state institutions. Nonetheless, it is ironic that these institutions are more likely to embrace more expensive assessment techniques, even though they have far fewer resources than do larger institutions. Thus, it is more likely that smaller institutions will engage in the use of external techniques because this reflects the greater emphasis that smaller, primarily undergraduate institutions place on teaching and learning, and these departments seek to go beyond merely employing the easiest assessment techniques to meet the "letter of the law."

As a greater number of political science departments adopt assessment plans, there will be more data available from a variety of different institutions. Perhaps, by documenting the kinds of assessment models that are currently available, this might facilitate greater discussion and more careful consideration of assessment as a useful tool in promoting student learning.

NOTES

1. This chapter is based on a version of the article by the author, "Assessing Assessment: Examining the Assessment Plans at 50 Political Science Departments" (*PS: Political Science & Politics* 41 (January): 167-170).

2. It is important to note that the Kelly and Klunk survey did ask whether departments had adopted the following two learning objectives: (1) "Students should be able to design and conduct political science research projects" and (2) "Students should be able to use quantitative and statistical approaches to political science." Although not entirely the same as the single-indicator methodology research skills (since they were separated into two indicators), their results are informative. They indicate that fewer political science programs emphasize designing research skills (40.2%) than in this study, and fewer still emphasize quantitative approaches (35.5%). The differences are likely due to the more general coding of political science methods I adopted—many departments include in their goal statements "training students in methodology," but do not interpret this to necessarily mean quantitative and statistical methods, nor specifically designing research projects (as in a senior thesis).

3. The Kelly and Klunk (2003) study did mention the use of "pre- and post-tests." In my view, these are not the same as the commonly used comprehensive senior tests that are often employed and produced by ETS (such as the Major Field Test) and hence I did not include their results in the table. Nonetheless, their findings are informative. In their study, they indicated that 24.1% of the study used post-tests of any kind (as compared to 34.7% reported in this study). This difference may be due to the more narrow definition of pre- and post-test as perceived by the survey respondents in the Kelly and Klunk study.

REFERENCES

American Association for Higher Education (AAHE). 1991. *Nine Principles of Good Practice for Assessing Student Learning.* Sterling, VA: Stylus.

Angelo, Thomas A. 1995. "Reassessing (and Defining) Assessment." *AAHE Bulletin* 48 (November): 7–9.

Deardorff, Michelle. 2005. "Assessment Through the Grassroots: Assessing the Department via Student Peer Evaluation." *Journal of Political Science Education* 1 (January): 109–27.

Deardorff, Michelle, and Paul Folger. 2005. "Assessment that Matters: Integrating the 'Chore' of Department-Based Assessment with Real Improvements in Political Science Education." *Journal of Political Science Education* 1 (September): 277–87.

Hill, Jeffrey. 2005. "Developing a Culture of Assessment: Insights from Theory and Experience." *Journal of Political Science Education* 1 (January): 29–37.

Ishiyama, John, and Marijke Breuning. 2008. "Assessing Assessment: Examining the Assessment Plans at 50 Political Science Departments." *PS: Political Science & Politics* 41 (January): 167–70.

Kelly, Marisa, and Brian E. Klunk. 2003. "Learning Assessment in Political Science Departments: Survey Results." *PS: Political Science & Politics* 36 (July): 451–55.

U.S. News & World Report. 2006. "America's Best Colleges." www.usnews.com/usnews/edu/college/rankings/rankindex_brief.php.

Wright, Barbara. 2005. "Assessment Methods—A Close-Up Look." www.apsanet.org/imgtest/Methodscloseup2.doc.

MICHELLE D. DEARDORFF, JACKSON STATE UNIVERSITY
PAUL J. FOLGER, HEARTLAND COMMUNITY COLLEGE

5

MAKING ASSESSMENT MATTER: STRUCTURING ASSESSMENT, TRANSFORMING DEPARTMENTS

Clear expectations from accrediting and legislative bodies, the development of a growing scholarly literature, and threatening conversations from within the Department of Education have forced most disciplines and institutions to recognize the permanence of assessment in higher education. Despite its ubiquitousness, denial of the need for assessing is commonplace. It is axiomatic in many circles that one of the primary barriers to effective disciplinary and departmental assessment has been the resistance of the professoriate. Chairs and assessment coordinators frequently note the resistance of their tenured faculty to any form of summative or formative evaluation as a primary concern. For many professors, the idea of assessment generates a pantheon of concerns: loss of professorial autonomy, distraction from primary departmental goals of teaching and research, and the creation of alien and artificial standards by administrators (Julian et al. 1991). For those of us who have lived through four or five different versions of a university's strategic plan, it is too easy to believe that the emphasis on assessment is simply the latest version of academia's fascination with intellectual fads.

While many chairs recognize the need for program assessment, to be truly effective they must emphasize how to integrate such assessment into the regular work of the faculty. Professors are most cooperative when we believe that assessment can provide tools that enable us better to practice our profession. A recent thread in political science research has been the recognition of the manner by which assessment can positively change an academic department and the educational environment that a department provides its students (Deardorff and Folger

2005; Deardorff and Posler 2005; Smoller 2004). Political scientists have become more accepting of assessment and have been willing to explore the ways in which it may enhance current departmental objectives and programmatic goals (Lasher and Kitts 1998). Some of the research has examined how to clearly and carefully take an articulated departmental goal, such as "excellent teaching," and evaluate that specific expectation (Fox and Keeter 1996). Other articles focus on specific assessment tools, like portfolios and standardized testing, and how best to integrate these elements into departmental norms and culture (Thompson 1991).

The literature demonstrates that faculty engagement in assessment is necessary for its success. We know that "[a]ssessment is most effective when undertaken in an environment that is receptive, supportive, and enabling" (Banta et al. 1996, 62). This requires both university administrative support and faculty engagement. The American Association for Higher Education in its *Principles of Good Practice for Assessing Student Learning* (1992) clearly indicates that assessment works best when the entire institution is committed and involved. They argue that assessment cannot be simply forced from a department chair onto his colleagues or from a higher administrator onto a department and be successful. Unfortunately, the assessment literature in its discussion of departmental assessment frequently ignores the quandary of the department resistant to assessment and instead focuses on idealized implementation processes. This more ideal model, referred to in this chapter as "Structural Implementation" or "Mission-Based" assessment, requires the department to identify key learning objectives that are reinforced through the curriculum and systematically evaluated. This approach is predicated upon departmental and university support (American Association for Higher Education 1992; Astin 1993; Banta et al. 1996; Palomba and Banta 1999).

A recent survey of political science departmental chairs found that over 50% of the responding undergraduate departments and 45% of responding departments with graduate offerings engage in some form of assessment (Kelly and Klunk 2003). However, it was also clear from this study that "the development of learning assessment strategies by departments does not seem to follow the 'ideal type' learning assessment models" (455). In fact, many of the respondents to the survey indicated that they implemented assessment instruments without adopting specific measurable learning objectives.

As anyone who has ever witnessed formal or informal faculty discussions of assessment plans realizes, one of the dominant critiques of assessment is that ideal circumstances frequently do not exist. Department chairs are often charged to produce assessment plans and measurable outcomes without collegial support or the resources necessary to garner such backing; little has been written on leveraging departmental energies for common assessment goals (Deardorff 2007). Regardless of the assessment environment in which a department operates, the only way in which a program will gain faculty cooperation for assessment is if it demonstrates how assessment can provide the tools to enable us to better practice our profession.

The assessment literature clearly demonstrates that there is no single way to create a compelling assessment plan. As Chapter 4 by John Ishiyama (in this volume) demonstrates, political science departments vary widely in the learning outcomes they identify and in the assessment techniques they use. Factors such as selectivity in admissions, existence of graduate programs, and the culture of the institution all impact the type of assessment engaged in or by the department.

Consequently, the process and structure of assessment must reflect the needs and idiosyncrasies of both institutional and departmental communities. Consideration of such characteristics as the percentage of tenured versus non-tenured faculty members in the department, the balance between recent hires accustomed to assessment and more cynical faculty members who have been through multiple university strategic planning cycles, and whether or not the university has a culture of assessment should inform the strategies developed by the chair in creating assessment plans. For example, if a university or college does not have a culture of assessment—forms are filled out, reports are filed, but decisions still appear to be arbitrary and not based on the assessment findings—a chair cannot pressure the department to comply with assessment on the grounds that they will receive external benefits. That approach, on the other hand, would be very effective in a university with a culture of assessment where well-implemented assessment plans result in additional faculty lines and departmental resources. The key to establishing buy-in is leadership from the departmental chair or another respected senior member of the department (see Chapter 6 by Hill and Pastors). The chair must see the potential of assessment in improving quality teaching, research outcomes, and student engagement, as well as departmental quality—regardless of the administrative response. If the chair does not see the transformative potential of assessment, it will be very difficult to convince the faculty.

IDENTIFYING THE APPROPRIATE ASSESSMENT MODEL

As many departments have discovered, a careful assessment plan can generate significant benefits for a department. It can expand our understanding of student learning, connect our departmental objectives to the larger institutional goals, link our students' co-curricular engagement to the major, improve departmental advising, enhance our appeal to external audiences through a more focused presentation, and allow ourselves to adapt rapidly to a changing environment (Smoller 2004). While the results of effective assessment may be universal, the paths departments walk in developing and implementing these plans vary dramatically. The key is to find an approach that best exploits a department's unique situation and opportunities.

This chapter demonstrates two distinct strategies toward departmental assessment. We are sure these strategies are not the only ones available; however, these approaches do demonstrate the variance available in planning for assessment. The *Structural Implementation* or "Mission-Based" approach begins with the establishment of a mission, learning objectives, and the implementation of a subsequent curriculum. This approach will be most effective in newer programs, smaller departments, departments where the chair possesses more authority (e.g., younger faculty, a higher percentage of adjuncts), undergraduate and liberal arts institutions, and in programs where assessment is part of the larger institutional culture. Such a strategy works in these circumstances because, generally, there are fewer faculty vested in keeping things as they are currently structured and more faculty who are willing to rethink the work of the department. The second approach, *Grassroots Implementation* or "Question-Based" assessment, creates an assessment program from the "bottom-up," focusing on concerns and questions emanating from the faculty and utilizes internal means of evaluation to begin building consensus for an assessment program. This approach demonstrates how simple course assessment techniques can easily become the core of a comprehensive departmental assessment plan. Building on successful classroom pedagogy, a department articulates a single shared objective and creates a simple, non-threatening assessment process that could pave the way for more integrated assessment approaches. Grassroots Implementation is most effective in departments where there is strong resistance from the faculty toward discussing issues of teaching and assessment, limited support or incentive provided by the larger institution for faculty engagement, and the chair has no resources to entice cooperation. This approach is less drastic and focuses on faculty buy-in to the assessment process through gradually integrating assessment techniques into the life of the department. If departments are able to identify which structure is most appropriate for their own cultures and circumstances, assessment may be more fruitful for the department. Clearly, there are times when techniques from either model may be valuable to the intrepid chair.

STRUCTURAL IMPLEMENTATION— "MISSION-BASED" ASSESSMENT

Structural implementation requires a department to integrate assessment throughout its curricular and co-curricular offerings. For many departments, reaccreditation or required program reviews are the only times when this sort of reflection and programmatic change occurs. If faculty use assessment to make more frequent, subtle improvements in teaching and to more closely achieve their mission, then specific benefits accrue. This approach to assessment forces faculty to rethink the meaning of the department, the purpose of assessment, and the significance of political science education. It makes assessment a basic part of a deliberately constructed culture—an assessment of intentionality. Assessment becomes part of the scholars' habit of reflection and refinement. We plan, we implement, we assess, and we plan again.

This form of "top-down" assessment requires a strong chair or assessment coordinator, who will be able to encourage or entice faculty engagement. Because this model requires faculty to be engaged or to accept the clear articulation of a mission that will be translated into learning objectives and tested through multiple assessment techniques, a strong institutional assessment environment is generally a prerequisite for this approach. This type of environment is more likely to be found in community colleges, liberal arts schools, or other undergraduate institutions, but may increasingly be found in state schools focusing on assessment mandates from their legislatures. Because of changes in academic socialization, younger faculty are less resistant to issues of assessment and are more likely to cooperate with these departmental initiatives. While having a large number of adjunct faculty is often a disadvantage for a department, it may help make this model more feasible.

Process of Implementation

To demonstrate the implementation of this assessment strategy, we will consider the life of a political science department located at a small private university (see Deardorff and Folger 2005 for a full discussion of this department). The department begins the assessment process by identifying a mission that embodies both the university's identity and the current strengths of the department. The creation of a clear mission ensures that teaching, scholarship, service, planning, and assessment are all evaluated and pursued in light of how each furthers the department's defined purpose. The written mission becomes the center of the department—not just a cliché on paper. This deliberateness (creating a clear vision, providing a written mission, articulating related objectives, defining subsequent values) has many benefits. First, the faculty will focus only on activities that will further their mission. Second, the program has a coherence that appeals to students and furthers the sense of departmental identity; this may have the additional benefit of heightening retention rates. Third, assessment is simple when what is being assessed and the indicators of its success have been identified prior to planning, performing, or evaluating. Finally, in an academic culture of scarce resources, a cohesive department with clearly stated and measurable goals may receive greater administrative support than the stereotypical department governed by the idiosyncrasies of individual faculty.

The department next selects specific goals following from both the departmental and university missions. These objectives focus on defining the knowledge, skills, and values students should possess prior to graduation. The faculty have also identified precisely where in the curriculum, culture, and assessment these objectives are pursued and evaluated. Communicating the mission and its justifications early, and frequently, is vitally important if the department will hold its students to this purpose. By keeping the mission close at hand and commonly understood, they are able to return to it as the yardstick against which all is measured. For example, when their students develop their required internship portfolio, they connect their internship expectations with the stated departmental objectives. This centeredness makes it much easier for faculty to parcel out precious time and resources to most effectively meet their goals, and serves as the touchstone by which they evaluate their process.

The department is able to begin the assessment process by evaluating their strengths and weaknesses in achieving specific learning objectives. Each year, they select one particular aspect of the program to assess in light of the departmental mission and university priorities. The purpose is not to demonstrate that all students meet all objectives; this is not a realistic target and it ignores student responsibility for their own learning. Instead, the program attempts to find ways to improve what the department is doing based not upon impressions but upon qualitative and quantitative evidence. For instance, in the second year, the department could evaluate its success in meeting their objective to develop research skills. To ascertain this, a group of faculty attends the sophomore Research Methods class where formal research presentations are made. By evaluating the students' work against their agreed-upon goals, they are able to improve their Methods instruction. However, they soon face the need for a more comprehensive program assessment, moving beyond mere learning assessment, and they begin the process of evaluating how successful they have been in fulfilling their departmental mission and meeting their overall programmatic objectives.

ASSESSING THE DEPARTMENT: COMPARING PERFORMANCE TO OBJECTIVES

The first step as they begin evaluating the program is to determine current strengths and weaknesses. The department does not want to change for change's sake, but needs to evolve in order to maintain growth and a strong departmental identity. The data they collect comes from a wide variety of sources across and beyond the institution. By making connections with different constituencies and different administrative offices, the department finds that these groups are now vested partners in seeing that their assessment and curriculum development process succeeds. Administrators have assessment reports of their own to make; the success and work of the department allows these administrators to accomplish some of their own goals. While there are many sources of data available to departments, the key is to harness the most valuable and easily accessible data for assessing their mission and program.

The department, cooperating with its Office of Alumni and Development, conducts a survey of alumni. The survey enables the faculty to see how political science alumni perceive the quality of the department's work. For example, the faculty discovers that more recent alumni are more satisfied with the department and major than earlier graduates. For alumni of all ages, one clear negative appears: a perceived lack of course diversity provided by the political science department. According to the alumni, the weakest area in the department is career counseling, matching the university's alumni survey that found dissatisfaction in career counseling and placement.

The second source of data is a survey of the satisfaction of political science majors. This survey asks questions about the majors' satisfaction with the political science curriculum, specific required and elective courses, advising, and the departmental culture in general. Professors selected questions that correspond with a student satisfaction survey annually conducted at the university level. By doing this, they receive comparative data ("Are political science majors more or less satisfied compared to students from the entire university?") and obtain specific opinions and suggestions from current students regarding their observations of the department. In addition, this research has the added benefit of helping students become more engaged in the curricular revision process.

The findings are very positive across the range of questions; the political science department is higher on *every* indicator than the university as a whole. Majors rate the department especially high on "faculty caring" and "accessibility," "rigor," "quality," and "reputation." Upon scrutiny, it becomes evident there are significant differences between students who work more than twenty hours outside of classes and those who do not work such extensive hours. Employed students rate the department lower on a wide variety of questions. This correlation does not occur with other factors (e.g., race, gender, socio-economic status, GPA). One of the strongest positive responses is to the question: "I seldom get the 'run-around' when seeking information from the department"—this is much higher than the whole campus response. The faculty believes that these findings demonstrate their success in creating an academic community, a primary goal articulated in their mission.

The registrar's office provides the numbers and sizes of all the courses that faculty in the Department of Political Science have offered over the past five years in the general and major curricula. These enrollment patterns help determine which courses need to be offered more or less frequently and which do not need to be offered at all. By identifying courses that do not make enrollment targets consistently or are typically oversubscribed, they are able to make decisions that maximize the potential for growth without compromising quality.

In many institutions, the Director of Institutional Research and/ or the Coordinator of Assessment can be a great source of additional data. For our hypothetical department, the university attrition statistics reveal that students switching from political science tend to transfer to majors in business and criminal justice. The department discovers political science majors withdraw from the university at a higher rate than students in other majors, generally citing financial reasons. Well above the university norm when it comes to financial concerns, political science students at this institution focus on getting jobs and being financially successful after graduation. National data demonstrates that the department's political science students are employed for more hours a week than the national norm and seem to have a greater financial need relative to the whole population. Consequently, these students are concerned about future employment and are worried that a political science degree is not useful in the job market. More positively, the department demonstrates through the data that several of their departmental goals are being met, especially when compared to national college student data and to their own university student body.

Through this process, the department changed and reimagined itself and its mission. The department's research demonstrates that it had constructed a strong departmental culture—supporting students through their pedagogy, advising, and providing a rigorous education experience. However, it is weak in one primary area. Both alumni and majors repeatedly noted concerns about their ability to find a job after graduation, despite the fact that students did find employment, albeit not as easily as peers graduating from other departments such as business. Although this theme was articulated in many different motifs, it was a constant message. To that end, the department revised its mission and objectives to focus more clearly on the intersections between theory and practice and to emphasize the development of portable skills. By creating a skill-based curriculum, professors believe students will be better equipped to perceive direct relationships between their career interests and classroom preparation. The faculty plans to develop career-focused departmental handouts and institutionalize annual career workshops with alumni panels. The department hopes that these steps will encourage students to see the relationship between their curricular/co-curricular experiences and their future objectives.

A good foundation to an assessment program is key to its long-term success, but like any form of excellent research, questions of validity and reliability must be continually addressed. Processes need to be implemented that will allow the department to make regular evaluations as to the impact and value of their new curriculum. The department now needs to receive feedback from sources external to the university; peer review of their work (outside evaluation by another political scientist) ensures better quality. While national data provides a good point of comparison, external review will enhance the value of the assessment.

STRENGTHS AND WEAKNESSES OF APPROACH

This strategy for assessment has high payoffs for a department. Department faculty talk to each other about what matters to them, students are brought into the assessment process, data designed to answer key questions is collected and evaluated—a culture of assessment permeates the department. Implications for other departmental duties are significant: specifically, the recruitment and retention of students and faculty, and the construction of annual reports and budgets. The department may become known within the institution as one that seeks continual improvement and excellence, and the administration may subsequently provide resources to the department over and above what might otherwise be expected. In these very specific ways, assessment has been worthwhile.

The key weakness of the approach is the amount of time and energy invested in the collection of data, the evaluation of findings, and the revision of programs. While the annual work is less labor-intensive, it does require an investment of departmental time, energy, and resources. To address the workload issue, the assessment coordinator could give individual professors responsibility for reviewing and analyzing one element of the raw data collected for program review (e.g., one writes a brief report scrutinizing the results of a majors survey, while another examines publication patterns of the department relative to student credit hours generated).

In undergraduate programs, it may be useful to integrate some of the survey development and interpretation into Methods (and other) courses. This lightens the load on the faculty, provides practical experience for the students, and engages students in the process of assessment. This process may, in some institutions, be of similar value with graduate students. In a departmental community where the labor can be shared, this is an ideal model—but it will not work for all departments or institutions.

GRASSROOTS IMPLEMENTATION— "QUESTION-BASED" ASSESSMENT

How can assessment occur in a department where faculty are less invested in assessment as a departmental or personal objective? There are multiple ways by which departmental leadership might transform assessment from an external chore to an internal quest to answer important curricular and pedagogical questions. However, it is essential to demonstrate how the discoveries provided by the assessment process can guide departmental decision-making in a curricular review process. One way of garnering departmental investment is to help faculty perceive how they can benefit from assessment. However, every department differs as to their triggering issues (American Association for Higher Education 1992). For example, members of one department might be curious to discover why their students are not going to law school as frequently as in previous years. To answer this question, they consider LSAT scores and matriculation patterns, performance of their majors compared to other majors in the university, contributing alterations in the department over the years, and how their program differs from others that appear to be more successful. These findings allow them to make adjustments designed to improve the success rates of their students' law school applications. In other political science departments, the salient issue may be how to improve the caliber of graduate students entering the program or how to enhance students' ability to serve as competent research assistants. Regardless of the issue, the key is to find a question or questions linked to an outcome in which faculty members are interested.

The Grassroots Implementation strategy hypothesizes that developing a shared teaching technique across the political science curriculum, evaluating a skill developed in a required course, or identifying a key question faculty want answered could potentially create a departmental environment more conducive to assessment. An effective course assessment technique can easily become the core of a comprehensive departmental assessment plan. By making parallel evaluations of students at different points in their career, comparing their responses and making changes, faculty can begin assessing departmental progress toward goals while improving student learning. More importantly, within this approach is found the beginnings of a departmental assessment plan.

What faculty hold in common in many institutions is an investment in teaching. If we can demonstrate that effective classroom pedagogical techniques can be used to assess departmental achievement of goals, it is possible to manufacture departmental buy-in on program assessment. Effective forms of student evaluation can be used to develop departmental assessment programs in a manner most faculty can endorse. The particular example demonstrated in this chapter is the use of systematic peer-evaluation techniques; such a pedagogy can assuage faculty fears of classroom co-option and performance evaluation, engage students in their own learning, and provide a systematic review of some departmental goals (Deardorff 2005). In addition to improving student learning, shared issues might include a desire to improve the quality of graduate students (Hamann 2007), internationalize the curriculum, encourage more students to participate in service learning, or garner more resources for the program. The process can begin with as few as one or two faculty, or more, depending on the engagement of the faculty in the department.

This form of "bottom-up" assessment often occurs in departments where there are limited resources for assessment, disengaged professors, or a faculty suspicious of assessment. This strategy might be most attractive to larger programs without clear state mandates to assess (mandated programs are generally told what to assess and how) or to state universities and research institutions. This approach may be particularly useful with teaching faculty who are absolutely not interested in engaging in assessment.

PROCESS OF IMPLEMENTATION—TRANSLATING CLASSROOM ASSESSMENT TO DEPARTMENTAL ASSESSMENT

A form of simple course assessment can easily become the core of a comprehensive departmental assessment plan, *especially in departments resistant to assessment.* Tom Angelo has noted the importance of building shared trust, shared motivation, and a shared language in creating meaningful assessment programs (1999). For many faculty, a collective interest in teaching and student learning might create a common motivation and language. For other faculty, a shared professional goal or objective can serve the same purpose. While many classroom pedagogies might provide this bridge, the example of peer evaluation is used to demonstrate how grassroots assessment can provide departmental feedback. In many departments, the key will be to select a pedagogy that may already be utilized by the faculty, so the new task is just collecting data and comparing findings.

Peer evaluation requires students to evaluate the work of their colleagues according to previously established guidelines. This pedagogy engages students in the process of evaluation and grading, motivates them as writers and scholars because audiences other than their professor will be assessing their work, and ideally forces them to be more deliberate in the construction of the outcome being evaluated. While the concept of peer review of scholarly work long has been accepted by academia, its application to students' learning has been limited. The use of peer critiques in the teaching of writing might be the most familiar approach (Dossin 2003); new technology such as Blackboard has enhanced strategies involving students in the evaluation of their peers' work. Concerns regarding self and peer evaluation have centered on issues of privacy and the technique's ability to provide statistical validity and reliability in the assessment of classroom assignments (Omelicheva 2005). Yet, scholars have emphasized its ability to engage students, reinforce classroom values, and monitor student improvement. Team-based learning approaches have also found peer-evaluation techniques invaluable for holding free riders accountable and for involving students in assessing outcomes of their own work (Michaelson et al. 2002).

In this departmental hypothetical, a political science professor at a medium-sized state university uses peer evaluation initially as a means of engaging students in their own learning process (Deardorff 2005). This technique also allows the faculty member to demonstrate how personal goals are met in the classroom. Because of promotion and tenure evaluations, post-tenure reviews, accreditation studies, as well as legislature and Board of Trustees' demands, many universities require some form of annual performance review. Peer evaluation can be an easy method for faculty to document what they are teaching in the classroom; all faculty *share* the concern of how to meet this documentation requirement. At this institution, for example, the performance indicators require a demonstration that the professor "utilizes creative and piloted teaching methods/skills (documentation required)." The use of peer evaluation in the classroom, easily documented by the matrices developed by the faculty member or the class, allows the professor to demonstrate student learning through the semester via a valuable learning strategy.

Besides the innate motivation of self-preservation, faculty might also share an interest in understanding student performance. What works and what does not? These conversations can provide common ground for the development of an assessment program (Maki 2002). The question for assessment-resistant departments has been: How do we begin these conversations in a manner that decreases resistance? Administrative requirements to create a departmental assessment plan may only fan resistance; a "grassroots" approach, stemming from classroom success, may be far more effective. A faculty member excited by a successful classroom technique can promote a less-threatening departmental conversation than a provost demanding a report. However, even for this approach, some form of departmental leadership is necessary to ensure that conversations advance to implementation.

The connection between classroom pedagogy and departmental goals must be clarified. Professors know what outcomes (knowledge, skills, and values) they wish to foster in their students. Goals that have the widest applicability to the most faculty members in the department should become the first that the department evaluates. For example, a political science department may have as a goal "to develop and hone students' skills in all forms of communication, from basic to sophisticated." Specific objectives of this goal might be to foster "skills such as writing, asking logical and coherent questions, working and deciding both collaboratively and independently, advocating a position, negotiating an outcome, and presenting professionally one's research and one's ideas." In order to assess the department's success in meeting these goals and objectives, the faculty need to 1) demonstrate how knowledge, skills, and value objectives are being emphasized and evaluated and 2) provide evidence that there is improvement over the career of the student. Clearly, *all* courses cannot equally emphasize *all* goals, and not *all* faculty focus on the same objectives in *all* of their courses. However, if professors can meet and discuss who is doing what in their classes, this becomes simpler. If there are two classes that emphasize questioning skills—one taught early and one taught later in the student's career—using a similar peer evaluation approach or other common pedagogical strategy in both, this may allow the department to evaluate its success in developing said skills.

For example, the first-year major course might emphasize the same small group discussion skills as the capstone. A matrix, which shares several identical characteristics, can be used for both classes. For the senior capstone students, the class collectively identifies what small group skills they wished to enhance in their last semester in college. For the first-year students, students compare their own and their peers' participation to the identified expectations four or five times during the course of the semester and students use it during most sessions in the capstone. The professors can also use the same expectations as the basis of their evaluation of student performance as well. To use this approach for departmental assessment, there must be some common indicators on both instruments. Ideally, in addition to the students' multiple evaluation within the classroom, members of the department observe and assess students' performance occasionally. By doing this, not only can the development of skills over time be demonstrated, *but also the department demonstrates a consistent focus on achieving this objective.* This same approach can be used to demonstrate the inculcation of values and the application of knowledge. This approach is less effective in the assessment of student comprehension of the knowledge goals articulated by the department.

In order for this technique to become a coherent assessment plan the department must meet annually to collectively discuss their findings from classroom assessment activities. If our departments are "[d]riven by compelling questions about how students translate what they have learned into their own set of practices, assessment promotes sustained institutional dialogue about teaching and learning" (Maki 2004, 3). By simply recording what they discovered in their classrooms that year and across the department, and noting what they would do the following year, the pivotal feedback loop will be closed. This means that the department does not simply gather information, but applies it to improve the program. This is what we generally do every semester when we personally evaluate the success and failings of each of our courses—we simply apply the identical process to the entire department.

Once faculty become confident and comfortable with the process of simple classroom assessment projects, they may begin to see how this process can document their efforts in the classroom and demonstrate progress toward departmental objectives and goals. If assessment becomes a way of receiving formative information rather than only a summative evaluation—a means of evaluating the success of individual and departmental approaches toward shared goals—it becomes less threatening. We are simply receiving guidance as to the relative utility of our methods, not being labeled a "success" or a "failure" in our classroom performance. As we discuss our teaching with each other, not only does the department become more focused on shared goals, but it may be willing to expand assessment activities beyond a shared pedagogical technique and new questions to answer may arise.

STRENGTHS AND WEAKNESSES OF APPROACH

While there is no panacea for recalcitrant tenured professors, the Grassroots Approach to assessment for these departments would be more successful than the traditional mission-driven strategy. By building on classroom assessment techniques, a department might discover shared objectives and create a simple, non-threatening assessment process that could pave the way for more integrated assessment approaches. While faculty might be concerned that this approach is very work-intensive, the opposite is true. Once common matrices are developed and the processes are made part of the life of the department, assessment becomes simple. While the paperwork may feel excessive, it is this very documentation that demonstrates to outside reviewers that assessment is generating feedback that can continually improve the department.

Assessment works best when it is done collaboratively. Thomas Angelo and Patricia Cross noted that they had initially assumed that faculty would want to work alone in the privacy of their own classes, without outside involvement. They found just the opposite; classroom assessment "gives [faculty] opportunities and stimulus for talking about teaching and learning and for sharing their assessment project designs, techniques, and experiences with colleagues. Faculty also mention the value of discussing their plans and findings with their students, and of involving students in all phases of the work" (1993, 11). Peer evaluation engages all of these constituencies in the collaborative endeavor of improving education and learning, but it is only one of the many possible classroom assessment techniques identified by Angelo and Cross and others that can be used as a starting point for departmental assessment.

Clearly, this strategy is limited in its utility. Departments that do not share a common interest in teaching or in the success of their students will not be motivated by this approach to begin any form of assessment. Other departments may be resistant to this particular pedagogical approach, but if this strategy is viable, any other shared, evaluated technique (simulations, service learning, research designs) should render the same outcome. The Grassroots Implementation approach demonstrates that by making similar evaluations of students at different points in their careers, comparing responses, and then making changes, faculty can begin assessing departmental progress toward goals, simultaneously improving student learning.

Conclusion

Assessment helps very little if the information does not influence decision-making processes or determinations. However, even if no one outside of the department examines the data, if the department learns from the assessment process and discusses their findings, they can benefit. The department (and the chair) must find ways to use the assessment findings to impact the graduate or undergraduate curriculum, departmental policies, or other aspects of departmental life. Regardless of the approach to assessment, one key to sustaining this process and minimizing its opportunity cost for the department is to imbed assessment as much as possible into the current work of the department. By making assessment part of classroom teaching, departmental service, and even undergraduate and at times faculty research, it will be less of an onerous task and more of an essential element of the life of the department. Assessment can transform the way we work. Our findings should inform future departmental decisions and encourage faculty to bring the same inquiring minds to their teaching and university life as they do to their research. If, annually, the department discusses what has been discovered through assessment and plans the alterations to be made in response, then the assessment process will be conducted for the good of the department, not for the external audiences that may have instigated it.

REFERENCES

American Association for Higher Education. 1992. *Principles of Good Practice for Assessing Student Learning.* Washington, D.C.: AAHE.

Angelo, Thomas A. 1999. "Doing Assessment as if Learning Matters Most." *American Association for Higher Education Bulletin.* 51 (May): 3–6.

Angelo, Thomas A., and K. Patricia Cross. 1993. *Classroom Assessment Techniques: A Handbook for College Teachers.* 2nd ed. San Francisco: Jossey-Bass.

Astin, Alexander W. 1993. *Assessment for Excellence.* Phoenix: Ornyx Press.

Banta, Trudy W., J.P. Lund, K.E. Black, and F. W. Oblander. 1996. *Assessment in Practice.* San Francisco: Jossey-Bass.

Deardorff, Michelle D. 2005. "Assessment Through the Grassroots: Assessing the Department Through Student Peer Review." *Journal of Political Science Education* 1 (January–April): 109–26.

———. 2007. "Methods of Effectively Leveraging Departmental Assessment Programs," in "Symposium: 2006 Workshop for Departmental Chairs—Planning for Assessment and Accountability Issues." *PS: Political Science & Politics* 40 (January): 100–01.

Deardorff, Michelle D., and Brian D. Posler. 2005. "The Mission-Driven Department: Benefits of Departmental Assessment." *PS: Political Science & Politics* 38 (April): 273–76.

Deardorff, Michelle D., and Paul Folger. 2005. "Assessment that Matters: Integrating the 'Chore' of Department-Based Assessment with Real Improvements in Political Science Education." *Journal of Political Science Education* 1 (September–December): 277–87.

Dossin, Mary Mortimore. 2003. "Among Friends: Effective Peer Critiquing." *Clearing House* 76 (March/April): 206–07.

Fox, J. Clifford, and Scott Keeter. 1996. "Improving Teaching and Its Evaluation: A Survey of Political Science Departments." *PS: Political Science & Politics* 30 (June): 174–80.

Hamann, Kerstin. 2007. "Presentation for Chairs' Workshop on Assessment, APSA 2006," in "Symposium: 2006 Workshop for Departmental Chairs—Planning for Assessment and Accountability Issues." *PS: Political Science & Politics* 40 (January): 101–02.

Julian, Frank H., Don H. Chamberlain, and Robert A. Seay. 1991. "A National Status Report on Outcomes Assessment by Departments of Political Science." *PS: Political Science & Politics* 24 (June): 205–08.

Kelly, Marisa, and Brian E. Klunk. 2003. "Learning Assessment in Political Science Departments: Survey Results." *PS: Political Science & Politics* 36 (July): 451–55.

Lasher, Kevin J., and Kenneth Kitts. 1998. "Coming Soon to Your Department: Institutional Effectiveness Plans." *PS: Political Science & Politics* 31 (March): 69–73.

Maki, Peggy L. 2004. *Assessing for Learning: Building a Sustainable Commitment Across the Institution.* Sterling, VA: Stylus Publishing.

———. 2002. "Moving from Paperwork to Pedagogy: Channeling Intellectual Curiosity into a Commitment to Assessment." *American Association of Higher Education Bulletin* 54 (May): 9.

Michaelson, Larry K., Arletta Bauman Knight, and L. Dee Fink. 2002. *Team-Based Learning: A Transformative Use of Small Groups in College Teaching.* Sterling, VA: Stylus Publishing.

Omelicheva, Mariya Y. 2005. "Self- and Peer-Evaluation in Undergraduate Education: Structuring Conditions that Maximize Its Promises and Minimize the Perils." *Journal of Political Science Education* 1 (January–April): 191–206.

Palomba, Catherine A., and T. W. Banta. 1999. *Assessment Essentials.* San Francisco: Jossey-Bass.

Smoller, Fred. 2004. "Assessment Is Not a Four-Letter Word." *PS: Political Science & Politics* 37 (October): 871–74.

Thompson, Joan Hulse. 1991. "Outcomes Assessment: One Department's Experience with Portfolios and Outside Evaluators." *PS: Political Science & Politics* 24 (December): 715–18.

JEFFREY S. HILL, NORTHEASTERN ILLINOIS UNIVERSITY

CHARLES R. PASTORS, EDUCATION DEVELOPMENT GROWTH
ENTERPRISES, INC.

6

WHO WILL BE THE ASSESSMENT CHAMPION? AND OTHER CONDITIONS FOR A CULTURE OF ASSESSMENT[1]

One of the wonderful science experiments of childhood is creating crystals. You gather the ingredients, mix the correct solution, and then just watch them grow. Unfortunately, building a culture of assessment is *not* like that, since it is more than a simple activity. It involves creating a new culture, changing established patterns, and overcoming people's very legitimate fears, while also teaching them what assessment is. You need gradual steps that encourage trust in the process and confidence in the ability to succeed in it.

Almost by definition, a "culture" of assessment requires grassroots support and activity. Building it is a bottom-up process that must be carried out by the people who will implement and learn from it. The reality is that initiative for assessment tends to come from administrators at the top of an institution, themselves often acting in response to the demands of boards of education, accrediting organizations, or other public/political demands for accountability (Banta 2001). There must be someone who will start the process and maintain it, but this is not what deans or provosts do when they require an assessment program. Unfortunately (or perhaps fortunately, depending on your viewpoint), upper-level administrators are not always obeyed. All of us recall examples of administrative initiatives that failed because of inaction (see Chace 2006). People do not actively oppose them; they just do nothing. While administrative policy may set the stage, by itself it is not able to get the process started. Someone else is needed to initiate activity. Who, then, should be the initiator of this activity and, once identified, what should this initiator do?

In the following pages, we address these two questions, based on our experience in the Department of Political Science at Northeastern Illinois University (NEIU). Borrowing from the literature on cooperation and policy implementation, we suggest that five conditions must be met in order to build a culture of assessment. These are:

1. Identify a "champion" or "fixer" to initiate activity and maintain momentum (Bardach 1977; Mazmanian and Sabatier 1983).

2. Overcome distrust and fear of the way assessment will be used (e.g., Axelrod 1984).

3. Make assessment tractable or "doable" (Pressman and Wildavsky 1979).

4. Build commitment, or "assent" (Bardach 1977), among the people you expect to be part of the assessment culture.

5. Prevent over-reliance on one person by developing a subgroup or subculture of champions and fixers.[2]

By a combination of learning, designing, and serendipity we were able to meet these conditions at NEIU, and formed the beginnings of a culture of assessment. In our department, we were helped in this by going through a period of design and implementation over several years, spanning the administrations of four deans and two chairs. This prolonged period is not necessary, but it provided an opportunity to explore the process and develop a better understanding of what we were trying to achieve.

CONDITION ONE: WHO SHOULD BE THE INITIATOR?

The first stop is the designation of an initiator. We use the word "designation" with some hesitancy since the choice involves a certain amount of self-selection by the individual as well as acceptance by the department. Accordingly, the initiator must be someone department members will listen to, and who is seen as having legitimacy in this area. This is someone who will not perform the activities but must make sure they get done. He or she may be involved *with* a committee, but cannot *be* the committee.

As we use it here, the concept of an initiator is similar to that found in the literature on implementation where the existence of a "fixer" was an important element in the successful implementation of programs (Bardach 1977; Mazmanian and Sabatier 1983). Fixers, or "champions" (the term preferred by Peters and Waterman, 1982, and the one we shall use here), do not rely on hierarchical controls. Rather, they act informally, encouraging activity and not just carrying it out themselves. They provide the start, help push progress when it slows, solve problems, and fill holes. But they do not do the job by themselves.

The history of assessment in the political science department at NEIU began with the chair accepting this role.[3] The chair already had an interest in assessment and saw the potential importance of it. When the university was looking for people to help start assessment plans within the departments, in response to accreditation demands, he had already begun the initial steps and was willing to continue. Thus, for us, the chair was an obvious choice for assessment champion.

Many people would see chairs, in general, as the people most likely to be the assessment advocates. After all, chairs are familiar with the department, with the curriculum, and with the field, and, in many instances, they are an excellent choice. But this is not always so. Consider that the person chosen must be someone with at least a minimal level of trust within the department. You cannot impose trust; it must be built and nurtured, and a chair that is not trusted cannot do that. But there is more to consider than this minimal requirement.

Within the literature on business and organizational development, a distinction is made between those who lead and those who manage (e.g., Zalenik 1992). Briefly, those who manage solve problems. They adopt impersonal, passive attitudes toward goals, and those goals come from necessity rather than desire. They tolerate mundane work with their focus being on survival. Leaders, on the other hand, are active, shaping rather then responding. They have a tolerance for a lack of structure. Mundane work tends to drive them crazy. Not all managers are leaders. And, as importantly, not all leaders are managers (Pastors 2002).

This leader/manager distinction has obvious relevance to business and organizational development in general (e.g., Burke 1995). And it is also important to consider this dynamic within a university attempting to build a culture of assessment. If a university normally expects all department chairs to fill the roles played by managers, it cannot expect that all of these people will then excel in the very different role of leaders. If a university's assessment plan implicitly assumes that chairs can play both roles, the risk of early failure can be high.

The relationship between assessment and the leader/manager distinction is seen in a survey of department chairs at NEIU (Pastors 2002; 2003). Chairs identified in a questionnaire as leaders or leader-managers were much more likely to have shown progress in developing assessment programs than were chairs identified as managers. More telling, however, is that only 13% of those surveyed were designated as leaders, with an additional 39% using a combination leader-manager style. Almost half of those surveyed (48%) fit the model of managers. For these individuals, requests to lead interfere with their primary responsibility of running a department. Choosing them as advocates is forcing on them a different role.

The implication of this study is that if you look only to chairs for leadership, you will be frustrated for at least two reasons. First, a majority of chairs are not likely to see their job as primarily that of leadership. Requests to lead will not be taken seriously by those who consider themselves to be managers. Further, they will likely not devote their first attention or highest energies to that leadership task. What they see as their primary responsibility—running (managing) the department—will occupy their time and their attention.

Second, those who would respond to the call to lead must still do the time-consuming work demanded by their management tasks. Running the department is a major part of their job, it takes a predominant amount of their time, and it is likely to be what their colleagues expect them to be doing. Thus, even chairs eager to take on leadership tasks may be unable to do so, as they do not have the time to fill both sets of responsibilities adequately. Asked to lead, and thwarted in their ability to respond, they may withdraw from the task in frustration, become more dissatisfied with the position of department chair, and seek the earliest possible time to leave it.

We have no easy solutions to this problem except to say that the champion does not have to be the chair. Others can be encouraged to accept the role since it requires persuasion rather than authority. It is an informal activity, usually done outside of ordinary channels. Thus, when the chair does not or cannot fill this role, administrators must encourage people to step forward. They may wish to look for an individual with a strong commitment to teaching, since such an individual would be more likely than others to see the value of assessment. But while possibly desirable, teaching commitment should not be seen as a necessary requirement. People may be committed to assessment for a variety of personal reasons. As long as the commitment is there, we suspect that the motivation does not matter. What does matter is that the champion possesses strong organizational and people skills. Organizational skills are needed since the champion must be someone who knows how to get things done. And people skills are needed since the job of the champion is not to do all the work, and certainly not to order others to work. The champion instead needs to be able to convince, persuade, and even cajole, but never to order.

CONDITIONS TWO, THREE, AND FOUR: BUILDING TRUST, MAKING IT FEASIBLE, AND GAINING ASSENT

EARLY STEPS IN BUILDING AN ASSESSMENT CULTURE

The early history of the department's assessment activities was relatively simple. We began with two non-comprehensive assessment instruments designed to determine how satisfied majors were with the department. Faculty members drew up a "Survey of Major Satisfaction" and an "Exit Interview." The survey, containing 28 items regarding student experiences and demographics, was administered during class periods to declared majors. To give students every opportunity to take it, it was administered in all classes for two days. Students were asked not to fill it out more than once and there was no evidence indicating this was a problem. Virtually all faculty members participated in administering it. There was no problem if a particular faculty member forgot or refused to cooperate as redundancy was built into the project.

The other instrument, an 84-item exit interview to be given to majors when they applied for graduation, was a failure. Students looking forward to graduation showed little enthusiasm for the interview. Moreover, administering it fell to only a few people, the undergraduate advisors. The multiple opportunities that assisted compliance with the satisfaction survey were not available here. A student's graduation could have been held up, but advisors were understandably reluctant to do this.

Few exit interviews were completed, and the instrument was dropped from the department's plans.

GAINING TRUST FROM SMALL STEPS

Even these small initiatives were met with great distrust. Assessment, in general, was seen as both threatening and impossible. Many faculty feared they would spend long hours producing still another report no one would read. Others were concerned that assessment would take time away from more valuable activities in research and teaching. Perhaps most important was the fear that assessment would be used against individual faculty members or against the department. Administrators assured faculty that data would not be used in this way, but verbal assurances are not sufficient if trust does not already exist.

The reason trust is such a problem is because participation in assessment is similar (but not identical) to the problem of the "Prisoner's Dilemma." That is, two people initially agree to cooperate with each other. They will both be better off if they keep this agreement. But after they separate from each other, they are faced with a problem. If one person maintains the agreement, that is, if one person cooperates, but the other does not, the one who is true to the agreement will receive great harm, known in formal terms as the "sucker's payoff." The damage from the sucker's payoff is so great that a player chooses not to risk this outcome and refuses to cooperate. The second player faces the same decision and makes the same choice. Accordingly, even though both parties know they would be better off keeping the agreement, both parties still choose to break it because one cannot trust the other. This applies to assessment as faculty members feared if they undertook assessment in good faith, and that faith was violated, then they could pay large costs in terms of promotions, replacement positions within the department, or academic freedom. Not cooperating would be the best choice at any *single* moment. However, there is a way out of the Prisoner's Dilemma if we see it as an exchange that will be played repeatedly (Axelrod 1984). If faculty members choose to cooperate with the assessment activities, and the administration also chooses to cooperate and does not use the data inappropriately, then trust is built up and cooperation is likely to continue.

Without any of us actually being aware of it, these small, non-comprehensive projects were serving to build up this sense of trust. The first one, the survey of majors, was a relatively easy step to take because the required effort was small (it took little time from teaching and research) and so was the risk. It examined the department as a whole and not its individual members. Moreover, it did more than simply produce another report. Faculty members found it helpful and used the results to make several small but significant changes, including increasing the number of night classes, writing and distributing a departmental handbook, and preparing a two-year course plan to help students in their own planning. All of these actions were seen as reasonable uses of the information. The administration did not blame the department for not having done these things before, and department members began to trust that additional material would not be misused. Ironically, the unsuccessful exit interview was also important for building up trust. First, it showed that there were no repercussions for failing. Second, it showed everyone that we could engage in assessment while still being sensitive to fears that it could drain time away from other activities. Certainly in the early stages, building a culture of assessment will indeed take time away from teaching and research. Denying this possibility, or dismissing it as selfish, is counterproductive. The time demands of assessment must be considered at all stages.

SOME LARGER STEPS

The relatively painless and generally useful initial experiences allowed the department to continue building its assessment plan. Department members drew up instruments for assessing the department's general education courses, Introduction to Political Science and American National Government. Committees devised two tests to assess students' mastery of the knowledge and skills they obtained from these two courses. In addition, there was a five-item survey of the attitudinal or behavioral impact of the course on the student. During selected terms, we administered these surveys as a pre-test and a post-test. Students were asked to complete it during the first or second meeting of a class, and to do so again during the next-to-last class period. Students were also asked to help us in our analysis by placing their ID numbers on the response sheets. With the information gathered, we could see how much the average student's knowledge had improved. We could also check the validity of the survey by comparing correlations of survey results with student performance in the course (as measured by grade) and with a separate

"Expectations/Experiences Survey." This latter survey was based on the idea that "amateurs" and "experts" differ in the ways they receive, store, organize, and retrieve information (Day 1996). The expectations survey was also initially administered the first day of the class. Instructors asked students: "List as many as twenty topics, concepts, ideas, terms, theories, etc., that you believe will be covered in this course." After a few minutes, students were asked to "group," or "cluster," what they had listed into related groups, or clusters, or piles—as hardware stores, grocery stores, or restaurants might organize the items they provide. The expectations survey was administered again at the end of the course. We could now compare the pre- and post-course "surveys," finding how the number and complexity of items listed was changed by the course. That is, we saw how much students had moved from amateurs to experts in their thinking.

BUILDING ASSENT AND MAKING IT FEASIBLE

Besides providing useful information, these initial assessment tools were helpful in constructing an assessment culture. Faculty in the department began to learn what assessment was, how it was done, and, as seen in the exit interview, how it should not be done. When additional activities were discussed, they seemed less overwhelming and more doable. Making assessment tractable (Condition 3) is vital if an assessment culture is to be built. Even a brief review of the literature on policy implementation will yield examples of people who sabotaged or walked away from tasks they found too overwhelming (La Porte 1975; Pressman and Wildavsky 1979).

Equally important is that these initial activities helped create a commitment, or at least acceptance, of assessment among the department members (Condition 4). This is what the literature on policy implementation calls "building assent" (Bardach 1977). Policy implementation is a gradual process in which agencies, groups, and individuals slowly agree to support a policy. It is a form of coalition-building in which education, negotiation, and coercion are used to convince actors that there is value in assisting (or at least not opposing) the program. The changes brought about by the early successes provided some evidence of the potential value of assessment, and the steady involvement of people in the regularized tasks of assessment (e.g., collecting surveys) helped to create support.

Finally, making each of these activities separate and distinct was also important for the continuation of a sense of trust (Condition 2). Assessment of the general education classes was potentially more threatening than the earlier survey of majors. The assessment of each course and instructor could have been used in performance reviews for tenure and promotion. When promises were made that they would not be used in this manner, those promises were more readily accepted. If the department had started with the general education survey, it is not clear if it would have been as readily accepted by the faculty.

CONDITION FIVE: DEVELOPING A SUBCULTURE OF CHAMPIONS

We continued our assessment activities following the same pattern of cumulative incrementalism seen in the earlier history. The university assisted us in building assent (Condition 4) with a series of meetings and workshops that were helpful in showing the advantages of assessment and also emphasizing that assessment was a large, but not impossible enterprise.

DESIGNING A COMPREHENSIVE PLAN: MEANS BEFORE ENDS

The department chair continued as one of the champions by initiating meetings and structuring the much larger tasks that remained. He started this stage by searching for a method to assess how well the department's goals were met, leaving until later any decision as to what the goals were. This seemingly backward process was intentional and helped to further assent. We addressed the relatively easier task before moving to the technically and emotionally difficult one of determining the goals of an education in political science. The department had already tried and rejected the use of an exit interview as a means to assess the major. Thus, this stage was seen as simply an extension of this earlier task.

The department chose a form of portfolio assessment in which papers would be collected and placed in a student's portfolio. Upon graduation, a committee of department faculty would review the earliest entry and the most recent entry in a student's portfolio, scoring them on a series of learning outcomes derived from the department's learning goals. This would be the primary data for any subsequent assessment decisions. The problem is that the department had not yet determined either the goals or the outcomes. We had selected the means before we decided on the ends.

DESIGNING A COMPREHENSIVE PLAN: THE GOALS AND OBJECTIVES COME LAST

We started this part with a review of the goals adopted by the university and by the Illinois Board of Higher Education. But this still left the department with the job of applying these to the discipline, devising measurable outcomes, and setting up a process for reviewing and applying the data. Not surprisingly, this was the longest, most difficult of all assessment activities—another reason not to make it a starting point. As in labor-management bargaining, a common tactic is to leave the most difficult issues to the end. We did the same.

The task entailed more than devising a series of goals. It included learning what assessment was. This was often frustrating. A group of individuals would develop an understanding of what assessment was, draw up a plan, and learn from various informal reviews that a portion was missing or wrong. This procedure of writing, review, and revision was repeated a number of times.

As before, the role of the champion was vital, but there were changes in the way the champion worked. There was no longer only one champion. The process was moved along by a group of people playing the role of serial champions. Not only were there more people in this role, but the way they fulfilled it also changed. They still made sure holes were patched and problems solved, but they were also actively involved in constructing the tools needed for assessment. They were no longer outside of the committee, and often became the major players in task forces and committees. At different times in the process, different people initiated activity and solved problems until a draft was written, reviewed, and approved by the department. Usually this was done with one person taking responsibility for ensuring one particular aspect was completed or reconsidered in light of subsequent decisions. No one was asked to fill this role; they simply assumed it when needed. We had developed a kind of subculture in which filling this role was seen as legitimate by all department members (Condition 5).

Having serial champions was an important development in creating a culture of assessment. In some ways, this made activity more difficult since there were now multiple and not always consistent visions of what needed to be done. These differences needed to be resolved in meetings and discussions. But, beyond this complication, multiple people playing this role signified that a culture had been generated. People began to see what assessment was and how they could do it. Rather than being a sign of inefficiency, it showed that a threshold level of assent had been achieved (Condition 4). People were talking about assessment and were actively engaged in it.

The final result of this stage was reached when we agreed upon and adopted four goals, a series of outcomes related to each goal, and performance criteria with scoring rubrics. The goals and related outcomes were as follows:

GOAL I: Students able to understand/comprehend and assess empirical political information, concepts, and analytical framework.

1. Able to understand/comprehend and assess important empirical information (features, events, trends, interactions, structures and processes).

2. Understand major concepts and theoretical frameworks as they are used to organize and clarify the empirical realities above.

GOAL II: Students develop an interest in and understanding of organizing, planning, executing, and participating in political activity.

1. Able to utilize theory to address problems and shape practice.

2. Understand historical and contemporary examples of political action at local, national, and global levels.

3. Able to analyze and discuss different kinds of participation and organizing strategies (both successes and failures).

GOAL III: Students able to understand the values underlying political choices.

1. Understand and clarify one's own and others' values.

2. Able to distinguish analytical frameworks and the values inherent in each.

GOAL IV: Students able to communicate in both written and oral forms and to demonstrate effective and critical use of information-gathering and research media within the broad context of social science.

1. Able to communicate in writing and speaking clear and accurate empirical descriptions, and to develop and express coherent arguments.

2. Able to demonstrate effective and critical use of information-gathering and research

3. media within the broad context of social science.

MAINTAINING A CULTURE OF ASSESSMENT: UNFORESEEN PROBLEMS AND SOLUTIONS IN IMPLEMENTATION

UNFORESEEN PROBLEMS

We adopted the plan and quickly encountered new problems, the most difficult being the retirement or pending retirement of several people. Included in those retiring were two of the four people who had, at various times, filled the role of champion. Taken together, we no longer had the staff necessary to carry out even the fundamental teaching and administrative workload of the department. The initial fear that assessment would take away from research and teaching had been realized. Assessment activity slowed to almost a standstill.

The biggest problem in our assessment plan was in the creation of the student portfolios. No one was doing it. Faculty were generally not collecting papers and no one was maintaining a file of collected papers. Even if people had collected papers, we soon realized we did not have the file space necessary to store them for several years. Our plan had tried to solve this problem by the use of a new capstone course. Students would be asked to submit papers from earlier courses, and papers from the capstone course would be the final part of the portfolio. But the loss of faculty made this option unworkable. Since students graduate both terms from both day and evening programs, we estimated we would have to offer the capstone course at least twice per year, and, more optimally, four times per year. With two retirements and three more expected within the next two years (in a department of nine faculty), we did not have the staff to offer the capstone course as frequently as needed. We were no longer meeting one of the five necessary conditions (Condition 3). The assessment plan was no longer tractable.

This problem might have been resolved in the past by the actions of the champions. But retirement led to a loss of one-half of the people who had served in this capacity. The remaining two were now responsible for other parts of departmental administration and no longer had the time. There was no one to make sure everyone was collecting papers, and that collected papers were being reviewed. While the portfolio plan would still have been unworkable, the discovery of the problem and the devising of a solution would have happened sooner had the serial champions been active. Again, one of the conditions necessary for assessment (Condition 5), was no longer being met. There was no subculture of champions. Virtually all activity stopped.

A second source of problems was found outside of the department. The dean and the provost who had helped to start assessment both left the university. Each one had been a strong advocate and had established some level of trust in its use. Thus, the people outside the department who may have been able to identify the lack of progress had also left. In essence, we had three problems: administrative turnover, inadequate staff, and an intractable plan.

INITIAL SOLUTIONS

The first problem, administrative turnover, was solved when a new dean and a new provost were hired. The task for them was to show support and reestablish the conditions of trust that had allowed assessment to be developed. Over time, they both showed a commitment to assessment and did not misuse the various assessment results that were delivered to them. They also helped resolve our staffing problem with authorizations to hire new faculty who quickly took an active role in assessment, revitalizing our efforts. Some of them had been exposed to assessment while in graduate school and came to NEIU expecting to participate in any assessment activities. Others were encouraged to participate by the activities of the administration. The more senior members of the department welcomed this enthusiasm since they still supported the assessment plan, but they simply had not had the time to invest. With the new faculty, the time demands on everyone decreased to a point where progress was again possible. New faculty began to participate as serial champions and they helped in resolving the final problem we encountered, the intractability of using portfolios. Our solution was to drop our dependence on the capstone course. We also abandoned the longitudinal analysis that used portfolios to assess the performance of individual students, replacing it with a cross-sectional design. In this new approach, we collect papers from students in introductory courses that are not general education courses. The vast majority of the students in these courses will be majors or minors. Their papers are scored according to how well they demonstrate mastery of our department goals and objectives. We then compare scores on these papers to scores on papers collected from graduating seniors in upper-level courses. In this way, we obtain an estimate of the value added from our program. We lose the ability to track each student, but we gain by making assessment "doable" again. Moreover, if one instructor fails to collect papers, there are enough sections and instructors to ensure this will not be a fatal error. As in the general education assessment plan, we have built some redundancy into the system.

Once per year, department members gather for one afternoon and score the collected papers for their level of achievement on one goal or two goals. So far, we have done this once and submitted a report with our results. Our current step is to examine the implications and make any appropriate changes in our curriculum.

MAINTAINING A CULTURE OF ASSESSMENT: A SELF-PERPETUATING SYSTEM?

This short history shows the difficulties of building a culture of assessment. Problems in the use of certain approaches, e.g., portfolios, must be expected. Thus, in some ways, we were not surprised. What we did not expect was how much retirements and changes in administration would undermine the conditions that led to our initial successes. When we lost our core group of champions, momentum was lost, problems went unaddressed, trust and confidence declined. Only when we reestablished these conditions were we able to make progress again.

But our assessment culture is still fragile, and the immediate threat at this point is burnout. A single champion is not sufficient to maintain the culture. Even with a rotation of responsibility among multiple champions, exhaustion and varying levels of commitment remain problems. But burnout is just a symptom of a deeper problem. We are in the early stages of a new culture, one where the activities are done episodically by a few individuals. Assessment is still "added-on" to regular activities, and it is not yet one of the regular activities of the department. We have what some describe as a "climate" rather than a "culture" of assessment. A culture requires assessment to be an integral part of the department and the university, protected by structures, policies, procedures, and behaviors (Hatfield 2002). Such structures require resources that encourage and reward the time invested in assessment activities. These rewards or incentives include a faculty support system of faculty development, coaching, and campus-wide programs through a "teaching and learning" center or similar structure. Also important are direct compensation, support for conference travel, local recognition, enhancement of prospects for promotion or tenure, and release time. Ideally, assessment activities should be included in the professional development criteria so that they become a part of salary, tenure, and promotion decisions. If some mixture of resources is not allocated, if assessment activities are not recognized in personnel decisions, then assessment will be seen as something that takes away from more important activities such as research or teaching. Supportive rhetoric without resources is meaningless.

At the same time, additional resources will not be enough. They are necessary in the sense that their absence can harm assessment efforts, but the presence of support or rewards will not be sufficient. In the short run, we can make people do things if we make it worth their while. Rewards work; they affect what we do. But what about the long term (Kohn 1993)? In other words, how do we stabilize our culture and make assessment a self-perpetuating activity?

We need to make assessment something that faculty see as valuable and worth doing for its own sake, for achieving the things faculty already find worthwhile. It must fit in with the already existing set of faculty goals. What are these goals? While they will certainly vary with the individual and the context, Wegrin (2001) suggests that faculty are motivated by desires for autonomy, community, recognition, and efficacy. He explains that faculty seek autonomy to experiment without fear of consequences and to be members of a community of scholars in which their work is valued. Expressions of value include receiving unsolicited compliments from students or colleagues, getting quoted, or fielding requests for assistance (Wegrin 2001). The key to making assessment a self-perpetuating culture is to show how it can help faculty meet the goals they already have. At Northeastern, we are still trying to make this connection, but probably the best way to do this is through its use in the classroom. If assessment solves the problems faculty face in getting a point across, in engaging students, or in finding which approaches keep material fresh, then it becomes self-reinforcing. Faculty do it because it helps them. It no longer is seen as taking time away from teaching and research. On the contrary, by providing solutions, it can free up time that would be spent searching for answers. In turn, more time is now available for research. There will still be time demands from assessment, but their function will be clear, and the time they require will be recognized and supported by the administration. They will likely be seen as worth doing. Once faculty become committed to its utility in their day-to-day teaching and personal satisfaction, they are much more likely to see it as non-threatening and beneficial in improving student learning in the department as a whole. The shift in focus from classroom assessment to program assessment becomes natural. At this stage, assessment becomes part of the culture of the department, and the motivation to engage in assessment becomes intrinsic.

CONCLUSION: FINAL THOUGHTS AND FUTURE THREATS

In these pages, we have suggested that a culture of assessment does not simply happen, and that there are five conditions that must be met before the beginnings of such a culture are possible. To restate these conditions in a slightly different manner, we see the first is that there must be someone who will initiate or "champion" assessment activity. Conditions 2 and 3 require that careful efforts must be made to assure faculty that assessment will not be harmful, and that it is possible or tractable. Without these basic conditions, faculty will be unwilling to commit themselves to participating in assessment (Condition 4) and, further, will not take a leadership role in maintaining, repairing, and preserving assessment (Condition 5).

These conditions are only the start and work does not end once they are met. Each one should be seen as a hallmark of an on-going process. Each step must be constantly reinforced by conscious action, a difficult and potentially exhausting task, or we must make assessment a self-reinforcing behavior in which the steps are met automatically. Only in the latter case does it truly become a culture.

Even a well-established culture is still vulnerable. Its strength is that it is valuable to its members. However, if it ceases to be valuable, then it is likely to disappear. One way to destroy this perceived value is for assessment information to be used in ways that are potentially harmful to faculty, eliminating the trust that was steadily nurtured. If it were broken by accident or for reasonable, important, but short-term reasons, then it would be permanently destroyed. Trust would end, the value found in assessment would be lost, and the intrinsic motivation to engage in it would disappear.

A second potential threat exists when people expect too much. People are excited by assessment, but there is danger in this excitement. Managers in both the public and private sectors are often exposed to new approaches or tools that promise to improve efficiency or forestall disaster, but expectations rise until they become unreasonable. When this innovation inevitably fails to meet these expectations, the whole approach is dropped and exhausted managers sigh in relief. Lost in this cycle is the energy and trust that went into this new "paradigm." Also lost are the less dramatic but still significant improvements that people would have valued, had expectations been more realistic. Assessment must be protected from a similar fate. It can be valuable, but it is not a solution for all our problems. In advocating it, we must not promise too much, and we must be sure of the strength of our own commitment before asking others to undertake it.

There is one last threat to assessment: validity. Implicit in all our plans is that our goals, objectives, and measurements all accurately reflect what a liberal education should be. In other words, we assume we know what we are looking for. But how sure are we that we are correct, especially considering that different schools come up with different goals and measures? Certainly, there is some overlap among us. We suspect an emphasis on writing, for example, will be found in almost all assessment plans. But there will also be significant differences. We cannot turn to a set of national or state government imposed goals to guide us, and the profession has not adopted a set of standards. Even if it had, this just moves the question of validity to a different level. Providing an answer is well beyond the bounds of this chapter, and we do not try to offer one. Still, everyone who uses assessment must recognize that, in the end, its worth lies not only in the method or techniques, but in the values and goals we adopt.

NOTES

1. This chapter includes updated and revised portions previously published separately in Hill (2005) and Pastors (2002; 2003). The authors wish to thank the members of the department of political science at Northeastern Illinois University for their work on assessment. This chapter would not have been possible without them. Thanks must also go to the editors of this volume for their hard work, gentle prodding, and editorial review. Finally, we wish to thank David B. Hill for his editing and assistance. Any errors and mistakes are, of course, solely our own responsibility. Authors are arranged alphabetically; there is no senior author.

2. An earlier version of these conditions can be found in Hill (2005).

3. The department chair who accepted this initial role was one of the authors, Charles Pastors. The other author, Jeffrey Hill, was one of the champions of assessment, although, at first, a somewhat reluctant one. Along with other members of the department, he experienced much of the distrust we describe in the article. When Pastors became acting dean, Hill became the chair of the department. We wish to thank the reviewer who suggested we reveal the roles we played in developing a culture of assessment.

REFERENCES

Axelrod, Robert. M. 1984. *The Evolution of Cooperation.* New York: Basic Books.

Banta, Trudy W. 2001. "Is External Encouragement for Assessment Essential?" *Assessment Update* 13 (November–December): 3, 10, 11.

Bardach, Eugene. 1977. *The Implementation Game.* Cambridge, MA: MIT Press.

Burke, W. Warner. 1995. "Leadership and Empowerment." *OD Practitioner* 8 (1): 8–16.

Chace, William M. 2006. *One Hundred Semesters: My Adventures as Student, Professor, and University President, and What I Learned Along the Way.* Princeton, NJ: Princeton University Press.

Day, Ruth S. 1996. "Cognition and Teaching: Part 2." Presented at the National 1996 Chautauqua Short Course Program, May 8–19, Durham, North Carolina.

Hatfield, Susan. 2002. "Creating a Department Culture of Assessment." Presented at the Pre-Conference Workshop, Nineteenth Annual Kansas State University New Chairs Conference, February 5, Orlando, Florida.

Hill, Jeffrey S. 2005. "Developing a Culture of Assessment: Insights from Theory and Experience." *Journal of Political Science Education* 1 (January–March): 29–37.

Kohn, Alfie. 1993. *Punished by Rewards: The Trouble with Gold Stars, Incentive Plans, A's, Praise, and Other Bribes.* New York: Houghton Mifflin.

La Porte, Todd R. 1975. *Organized Social Complexity: Challenge to Politics and Policy.* Princeton, NJ: Princeton University Press.

Mazmanian, Daniel A., and Paul A. Sabatier. 1983. *Implementation and Public Policy.* Glenview, IL: Scott Foresman and Company.

Pastors, Charles. 2002. "Assessment: Program Reviews and Curriculum Revision— One Long (Forced?) March." Proceedings of the Nineteenth Annual Kansas State University New Chairs Conference, February 7–9, Orlando, Florida.

———. 2003. "Department Chairs' Leadership Role in Program Assessment." *The Department Chair* 14 (1): 16–18.

Peters, Thomas J., and Richard H. Waterman, Jr. 1982. *In Search of Excellence.* New York: Warner Books.

Pressman, Jeffrey L., and Aaron Wildavsky. 1979. *Implementation.* 2nd ed. Berkeley: University of California Press.

Wergin, Jon. 2001. "Beyond Carrots and Sticks: What Really Motivates Faculty." *Liberal Education* 87 (Winter): 50–53.

Zaleznik, Abraham. 1992. "Managers and Leaders: Are They Different?" *Harvard Business Review* 70 (March/April): 126–36.

CANDACE C. YOUNG, TRUMAN STATE UNIVERSITY

PROGRAM EVALUATION AND ASSESSMENT: INTEGRATING METHODS, PROCESSES, AND CULTURE

This chapter explores the methods, processes, and cultural dimensions associated with effective assessment. It also offers strategies to help integrate the three dimensions and presents an assessment model that is simple, feasible, and effective. The recommendations offered regarding these three assessment dimensions are based on more than 25 years of participant observation at a university that used assessment to transform itself.

By the time I arrived at Truman State University[1] in 1980, the university already had begun to escalate its effort to assess student learning. Over the next decade, skillful leadership and assessment transformed the university from a comprehensive regional institution to the state's liberal arts and science university for high-ability students. Its leadership in the assessment movement led numerous other schools to request assistance, and I was among a group of faculty members who agreed to work with other institutions who were seeking help. Thus, I had the opportunity to observe numerous schools, public and private, two-year and four-year, comprehensive and specialized, as they were designing and implementing their own assessment systems in response to various pressures in the rapidly changing higher education environment of the past quarter century.

In the mid-1980s, the entire country was caught up in the critical examination of higher education (National Commission on Excellence in Education 1983; National Institute of Education 1984; Association of American Colleges 1985). No longer did the public presume quality at the country's universities. Concerns for quality and calls for outcomes assessment were the order of the day. The report from the National Governors' Association, "Time for Results," reflected public sentiment of the time, saying that "the public has the right to know and understand the quality of undergraduate education that young people receive.... They have a right to know that their resources are being wisely invested and committed" (National Governor's Association 1986, Preface). For the nation, these reports signaled a substantial change in public expectations for universities.

While many in the higher education community hope that assessment is just another fad, I assume that the calls for assessment of student learning will not pass soon. In fact, the Spellings Report signals renewed energy in the demands for assessment, and a critical view of higher education is likely to continue in the future, given the public's concern with rising costs and increasing global competitiveness.

The purpose of this chapter is to develop a model that will meet "best practices" while also recognizing the compliance orientation and resource limitations of most departments. It also advances process and cultural issues that will influence whether a department can get benefits from its assessment system.

CASE EXAMPLE

While the reports of the 1980s placed other universities in a defensive position, Truman State University benefited from having had over a decade to assess, evaluate, and revise curriculum. When the reports called for increased quality and accountability, they validated the university's dialogue and assessment innovations of the prior decade. For example, when the American Association of Colleges (AAC) "Wahlke" report on the political science major (1991) was published, Truman had already implemented many of the same conclusions over the prior decade as a result of sustained attention to quality initiatives and data generated by its assessment program. Initially, the data gathered in the assessment effort at the program level offered a number of negative data points on student performance in political science. However, a low-key reporting process and non-punitive assessment environment permitted political science faculty to treat results rather passively. University leaders, including the President and Vice-President for Academic Affairs, patiently nudged the campus to engage the evidence and within a few years our egos got the better of us. Students reported high satisfaction with the program, but even those with high GPAs were underperforming on a nationally recognized exam. Eventually, we resolved to spend the time necessary to investigate the discipline's mix of assessment data. Several negative data points caught our attention: poor results on the national exam, several years of bookstore data showing that a significant proportion of students did not buy assigned textbooks, and lower-than-expected self-reported study time (most students spent 6–10 hours a week, total). Of importance to note is the likelihood that had we been placed in a high-stakes reporting environment, we probably would have emphasized student satisfaction data which "showed" we had a great program.

As a group, the political science faculty decided to review the national exam, which at the time was the Graduate Record Examination field test in political science. We concluded that it was very challenging and covered the vast array of the discipline, but since students only had to get 60% correct to score at the 99th percentile, we felt it was a reasonably good fit with the content of our curriculum.

Our discussion following the review of the exam led to a decision to inquire of students and to analyze transcripts to try to understand course choice patterns within our distributional curriculum. When we went back to the classroom, we asked students to discuss concepts that we knew they had covered in more than one prior course. Their inability to do this even marginally well had the effect of persuading us that the weak exam results reflected the tendency for students to study for exams without really engaging or internalizing the concepts. Our transcript analysis showed that students were frequently taking very specialized courses that left huge holes in their understanding of the general concepts and models of the discipline. We concluded that there was nothing in our current curricular design that challenged the short-term learning practices of our students.

While we became convinced that the national exam provided a reasonably good measure of the content knowledge of the discipline, we also concluded that the research and higher order thinking objectives of the program were not adequately measured in the current assessment system. We resolved to restructure our curriculum and to develop a way for the faculty to collectively assess students' higher order thinking skills. What emerged was a sequenced curriculum that required students to take introductory coursework, a foundations course in three subfields, a methodology course, and a newly created capstone course. With this curriculum, we were able to get all students in the major to learn the key concepts and approaches of the discipline. Plus, we agreed to assign specific types of research and skill development in each of the required courses. Under the new curriculum adopted in the mid-1980s, students in political science systematically progressed through assignments designed to develop higher order thinking, research, and writing skills. Their final course in the sequence, a senior seminar, generated student work that enabled faculty to assess knowledge and skill achievement by graduates.

Thus, when the Wahlke report came out in 1991, reading it was an eerie encounter. Virtually everything in the report had been discussed in our campus meetings, and the recommendations for the major closely matched our own decisions. While we had already gotten positive assessment feedback from the changes to the program, the Wahlke report served to authenticate our structured curriculum and capstone requirement. Significant improvement in student performance on quantitative and qualitative assessment measures also provided evidence that our changes were successful. Finally, campus values and discussions that encouraged students and faculty to focus on student learning and quality rather than traditional efficiency data helped motivate us.

A number of assessment scholars have argued that the source of pressures for campus assessment makes a difference in its potential for impact (Aper, Cuver, and Hinkle 1990, 471; Banta and Moffett 1987; Banta, Rudolph, Van Dyke, Fisher 1996; Wright 2000). Internal initiatives are given a better chance of success than external mandates. However, even at Truman, where pressure for assessment came from within the university, faculty felt it was being forced on them by the administration. It was only through the administration's patience that the majority of us were persuaded to embrace the assessment enterprise. Administrative decisions, such as increasing the number of faculty while reducing administrative positions on campus, and promising to never use assessment punitively, elevated trust, as did the persistent drumbeat for the faculty to "think better, not bigger." The focus was on the quality of student learning rather than on numeric efficiency.

Unfortunately, many of the campuses we worked with over the next two decades did not have supportive environments to complement assessment demands. In these situations, the most promising message is probably the following: Since faculty have the prerogative to contribute to the design of the assessment system, they can identify ways to use assessment to yield information on issues they care about at the same time as they meet external accountability requirements. For example, even if the university is required to use national exams, they can place the exams in a larger system of mixed measures and evaluative processes that offer the potential for both accountability and improving programs. Since Truman's experience was that poor performance on the national exams forced us out of our complacency, Truman faculty were able to speak to the utility of its inclusion in an assessment system. We were also able to highlight that other assessments, such as survey data and capstone projects, can play a vital role in guiding reform strategies.

RESPONSES TO ASSESSMENT PRESSURES AND CHOICE OF ASSESSMENT METHODS

Rather than advocating the use of specific assessments, it is more useful to identify some general considerations for building effective assessment systems. While regional accrediting agencies and states have been mandating assessment in various forms for several decades, their implementation of the requirement has varied in content and timing. Even though most states permit universities to design their own assessment systems within certain constraints, by the time accreditors, state mandates, and administrative decisions make it to the faculty, the overhead weight can be very heavy. Thus, it should not be a surprise that on most campuses faculty energy is focused on resisting the mandates to assess rather than on designing a system that will provide useful feedback. This pushback by faculty helps to explain why a number of schools are still in the early stages of building an assessment system. At the same time, as more campuses have established assessment processes, there are more faculty voices in the higher education community offering evidence of the positive results that can come from assessment.

This range of reactions to demands for assessment is reflected in the assessment papers presented over the past several years of the newly established APSA Teaching and Learning Conference (American Political Science Association 2008). Those who have found assessment an intrusion, cite limited resources, imperfect measures, unclear directives, non-enthused colleagues, and fear of misuse as a few of their concerns. At the other end of the spectrum, there are a number of papers that communicate how campuses derived positive results from their initiatives to comply with assessment demands. My conclusion is that in most cases, faculties can find ways to derive advantages from assessing, even when they are initially motivated by compliance rather than improvement.

For departments that are struggling to get colleagues to pay attention to assessment, it is important to suggest ways that they can make assessment more than a bureaucratic activity. Patient but persistent nudging is usually necessary to get colleagues to establish and maintain a comprehensive assessment system. However, the deadlines attached to accreditation processes may be your best friend for beginning an initial assessment cycle. This deadline can be used to get the effort and support (or quiescence) necessary to move forward with a first round of assessment. Every university has unique cultural elements that must be considered. However, an overview of the wide array of potential methods should help those who are responding to assessment mandates. With such a large assessment tool box, faculties have the opportunity to tailor practical, useful responses to the needs of their programs. Upon perusal of what is admittedly not a comprehensive list (see Table 7-1), you can probably find several methods that are likely to be acceptable and affordable. This is the first step.

Table 7-1 Overview of Assessment Methods*	
TRADITIONAL PROGRAM DATA	Student–Faculty Ratio
	Retention to the Major
	Number of Majors/Minors
	Grade Distribution
	Transcript Analysis
	Syllabi Review
ATTITUDINAL AND SELF-ASSESSMENT INSTRUMENTS	Surveys (e.g., behavior inventories, self-assessments, satisfaction) • Alumni • Enrolled Students • Graduating Students • Employers • Faculty
	Interviews (e.g., exit, entrance, rising junior, employers)
	Focus Groups (e.g., employers)
	Nationally Recognized Surveys (e.g., NSSE, CIRP)

COURSE-EMBEDDED ASSESSMENTS	Collective Scoring of Student Presentations/Papers
	Simulations (e.g., team scoring of problem solving/interpersonal skills)
	Portfolios
	Capstones as Assessment
COMPREHENSIVE EXAMS	Nationally Recognized Exams in the Field (e.g., ETS Major Field Test)
	Nationally Recognized Exams in Critical Thinking/Problem Solving (e.g., Collegiate Learning Assessment)
	Locally Developed Examinations (could be embedded in a capstone)

*To see campus' experiences with these methods see Banta, Lund, Black, and Oblander 1996.

REVIEW EXISTING DATA

The initial stages of preparing a program assessment plan should include review of data that already exists. Often this requires accessing a number of different offices on a campus and thinking creatively about how one can mine the data. Traditional data provides the opportunity to compare the program to the university on items like retention, major migration patterns, graduation rates, number of transfer students, number employed following graduation, number enrolling in graduate or professional programs, and number doing internships, service learning, undergraduate research, and studying abroad. It is also important to identify any university-wide assessment instruments that the program could incorporate into its assessment. For example, if the university uses any of the nationally recognized surveys for incoming freshman or student engagement, the department can use them for very productive evaluations of the types of students in the program, their backgrounds, habits, and expectations. While these are not direct measures of student-learning outcomes, they provide important information for understanding how students approach learning. Some of the engagement surveys have numerous questions about students' study practices, class preparation habits, and faculty–student interaction opportunities that would be very helpful to review. Even if the data is a sample of the whole campus and data is not broken down to the program level, it still can be a very helpful place to start the program's review. Getting the university to provide data on the program's students may be possible, especially if several years of data can be aggregated to create a sufficient number of respondents from the major. Some of the same variables can be studied in a locally developed departmental survey which can then be analyzed and compared with campus and national data.

PROGRAM PURPOSES: STATEMENT OF GOALS AND OBJECTIVES.

Accreditors usually expect departments to begin with a statement of goals and objectives about the intended purposes and expected results of the program. Goals are considered broader and more general. Objectives are supposed to target specific learning outcomes that the program develops in its students. I recommend that departments not let this become too time-consuming an effort. Looking at the websites of other universities and keeping the statement of goals and objectives pretty simple can assist in moving on to assessment without getting bogged down. Make it clear that the program will revisit the goals and objectives statements as faculty continue their discussions. Many programs find it most helpful to develop a more complete statement of goals and objectives after their discussion of assessment results because this dialogue grounded in the assessment experience almost always produces a more substantive discussion of what the faculty wants its students to know and to be able to do.

MULTIPLE MEASURES

Recommended methods range from quantitative to qualitative and from assessing individual students to evaluating programs and campus environments. While Table 7-1 (above) includes a lot of specific examples of various types of assessments, it is not an attempt to provide an exhaustive list. Rather, the table seeks to help readers understand several types of instruments that fit under each of the categories.

Whether the program is hurriedly crafting an initial cycle of assessment to meet a self-study deadline or is developing a comprehensive, long-term assessment system, using multiple measures is essential. For example, accepting a national exam as your entire assessment system will provide you with a summative evaluation of student knowledge. However, the program needs additional types of assessment information to know how to interpret the results and what reforms to advance. By using multiple measures, you can get information on both educational processes and outcomes. One without the other is not nearly as useful. Politically, multiple instruments help the program respond to the methodological preferences of faculty. It is also helpful to assure faculty that no decisions will be made based on a single data point, thus reducing the opposition of faculty to assessment. When the results of several assessments reinforce each other, it becomes simpler to convince people that the findings are valid and proposed actions are warranted.

Scenario One: Quick Response

Let me propose one possible combination of methods as a simple and effective scenario for an initial assessment cycle. Assume that most faculty in the program highly value teaching students how to conduct research. For an initial assessment effort, the program could get a group of faculty to collectively review a sample of student research papers. This could be supplemented by a syllabi study to reveal the role research assignments play in courses, a transcript study to show how many research courses students take and in what order, and a student "self-assessment" questionnaire covering various elements of the research and writing process as well as their evaluation of resulting papers.

Direct and Indirect Measures

The scenario above would meet accreditors' expectations that the program look at both direct and indirect measures of student learning. Direct measures actually look at student work and in this example meet assessment standards by having faculty members beyond the classroom teacher evaluate them based on the program's knowledge and skills objectives. Indirect measures are a second important strategy, as they have the potential to provide information on behavioral and affective traits that are believed to affect student performance. Pat Hutchings (1989) articulated years ago that just measuring outcomes is insufficient. Looking at faculty expectations and student learning behaviors that underlie student performance through indirect measures is also essential. Information from indirect assessments, like student surveys or transcript studies, also provides vital information conducive to identifying strategies for improvement. For example, in the above scenario, the syllabi and transcript reviews and the student survey responses would provide insight into what students were asked to do and how they evaluated their own research and writing habits and results. This knowledge will complement the direct measure and assist in reform efforts.

Internal and External Measures

Another enhancement in the choice of methods is to combine internal and external assessments as well as direct and indirect measures. Thus, in the scenario above, external examiners from other universities could be incorporated into the reading process to provide an external perspective. Or, several members of the faculty could get together to organize a conference-like event on campus where external examiners are invited to review the student's work. To add an external dimension to the indirect measures, the department could administer a survey for which there are external benchmarks.

Some might wonder why external measures would enhance an assessment system. At the top of the list is that external measures permit the program to make useful comparisons with other programs and to examine other approaches to achieve program objectives. An external examiner process is one means for doing this. Many faculty find the expectation for external assessment intrusive. It can be very stressful to have outsiders evaluate programs or student work. However, without an external perspective, there is a tendency for programs to fall into the Lake Wobegon syndrome where all students and all programs are judged to be above average. At Truman, President Charles McClain challenged faculty to view external measures as similar to the British model of education where students' degree programs culminated with exams written and scored by external examiners (McClain and Krueger 1985; Young and Knight 1993). He saw this as placing the emphasis on long-term learning, the ability to integrate learning over time, and an overall understanding of the field. He also believed the system was more likely to place the faculty member in the role of the students' coach rather than an adversary. Our experience has been that including external measures in a program's assessment system causes faculty to examine what others believe to be important to a particular major or general education program. We don't always agree, but at least faculty discussed the issue and arrived at a conscious decision of what to include or leave out of their program.

National surveys are another type of external measure that provides various opportunities for national benchmarks. For example, the surveys of student engagement provide very promising external measures that permit a broader analysis of student learning behaviors. These surveys give programs comparable information on everything from the student course reading habits to student feelings of belonging at the university. A more controversial but frequently used external measure is a nationally recognized exam. Nationally recognized exams in the field provide helpful feedback in terms of assessing whether students are meeting knowledge goals for the program. The exams provide the program with overall and sub-field scores and provide information on how students compare with others in the country. The exams are written by national panels of scholars so it is also possible to evaluate how closely campus program objectives compare with the expectations of a national panel of scholars. Student results on this type of assessment are very easy to aggregate and report, but this is not sufficient. It is essential to get faculty to examine and discuss the results in order for the assessment process to contribute to improvement.

One ancillary activity that was very helpful to faculty at Truman was for faculty members to review the exam and to discuss how well it fit the local curriculum. As noted earlier, it is important to know the percent of questions students must get correct to score highly on the exam; otherwise, the exams will be seen as too difficult. Remember, it is not bad for a local curriculum to differ from the view of the national panel as long as the program has a good rationale for its design. After taking the time to examine how others see the discipline, faculty must decide whether they agree with the national emphases or not. This discussion can be a powerful catalyst for producing a more intentionally designed curriculum (see Young and Knight 1993; Magruder, McManis, and Young 1997). For students, these national exams also provide an alternative measure of individual achievement to supplement the feedback they receive through traditional grades.

Somewhat surprisingly, one program I worked with proposed using two external measures, a national exam and a national survey, and no internal measures. Faculty were not interested in investing time in the process, had university resources to pay for the assessments, and wished to put forward a plan that provided minimal compliance. In addition, several of the program's faculty members had become quite critical of rubric-based scoring systems, believing them to lack validity. They thought that only measures that met sophisticated psychometric and methodological review could provide legitimate information beyond course grades. While this design had several positive attributes, it needed to incorporate strategies for "closing the loop." Generally, this requires faculty conversations to review the evidence these instruments produce.

Internal measures are measures derived from assessment instruments that have been developed locally by the campus. They are important in part because they require faculty members in the program to invest time in developing and implementing them. They also permit more opportunities for meaningful involvement of students in the design of assessment. Another advantage is that local measures provide programs the opportunity to design assessments tailored to unique elements of the local curriculum, goals, and objectives. Techniques like exit interviews and collective scoring of student papers require faculty to get together to discuss the nature of their program, courses, and assignments. At times, faculty are able to raise ideas for programmatic change as they sit around the table discussing observations of student work. Other times, changes are more individualistic in nature. For example, a faculty member who reads portfolios might adapt an assignment that the faculty member found to produce high levels of student thinking. One disadvantage of this type of assessment is that the results are often harder to communicate to those who were not part of the assessment process since there are no national norms to simplify interpretation of results.

Ideally, assessment plans will include elements that fit each of the four quadrants in Table 7-2, below. This ensures that the program gets multiple types of data. It also enhances the opportunity to respond to the dual purposes of assessment for improvement and accountability. (For more information about assessment strategies see Banta, Lund, Black, and Oblander 1996.)

Table 7-2. Examples of Direct/Indirect and External/Internal Measures		
	External Measures	Internal Measures
DIRECT MEASURES OF STUDENT LEARNING (requires looking at actual student work: exams, papers, presentations)	• Nationally Recognized Exams (e.g., MFT, PCAT, CLA) • External Examiners Review Student Work (e.g., senior theses, presentations, papers, simulations)	• Portfolio • Team Scoring of Student Work • Problem-Solving Simulations • Capstone Course Assessments • Locally Developed Exams
INDIRECT MEASURES OF STUDENT LEARNING	• National Surveys of Student Engagement • Time spent on course and non-course activities • Percentage of students studying abroad, interning, volunteering, conducting undergraduate research	• Student Interviews (e.g., exit, rising junior, or issue-specific interviews) • Focus Groups • Surveys • Syllabi Analysis of Course Assignments in the Program • Percentage of Students Who Go to Graduate/Professional School • Percentage of Alums Who Donate to the University

Virtually all types of campuses can find a system with the recommended mix of assessments that will be compatible with the campus culture and public expectations. Depending on process and culture, each of the techniques has the potential to make important contributions to an effective assessment system. The effect that assessment has on improving the curriculum and student learning is more likely to be related to the role of leadership and culture than to the specific methods chosen. However, having external methods included somewhere in the system is likely to help its perceived legitimacy for those outside the university.

PROCESS

For many programs, assessment demands are not taken very seriously until a deadline is imminent. It is quite typical for requests for assistance to come in this form: "Is it possible to assess students this semester and meet a reporting requirement six months from now?" While "assessment works best when it is ongoing, not episodic" (American Association for Higher Education 1992), it is conceivable that a program could do a decent—even good—first cycle of assessment in six months. Furthermore, if the effort is successful, there is a greater chance for faculty to support future assessment efforts. As a result, integrating consideration of assessment methods with a concern for process is essential. Issues of process cover everything from how assessments are developed, adopted, implemented, and reported to the need for involving faculty, students, and external constituencies. Many process issues are dramatically affected by organizational cultures of the individual campus. Thus, just as process is a consideration in the choice of methods, cultural attributes of the campus will affect assessment processes.

DEFINITION OF ASSESSMENT AS A PROCESS

Barbara Wright, a former director of the AAHE Assessment Forum, emphasizes the "process" of assessment. She defines assessment as "a process of 1) *setting goals...*; 2) *gathering evidence...*; 3) *interpreting* the evidence...; and then 4) actually *using* those discoveries to change the learning environment so that student performance will be improved" (Wright 2000, 2). The important element of this definition is that it recognizes that assessment methods employed are not the key feature of an assessment system. You can generate the best evidence possible, but if there is no serious consideration of the evidence, the potential for evidence-based change to curricula, courses, and pedagogy is minimized. Peter Ewell, one of the leaders in higher education assessment, challenges campuses to create "data dialogues" not "data dumps" (Ewell 2005). To accomplish this, strategic consideration should be given to embedding collegial discussions into the process of assessing. Many campuses have "picture-perfect" models, but the process stops after the second stage in Wright's definition—"gathering evidence." Some methods, like interviews and portfolios, finesse this concern because if faculty conduct the interviews and score the portfolios, they will inevitably integrate the assessment with contemplation of changes in their courses. However, even in these methods where faculty members serve as assessors, assessment will have an even greater impact when there are standard processes for program-wide discussions of the implications of the evidence.

INCORPORATION OF COLLEGIAL DISCUSSION

What, then, are some successful means for integrating assessment methods with the generation of collegial evidence-based discussions? A department chair, dean, provost, or president can each be pivotal influences in generating more collegial discussion. For example, if the provost requires all budget requests for additional funding to include evidence-based rationale, the likelihood of evidence-based discussions goes up. If department chairs know the data and bring agenda items to department meetings based on it, there will be more evidence-based discussions. If there are annual processes for departments to report continuous improvement plans, the likelihood of evidence-based discussion goes up. If faculty are expected to demonstrate involvement in assessment for annual reviews, or at least are rewarded for it, the number of administration–faculty collegial discussions incorporating assessment will increase.

One question that I have been asked on a number of occasions is whether a department can be successful in completing the full cycle of the program assessment process if there is little in the campus culture to reinforce it. This is an excellent question. Of course, there is always a possibility that leadership at the program level plus a cohesive group of faculty can pull it off. However, it is extremely challenging for a department chair and faculty to maintain the enthusiasm to go beyond a compliance approach to assessment if the university president or chief academic officer is not engaged and reinforcing the effort. In these instances, compliance in the form of collecting the data will be the most likely result (Cartwright and Young 2000).

KEEP IT SIMPLE AND FOCUSED

Let's go back to the question at the beginning of this section. Is it possible to conduct a program assessment in six months? In some ways, a tight deadline can be seen as a positive circumstance. Expediency is essential to the effort and thus avoids the pitfall of many assessment efforts that fail as a result of creating too many objectives and too many measures. The tight time frame may help keep the process simple and focused. Using Table 7-2, choose a mix of techniques that will generate evidence to illuminate issues of interest to program faculty. It is more important for the process to go completely through the cycle than for the assessment system to be a path-breaking, comprehensive model.

When putting the assessment plan together, think about a couple of targeted projects where the program can produce quick useful data to address a collectively perceived problem or question of importance. The scenario provided in the methods section above is one that provides direct and indirect evidence of student learning. It also holds the potential to incorporate an external measure either through the use of an external examiner or survey questions with national benchmarks, thereby giving the plan an external as well as an internal point of view. If well crafted, the evidence can be gathered with a minimal amount of time invested and should yield several actionable results based on the "triangulation" of multiple types of data (Young 1996). A single data point is not usually the basis for departmental change, but if several data points reinforce a conclusion, faculty will be more likely to accept the diagnosis and to support change. For example, at Truman, weak performance on national exams, weak retention of important discipline content from one course to the next, inadequate student self-reported study time, and lower-than-expected successful placements in graduate and professional programs caused the department faculty to propose substantial reforms. Thus, it is essential to remember that one of the most important and often overlooked elements in planning program assessment is to structure into the plan occasions for the analysis and discussion of several types of assessment data as they relate to specific department issues.

INTEGRATING STUDENTS AND EXTERNAL CONSTITUENCIES WITH ASSESSMENT PROCESSES

Students and external constituencies should be included in the planning and data interpretation processes of assessment whenever possible. This integration of additional constituencies yields many benefits, such as communicating to these constituencies that the department values their input. Students have the ability to provide helpful interpretations of survey data and can give faculty important insights into what is behind the data. Involving students in the planning and interpretation phases can also help symbolize the intended purposes of the curriculum as well as the purpose and importance of assessment. Student acceptance of assessment is best when it is embedded in courses in ways that make it relatively invisible to students. For example, a program that chooses to team-score student research papers as a direct measure in an assessment plan lessens what students must do for assessment. For non-embedded assessments, keeping the amount of time and effort to complete them to a minimum is also helpful.

External constituencies, such as employers and professionals in the region, may be effectively involved in the process. A number of campuses have found that professionals from the community are especially helpful as external examiners for the evaluation of complex simulations, research papers, and project presentations. In addition, these community professionals tend to increase their support of the college. It allows them to see that the institution is serious about student learning, and they become aware of the capabilities of its students.

REPORTING

In general, reporting of assessment data should integrate the various types of assessment data as they relate to various program and university goals. Data that is merely catalogued and not connected to program goals stimulates less use (Banta and Moffett 1987). Reporting also needs to incorporate a report of the processes that were employed to get the data considered by faculty and other decision makers. By doing so, the program demonstrates its investment in "closing the loop." Finally, programs need to report improvement strategies that are being advanced as a result of collegial discussions of the data. In the initial cycle of assessment, it is very common for the data to raise more questions than they answer. In this case, it is useful to applaud what is found and to then identify several new projects for the next assessment cycle. Often, the conversations that are part of the assessment cycle contribute to increased enthusiasm of program faculty and give them a clearer sense of the program's goals and objectives. If so, these outcomes should be touted. Other positives that can be highlighted are that the program increased what it knows about its students and that several faculty members are making adaptations to assignments, pedagogy, and/or advising. Curricular modification is a possibility, but a change at this level is much rarer than the types of smaller adjustments noted above. Even if each change seems small, the number of students affected and the cumulative impact can add up to significant change.

CULTURE

For centuries, the quality of higher education was assumed. However, criticisms and demands for increased accountability became very loud beginning in the mid-1980s. How campuses have responded to these pressures is a vital cultural influence on campus responses to demands for assessment. Many hoped the criticism and corollary demands for assessment would dissipate, but the recent reports from the commission on the future of higher education appointed by Secretary Spellings have actually increased the intensity of the calls for improvement and accountability (U.S. Department of Education). After describing the great historic successes of U.S. higher education, the commission's final report proceeds to describe substantial problems in the system. It documents a number of negative findings regarding student learning and then asserts, "Compounding all of these difficulties is a lack of clear, reliable information about the cost and quality of postsecondary institutions, along with a remarkable absence of accountability mechanisms to ensure that colleges succeed in educating students." (12) If the calls for increased quality and accountability were isolated, there would be less for the higher education community to worry about. However, that is not the case. The 2007 rankings by *U.S. News & World Report* is prefaced by another example of public concern. While the magazine accepts that their measures are not perfect, it notes high levels of favorable public feedback as support for ratings like theirs. The magazine also reminds its critics that the measures were constructed with the assistance of those in the higher education community. Of particular note is Editor Brian Kelly's assertion that the higher education system continues to be "largely unaccountable." Thus, the reputation and respect for higher education among higher education's attentive public and the public at large continue to show troubling signs. Given these concerns and increasing economic and educational competition from other countries, it would be imprudent for us to expect the demands for assessment to disappear in the foreseeable future.

LEADERSHIP AND FRAMING

If one accepts that accountability-based assessment mandates are not going away, higher education's collective interest would best be served if campus leaders are able to find ways to integrate measures that meet accountability requirements with measures of interest to the campus for improving the learning process. Assessment resisters and some assessment advocates view assessment for accountability as irreconcilable with assessment for improvement. Truman's experience and the experience of many other campuses suggest otherwise.

While assessment for accountability and improvement are usually seen as two opposing ends of the assessment continuum, each incorporates elements of the other. To be genuinely accountable, higher education must seek continuous improvement. The public would not easily accept a posture of "we've arrived and need no further improvement." Similarly, improvement without any understanding of how the program compares with others is underwhelming. External benchmarks that show deficiencies in your program may be exactly what is needed to get faculty to commit to improvement. For Truman, seeing evidence that our program was performing below our expectations led us to change, and these changes have resulted in a demonstrably better program. Thus, the more we view the improvement and accountability objectives as conceptually related and intertwined, the less the assessment debate will fall into the accountability versus improvement trap. The burden for resolving this accountability/improvement paradox rests on leaders at all levels of higher education.

Assessment models cannot be successful in a vacuum. Leadership is essential. How assessment is discussed and used sets the tone for the enterprise. Department chairs will be most successful when the president, provost, and deans generate enthusiasm for improvement and use data to validate the effort. If campus leaders characterize the effort as an illegitimate intrusion in the affairs of the campus, resistance to the mandates from accreditors and the state will be more likely. Alternatively, if campus leaders place emphasis on the centrality and quality of student learning and frame assessment as an essential scholarly activity, there is an increased chance for productive faculty efforts. A particularly successful strategy for leaders from department chairs and faculty entrepreneurs to provosts and presidents is one of patient persistence. Applaud honest efforts, support ongoing engagement in the assessment process, and encourage successive improvements to the assessment system. If campus leaders do this, they will enhance the likelihood of a productive response (Cartwright and Young 2000).

CULTURAL CONDITIONS THAT ENHANCE THE CHANCES OF EFFECTIVE ASSESSMENT

Over the years of working with multiple campuses, I have found a number of campus conditions to be characteristic of effective assessment systems:

1. Presidents, chief academic officers, and other campus leaders know the data and use it to raise questions and set agendas.

2. Assessment is integrated into strategic and long-range planning.

3. Leaders from the president down to program chairs emphasize the student learning goals that are being assessed; assessment is not the goal in and of itself.

4. Leaders do not use data punitively against members of the university community.

5. Decisions are made based on multiple measures.

6. Faculty are entrusted with the design and implementation of assessment.

7. Success stories are highlighted at campus forums and in campus communications.

8. Leaders introduce assessment in hiring interviews and faculty orientation; this helps communicate its importance to new hires while at the same time offering a more precise picture of the campus.

9. Students are introduced to the role assessment plays in improving the campus and to the opportunity it gives them to receive feedback beyond grades on their performance.

10. Students are members of assessment committees.

Where assessment works well, it symbolizes the shared vision of the university. This integration of assessment and cultural cues is one of the most beneficial results of assessment efforts. Faculty interests are enhanced when assessment elevates the visibility of student learning as a campus priority (Magruder, McManis, and Young 1997; Young and Knight 1993). As assessment evidence becomes an expected part of deliberation of campus issues, the campus culture and processes are enhanced. Faculty will be less fearful of misuse of the data when the process reports data for the whole department or subunits rather than by individual faculty member.

My experiences suggest that campuses should think in terms of three dimensions when developing program assessment. First, keep the assessment methods relatively simple and focus on topics of interest to faculty. Ideally, this system will include a mixture of direct, indirect, internal, and external measures. Second, assessment processes need to be developed that give faculty members ownership and occasions to be involved in evidence-based dialogue. Various techniques, such as requiring evidence as part of budget requests and planning processes, are helpful in taking assessment efforts beyond a disposition of compliance. Third, leadership needs to frame assessment in such a way that improvement and accountability are effectively blended. Enhancing the quality of higher education programs must be seen as the primary objective. Assessment systems that integrate collegial processes, enhance evidence-based discussions, and use willing faculty in assessment processes have the potential to enhance the quality of assignment prompts, the centrality of student learning, the purposefulness of the curriculum, and the cohesiveness of the department. Thus, assessment originally designed to achieve an adequate level of compliance may achieve far more.

Most universities still have an amazing amount of flexibility in the methods they can use to meet accreditation and state requirements. Seizing this opportunity to produce effective assessment systems makes it more likely that universities will influence future mandates and potentially receive fewer of them. Institutions and their subunits that make the most of the assessment process can significantly buffer narrow and specific mandates by presenting required data in the context of additional findings. Choosing from the wide variety of assessment methods available, it is possible to implement assessment that aligns with the values and needs of the department and campus. If successful, higher education may find it much easier to "tell its story" better and to improve both student learning and the critical posture the public currently possesses of higher education.

NOTE

1. At the time, the university was named Northeast Missouri State University. The legislature passed legislation in 1985 giving the university a new mission as the state's liberal arts and science university. In 1995, the state changed the name of the university to Truman State University.

REFERENCES

American Association for Higher Education (AAHE). 1992. *Principles of Good Practice for Assessing Student Learning.* Washington, D.C.: AAHE.

American Political Science Association. 2004–2008. Conference on Teaching and Learning, Papers on Assessment. www.apsanet.org/content_39495.cfm.

Aper, Jeffrey P., Steven M. Cuver, and Dennis E. Hinkle. 1990. "Coming to Terms with the Improvement Versus Accountability Debate in Assessment." *Higher Education* 20 (December): 471–83.

Association of American Colleges. 1985. *Integrity in the College Curriculum: A Report to the Academic Community.* Washington, D.C.: Association of American Colleges.

Banta, Trudy, and Marian S. Moffett. 1987. "Performance Funding in Tennessee: Stimulus for Program Improvement." In *Student Outcomes Assessment: What Institutions Stand to Gain. New Directions for Higher Education, no. 59,* ed. D.F. Halpern. San Francisco: Jossey-Bass, 35–44.

Banta, Trudy W., Jon P. Lund, Karen E. Black, and Frances W. Oblander. 1996. *Assessment in Practice: Putting Principles to Work on College Campuses*. San Francisco: Jossey-Bass.

Banta, Trudy W., Linda B. Rudolph, Janice V. Van Dyke, and Homer S. Fisher. 1996. "Performance Funding Comes of Age in Tennessee." *Journal of Higher Education* 67 (January–February): 23–45.

Cartwright, Debra, and Candace Young. 2000. "Assessment Measures Leading to More EffectiveAssessment Programs." In *Papers on Self-Study and Institutional Improvement*, ed. Susan E. Van Kollenburg. Chicago: North Central Association, 103-07.

El-Khawas, Elaine, and Linda Kopp. 1986. *Campus Trends 1986: Panel Report No. 73*. Washington, D.C.: American Council on Education.

———. 1996. *Campus Trends 1996: Adjusting to New Realities*. Higher Education Panel Report, No. 86. Washington, D.C.: American Council on Education.

Ewell, Peter T. 1991. *To Capture the Ineffable: New Forms of Assessment in Higher Education. Reprints of Two Papers Treating Assessment's History and Implementation*. Washington, D.C.: AAHE Assessment Forum, 1–46.

———. 1997. *Quality is Inside-Out: Re-Thinking Priorities for Assessment and Quality Assurance*. Boulder: NCHEMS.

———. 2005. *Assessing Assessment: Successes, Failures, and the Future*. Boulder: *NCHEMS*.

Hutchings, Pat. 1989. *Behind Outcomes: Contexts and Questions for Assessment*. Washington, D.C.: AAHE Assessment Forum.

Ishiyama, John, Paul Parker, John Quinn, and Candace Young. 2007. "The Capstone Course as Program Assessment." Paper presented at the American Political Science Association Teaching and Learning Conference. Charlotte, NC. http://apsanet.org/content_39495.cfm.

Kelly, Brian. 2007. "The Story Behind the Rankings." *U.S. News & World Report*, August 27.

Magruder, Jack, Michael McManis, and Candace Young. 1997. "The Right Idea and the Right Time: Development of a Transformational Assessment Culture." In *The Campus-LevelImpact of Assessment: Progress, Problems, and Possibilities. New Directions for Higher Education, No. 100*, ed. Peter J. Gray and Trudy Banta, 17–29.

McClain, Charles J., and Darrell W. Krueger. 1985. "Using Outcomes Assessment: A Case Study in Institutional Change." In *Assessing Educational Outcomes: New Directions for Higher Education*, No. 17, ed. Peter T. Ewell. San Francisco: Jossey-Bass, 33–46.

National Governors' Association. 1986. *Time for Results: The Governors' 1991 Report on Education*. Washington, D.C.: National Governors' Association.

National Institute of Education. 1984. *Involvement in Learning: Realizing the Potential of American Higher Education*. Washington, D.C.: U.S. Government Printing Office.

Northeast Missouri State University. 1984. *In Pursuit of Degrees with Integrity: A Value-Added Approach to Undergraduate Assessment*. Washington, D.C.: American Association of State Colleges and Universities.

National Commission on Excellence in Education. 1983. *A Nation at Risk: The Imperative for Educational Reform. A Report to the Nation and the Secretary of Education*. Washington, D.C.: U.S. Government Printing Office.

National Survey of Student Engagement. 2000. *The NSSE 2000 Report: National Benchmarks of Effective Educational Practice*. Bloomington: Indiana University Center for Postsecondary Research and Planning.

U.S. Department of Education. 2006. *A Test of Leadership: Charting the Future of U.S. Higher Education*.Washington, D.C.

Wahlke, John C. 1991. "Liberal Learning and the Political Science Major: A Report to the Profession." *PS: Political Science & Politics* 24 (March): 48–60.

Wright, Barbara. 2000. "Assessing Student Learning." In *Learning from Change. Landmarks in Teaching and Learning in Higher Education from Change Magazine, 1969–1999*, ed. D. De Zure. Sterling, VA: Stylus Publishing, 299–304.

Young, Candace Cartwright, and Michael E. Knight. 1993. "Providing Leadership for Organizational Change." In *Making A Difference: Outcomes of a Decade of Assessment in Higher Education*, ed. T. W. Banta and Associates. San Francisco: Jossey-Bass, 25–39.

Young, Candace Cartwright. 1996. "Triangulated Assessment of the Major." In *Assessment in Practice: Putting Principles to Work on College Campuses*, ed. Trudy W. Banta, Jon P. Lund, Karen E. Black, and Frances W. Oblander. San Francisco: Jossey-Bass, 101–03.

SCOTT ERB, UNIVERSITY OF MAINE – FARMINGTON

POLITICAL SCIENCE AND GENERAL EDUCATION ASSESSMENT

Political science courses serve at least two functions in most universities. For most faculty members, the goal of a course is to provide majors with core understandings of the discipline and give non-majors a sense of how political scientists think and understand the world. However, especially in schools with small programs like the University of Maine at Farmington, administrators also view political science courses as serving the general education mission of the school. General education has, in fact, taken on new importance for accrediting agencies, regents, and boards of trustees. One way political scientists can make a statement about the value of their program is to provide evidence of how political science courses meet and promote general education goals. In this chapter, I describe the assessment program in its initial stages at Farmington, designed to measure how well political science course work meets the university's stated general education goals, and to provide preliminary evidence on student performance in specifically defined general education skills: writing, public presentation, technology, and research. The Farmington experience so far suggests that an assessment program can provide information to improve teaching and learning, generate data showing the efficacy and importance of the political science program, and promote critical reflection on the content and purpose of political science course work.

WHAT IS GENERAL EDUCATION?

The political science program at Farmington is relatively small, meaning that in introductory classes often 90% of the students are non-majors taking the course work as electives or for general education purposes. Even upper-level courses are generally half major and half non-major. According to Nichols and Nichols, "General education relates to the concept of communication of a common body of knowledge, skills and perspectives/values regarding civilization from one generation to another" (2001, 11). Traditionally, this meant defining a core (common courses for all students) or a distribution requirement (a menu of courses designed to provide breadth and allow student choice) in order to ensure student access to the most important aspects of the academic tradition. As a result, general education tended to be reduced to a set of requirements that students had to fulfill in order to graduate–annoyances on the road to a major. Beginning in the 1990s, a sea change in thinking about general education began to take place as accrediting agencies and scholars started to question the efficacy of reducing this important function to a set of requirements that may have more to do with turf battles than actual concern for student learning. The result was that since 1990 general education curriculum has been changing rapidly (Johnson, Radcliffe, and Gaff 2004, 9).

The New England Association of Schools and Colleges (NEASC), the accreditation organization for Farmington, demands that "the general education requirement is coherent and substantive. It embodies the institution's definition of an educated person and prepares students for the world in which they will live. The requirement informs the design of all general education courses, and provides criteria for its evaluation, including the assessment of what students learn" (2005). NEASC goes on to require that at least 40 credit hours be spent in general education, and that "graduates successfully completing an undergraduate program demonstrate competence in written and oral communication in English; the ability for scientific and quantitative reasoning, for critical analysis and logical thinking; and the capability for continuing learning, including the skills of information literacy. They also demonstrate knowledge and understanding of scientific, historical, and social phenomena, and a knowledge and appreciation of the aesthetic and ethical dimensions of humankind" (2005). Moreover, institutions are expected to develop a culture of assessment and provide evidence on how well they are achieving these goals. General education can no longer be seen as just a set of diverse requirements, but rather as a cohesive program yielding measurable results. This creates an opportunity for political science, as our discipline combines issues and perspectives in a manner easily congruent with most general education goals.

General Education Reform and Assessment at Farmington: Trial and Error

In 1998, Farmington made its first major change of the general education curriculum in decades. Since then, the program has been in constant flux, with revisions nearly every year. One change put in place in 1998 was to add four skills–writing, public presentation, research, and technology–as general education goals. Summer committees composed of faculty members from a variety of disciplines drafted the criteria courses had to follow in order to be designated a "skills course." Unfortunately, this plan proved unworkable. Faculty members resented having to fulfill specific course criteria often out of step with the standards of their disciplines, while students were faced with a hodgepodge of letter codes to designate skill courses, making it virtually impossible for the Registrar's office to verify student compliance with the requirements.

In 2002, the Faculty Senate eliminated the skills designations, but maintained skills courses as general education requirements. Rather than verify that students took a certain number of skills courses, programs were expected to monitor and assess skill development within their program. This charge was accompanied by an institutional effort to help programs assess general education skills; this help included a website with examples from five different programs, including political science. We realized that even for general education there needs to be a two-track approach. While the institution defines overall goals and outcomes, disciplines define how their assignments address these goals and learning outcomes. Although the university website was meant to provide models for other programs on campus and was presented as an example of innovative thought in general education at a variety of conferences, including the American Political Science Association's Teaching and Learning Conference and the NEASC/NEEAN (New England Educational Assessment Network), most programs on campus did not undertake an effort to develop their own plans to monitor and assess general education skills, and progress stalled. Then, after a year of study and debate, the faculty at Farmington voted to switch the three-credit-hour per course system requirement to four credit hours. Included in this plan was a commitment to enhance both general education and assessment.

The Interdisciplinary and General Education (IGE) Committee developed a set of general education goals that were presented to the campus community in the fall of 2005. After discussion, debate, and redrafting, the Faculty Senate adopted them in the spring of 2006. This list included the earlier skills, but embedded them in a broader set of institutional goals. Programs were asked to identify general education goals fulfilled in each course and put that information in their course descriptions. Assessment remained a priority, but shifted to the Academic Planning and Assessment Committee (APA), which built on the work done in the past to create a new and vastly improved assessment website to help faculty develop and communicate assessment plans (http://assessment.umf.maine.edu/). Thus, nearly ten years after a new general education curriculum was implemented by trial and error, Farmington has moved toward a formal set of goals and a coordinated effort to develop a culture of assessment.

Many issues remain unresolved. General education assessment is usually thought to be a university-wide process. General education is interdisciplinary and presumably bears fruit later in the student's academic career as the various general education courses and activities accumulate and students learn to transfer knowledge from one course or setting to another. Yet, designing tools to assess that effort is a very difficult task, which we at Farmington have not figured out how to accomplish. An alternative is to examine general education outcomes within disciplinary courses, since presumably the impact of general education should show itself in all courses a student takes, and thus can be assessed. That is the model operating at Farmington, with the political science assessment program starting with an emphasis on writing, web design, public presentation, and research skills as reflecting general education development.

This process is continuing, and in 2007 a summer task force prepared recommendations to move to a coherent general education program that goes beyond the traditional distribution requirements now in use. This creates a double opportunity for the political science program. We can demonstrate our efficacy at general education through assessment, ensuring that any change in general education does not diminish the perceived importance of the political science program on campus. Moreover, this offers an incentive to thoroughly critique our own practices and course structure to explore strengthening them by taking interdisciplinarity seriously and developing new approaches to traditional questions investigated within political science.

POLITICAL SCIENCE AND GENERAL EDUCATION ASSESSMENT

Rather than approach assessment as a task designed to generate evidence for administrators to prove that students are learning, we decided to approach it as a research project to enhance effective teaching and learning. Farmington embraces the Scholarship of Teaching and Learning (SoTL) as being as significant as disciplinary scholarship for the purposes of promotion and tenure, demonstrating that the university values using faculty using their research skills and time to improve their teaching. The scholarship of assessment, as described by Thomas Angelo, "holds great promise for engaging faculty in activities to document and improve teaching effectiveness and student learning quality that are both institutionally and individually valuable" (Angelo 2002, 191).

How can this be applied to general education? In the myriad of influences facing students, how can one determine and measure what developed a student's writing skills or increased a student's respect for human diversity? Most assessment programs follow a similar strategy, articulated succinctly by Barbara Walvoord as a three step process: articulate goals for student learning, gather evidence on whether students are meeting these goals, and use the information to improve educational efforts (2004, 3). The goals already existed in the identification of the skills each program is required to assess, and in the specific general education goals passed by the Faculty Senate in 2006. The next step is to gather evidence. To that end, we undertook two initial assessment tasks: 1) to match our courses with specific general education goals in order to create a template of how our courses address university goals; and 2) to assess the four general education skills required by the Faculty Senate. We have collected data for each for the year 2006–07, yielding interesting results as well as providing lessons to consider while moving forward.

COURSES AND UNIVERSITY GENERAL EDUCATION GOALS

One easy way to assess how the program advances general education goals is to analyze syllabi from recently taught courses that service general education and match them to the university goals. The general education goals were agreed upon in the spring of 2006, and the new four-credit curriculum was implemented in fall 2006. This meant that all courses could be refashioned with the general education goals in mind.

The goals approved by the Faculty Senate are listed below. Each goal has a full description, a list of which is too lengthy to include here. Instead, example descriptions will be given for three of the goals (1a, 1b, and 1e) to demonstrate the kind of thinking behind the goals.

1. Students will acquire the concepts, literacies, skills, and habits needed as a foundation for their lives as students and for life-long learning.

   a) Mathematical literacy. Students will be knowledgeable about math, not merely as a utilitarian technique, but as a way of thinking that underlies and expresses a range of ideas in a variety of academic disciplines (e.g., economics, biology, music). They will be fluent in basic mathematical operations, think critically about statistical information, and be able to use these skills to solve real problems, in both academic disciplines and in their day-to-day lives.

   b) Science as a way of knowing. Students will understand the scientific method in terms of its processes, its historical significance, its power to reveal knowledge, and its ethical challenges. Students will be able to apply the scientific process by observing natural phenomena and developing, testing, and evaluating hypotheses. Students will be able to think critically about scientific results and claims, both for their intrinsic value and in the context of political, social, and environmental issues.

   c) Critical thinking and decision making.

   d) Habits of inquiry, invention, and reflection.

   e) Reading, writing, and speaking. Students will know how to do a close reading and how to progressively improve their interpretations of difficult texts. Students will be able to use writing not only to communicate information but also as a powerful mode of gaining access to, interpreting, and reflecting on the knowledge that evolves in their personal, academic, and discipline-specific experiences. They will know how to recognize different written forms and be able to adapt their writing to accommodate such forms (as in the various forms of papers in different disciplines). Students will be able to listen and speak effectively in a discussion group and to present their work to audiences, using technological innovation where appropriate. In all of these forms of expression, students will be able to formulate and defend a thesis.

f) Information research skills.

g) Health and wellness.

2. Students will have the capacity for both breadth and depth in their thinking.

    a) Knowledge of the intellectual and aesthetic heritage of human-kind.

    b) Literacy in disciplines.

    c) Interdisciplinary thinking beyond that provided by the major.

3. Students will be responsible local and global citizens.

    a) Respect for human diversity.

    b) Environmental stewardship.

    c) Ability to collaborate.

In 2006–07, we taught eight different courses that can be used as part of the general education curriculum (currently courses that count for a social science distribution requirement).[1] Each assignment was scrutinized to determine which goals were addressed and how. At this point, we did not including midterm and final examinations in our general education assessment program, based on a belief that those are most likely to test disciplinary knowledge. Information about the assignments was documented in a general education folder that demonstrates how our assignments address the goals; the process is ongoing, updated every semester. Starting in the fall of 2007, we began to collect evidence of student work to illustrate how the assignments address various general education goals from a political science perspective.

Table 8-1 summarizes the general education goals addressed by the courses taught in 2006–07, listing the number of assignments that in some way addressed each goal. After that is an example of the way

Table 8-1. Summary of General Education Goals*													
	GOALS												
Courses	1a	1b	1c	1d	1e	1f	1g	2a	2b	2c	3a	3b	3c
POS 101	1	2	3	3	3	2			3	1	1		1
POS 121	1	1	3	2	4	3			3	1	3		
POS 136		1	3	3	3	2			2	3	4	1	1
POS 177		1	3	2	3	2		2	3	2	3		
POS 210	2	1	3	2	3	3			2				1
POS 225	2	1	2	3		2		1	1	1			1
POS 231	1	1	5	5	5	1					1		1
POS 255		1	3	3	2	2			2				
POS 332	0	1	1	2	1	1			1	1			1
Total	7	10	26	25	24	18	0	3	17	9	12	1	6

*Addressed by assignments not including examinations and quizzes from each course

assignments are documented in the political science general education folder: each assignment is listed, followed by an explanation of how that assignment addresses various general education goals. The data shows room for improvement. Although our coursework includes considerable material meant to foster respect for human diversity, promote environmental stewardship, enhance knowledge about the intellectual and aesthetic heritage of human kind, explore science as a way of knowing, and develop interdisciplinary thinking, Table 8-1 shows that these goals are not made the subject of many assignments. Existing assignments are weighted heavily on skills, critical thinking, research, reflection, and styles of inquiry. Although it is tempting to point to course material (reading and lectures) as addressing the other goals, not having assignments where students actively engage the subject is less effective as a learning tool, and more difficult to assess.

Figures 8-1 and 8-2 give examples of how assignments can be assessed in terms of their fit to general education goals. While this documentation is a good start in assessing what the courses offer and require, assessing learning outcomes for general education goals is more difficult. Assessment tools for outcomes within the major (portfolios, matrices, etc.) could help, and this information would give the APA and IGE committees data to help build a university-wide general education outcomes assessment program.

Figure 8-1. Example of Assignment Documentation

COURSE: POS 277: Islamic Politics
Assignments 2 & 3 (research papers)
Major/Non-Major Count: 15 majors, 13 non-majors

General Education Goals Met: 1c, 1d, 1e, 1f, 2a, 2b, 2c, and 3a

Assignment: Research Papers (30% each, 60% total)

Students will write two research papers (6–8 pages) on a Muslim country or community of their choice. These papers are intended to give students an opportunity to focus their research on a topic of interest under the two different sections of the course (e.g., paper one on democratization and the Egyptian Muslim Brotherhood and paper two on the impact of State feminism on the status of Egyptian women). Students are strongly urged to write both papers on the same Muslim state or community (e.g., Muslims in France). Papers will be presented orally in class in order for fellow students to gain greater breadth and depth from the research of others. Topic proposals and initial bibliographies (1 page) are due October 4 and November 8. Papers are due in class on the day of the paper presentations: October 25 and December 13. With the exception of a documented health or family emergency, the grade on late papers will automatically be lowered by 1/3 of a grade per 24-hour period past the due date.

Figure 8-2. Explanation of Fit to General Education Goals

1c: This supports critical thinking and decision making as students must choose two topics concerning a Muslim community (decision making) and address complex issues (critical thinking). Students are required to submit topic proposals and bibliographies, designed to improve their decision-making skills in terms of completing assignments.

1d: The design of the assignment gives the instructor the ability to guide how students approach the research, working on developing solid habits of inquiry and helping students reflect on their methods and findings.

1e: Writing skills are developed by putting together two papers, with bibliographies and proposals due ahead of time. Speaking skills are developed by an oral presentation of the papers, with a rubric provided and time spent in presentation preparation.

1f: Information research skills are developed by researching these two topics and developing a research paper. A rubric is provided, as well as aid in the research process.

2a: Knowledge of Islam and the role of Islamic culture in various societies is an important part of the intellectual and aesthetic heritage of humankind.

2b: Students will be given political science concepts and research tools to use in order to investigate these issues, which are at the forefront of the discipline given current issues involving Islam and both world and domestic politics.

2c: The questions to be researched create obvious opportunities to link with other disciplines, including religion, sociology, philosophy, etc.

3a: Knowledge of Muslim communities in various countries and involving particular issues concerning their activity promotes learning about human diversity, with the assignment designed to foster respect.

Political science faculty members have also taken a leading role in interdisciplinary efforts, as interdisciplinarity is a core component of the general education goals and general vision for the future. This includes team teaching courses and working with other disciplines such as education, women's studies, business/economics, and history to develop innovative teaching methods. In political science courses, we also try to integrate the natural sciences (global warming, environmental and energy issues, and the relationship between science and politics), the humanities (consideration of novels as political, the importance of religion in politics, and investigations of politics and the arts), and of course other social science disciplines such as economics and geography. Although it was feared that embracing the interdisciplinary nature of the general education goals would detract from our ability to adequately teach political science, the opposite has happened. By injecting ideas from other disciplines and approaches, we are able to think about the issues of political science in new and creative ways both in the classroom and in scholarly research. The impact of taking general education seriously can go beyond simply serving the institution and in fact help enhance disciplinary work.

SKILL ASSESSMENT

Assessing skill development in writing, public presentation, research, and technology is a daunting task. Subjectively, we know that student presentations in their senior year are better than in their first year, but how do you measure that or determine causality? We decided to ignore the question of causality for now. Following the example of *grounded theory*, assessment can be seen as building a theory of learning by first gathering data and then searching for connections and interesting insights. This is, in essence, a continuing research project, with a goal of increasing sophistication and quality as data is gathered and methods are improved each year (for a description of grounded theory see Glaser and Strauss, 1967) . The starting point is a tool designed to assess each of these skills across courses and in different contexts with a goal of improving feedback to students and generating assessment data.

For each assignment to be assessed, students are given a sheet listing and explaining the criteria to be used for judging their work—a rubric. Each rubric states the expectations for superlative work in each component of the rubric. This differs from rubrics that delineate different outcomes for different grades ("A," "B," "C," etc.) or levels of quality.

Such efforts usually involve modifying the ideal downward, or giving the best and worst descriptions of student performance as bookends.[2] The language of the gradations is problematic and inherently vague. There is a level of subjectivity in making judgments in most assignments that needs to be acknowledged. For the purposes of cross-course comparisons between upper-level and introductory course work on the same scale, it made more sense to set a standard for ideal work and allow faculty members to determine how close they believe a student is to that standard.

Faculty members measure student performance by assigning assessment control points (the ACP score) to each component of the rubric on a 0–10 scale, with ten indicating full achievement of the ideal. Components include: 1) *Public Presentation:* organization, style, content, communication aids, personal appearance, and responsiveness; 2) *Short Papers:* thesis, structure, use of evidence, analysis, logic and argumentation, and mechanics; 3) *Research Paper:* thesis, structure, use of evidence, analysis, logic and argumentation, mechanics, quality of research sources, quantity of relative research; and 4) *Web Design:* content, originality, organization and navigation, presentation, enhancements, integration, and documentation. Although there isn't enough space to give the specific description of each rubric component, descriptions of each component can be found at: http://academic.umf.maine.edu/~erb/rubrics.htm. This is the same rubric given to students, and the web page will be updated as rubrics change. The total ACP score for the assignment is the sum of the rubric components.

ACP scores are generally not used in determining grades but rather as an assessment tool, comparing ACP scores over courses and assignments (an ACP of 7 on a writing assignment in a 100-level course may be an A; it could be a B or C in a 300-level course). Also, different instructors may weigh the components of the rubric differently in determining a grade, and some assignments may emphasize certain aspects of a given rubric. The ACP is a subjective measure to compare student performance across time and in different courses. In that sense it is much like how doctors ask patients to give their level of pain a number; the number may be subjective, but presumably the patient is relatively consistent in how that number is applied, meaning that it is valid to track relative changes in a patient's pain level. Starting in the fall of 2007 students kept their feedback sheets in portfolios documenting their progress and development.

IMPLEMENTING THE ASSESSMENT PROGRAM

The first task was to develop common rubrics, which required considerable web research, as rubrics and assessment plans from various institutions are readily available online. We also consulted other resources to help us understand how to develop skills like writing and public speaking. We investigated numerous online and published rubric guides pertaining to writing, speaking, and research skills (for examples, Singer 2006; Atkinson 2004; and White, Lutz, and Kamusikiri 1996). At this point, we have data from eighteen assignments covering five courses (two of them with multiple sections for eight total classes).[3] All the data comes from courses I taught; we do not yet have a cross section of data from different instructors. One reason for this was confusion on how to implement the program and how it would work in practice. After much discussion, we agreed that I would do the data collection of ACP scores to undertake a pilot study of how the assessment method would operate.

There was universal agreement by the students to have their data included in the project, so the results are based on full student participation. Table 8-2 presents a comparison of each skill by year (first year, sophomore, junior, etc.), clearly demonstrating higher scores by experienced students in three of the four skills. The exception was web-page assignments, where first-year students actually had the highest ACP score. However, web-page design was only used in POS 136, World Politics, an introductory course with a majority of first-year students. The N for this sample is only 45 (as opposed to 237 short papers, 85 research papers, and 137 public presentations). More data and web-design assignments for upper-level courses will be needed to see if this trend holds; since web design is not commonly required, it may be as new a task for a senior as for a first-year student. On the other hand, this could indicate a trend for increased computer proficiency among incoming students.

Table 8-2. Comparison of Average ACP Scores				
	Research Paper	Web Page	Short Paper	Presentation
First Year	N = 36 46.2	N = 24 49.5	N = 82 39.6	N = 63 47.2
Second Year	N = 11 55.3	N = 9 47.1	N = 48 40.8	N = 21 49.9
Third Year	N = 17 55.7	N = 3 47.0	N = 49 44.7	N = 49 55.1
Fourth Year	N = 21 59.6	N = 9 48.3	N = 58 45.1	N = 58 55.0

Table 8-3 compares the average ACP score for each skill in each course (combining short-paper assignments into one average for courses with multiple short papers) to the average grade, with grades given on a 0–4 scale (4.0 = A, 3.7 = A-, 3.3 = B+, 3 = B, etc.). The numerical value of grades reflects the GPA scale at Farmington. This was chosen to accommodate different grading scales (i.e., not everyone grades an assignment from 0 to 100). The data suggests that while quality of work was lower in introductory courses, it was easier to get a good grade. There does not seem to be a difference between 200- and 300-level courses in terms of the relationship between ACP and grades. This is an example of how the data will generate faculty discussions: should introductory-level courses be graded more leniently than upper-division course work? It will also be interesting to see if other instructors have the same kind of result.

Table 8-3. ACP Score vs. Grade by Course					
	FYS 100	**POS 136**	**POS 225**	**POS 231**	**POS 332**
Research	44.6 – 2.7	N/A	57.8 – 3.1	54.2 – 3.0	59.6 – 3.4
Presentation	46.2 – 3.3	49.2 – 3.4	56.8 – 3.4	52.8 – 3.3	55.1 – 3.4
Short Paper	N/A	40.4 – 3.2	43.7 – 3.0	44.2 – 3.2	47.8 –3.4
Web Design	N/A	48.6 – 3.1	N/A	N/A	N/A

One interesting question to ask is whether there is discernable improvement within the semester if types of assignments are repeated in the same course. Table 8-4 presents data from three different classes (two sections of POS 136, and one section of POS 231, European Foreign Policy), comparing scores on short-paper assignments. Each of these courses required three short papers. While there is significant improvement in the ACP scores from assignment one to assignment two, there is a slight drop off in assignment three. This is true for each section taught. This could be an indication that students learn how to improve after their first assignment, but then get so busy that they do not spend as much time on the final assignment. It also is not clear if the improvement from assignment one to assignment two reflects real skill improvement or just knowledge of how the papers will be assessed. It will be interesting to track individual student scores to see if this trend continues. Of course, people who did very well in early assignments may shift priorities to other classes if they think they have leeway, which is rational, if not optimal.

Table 8-4. Semester Progress: Short Paper			
	Paper One	Paper Two	Paper Three
POS 231	42.3	47.4	43.0
POS 136 (Fall '06)	37.6	41.8	40.0
POS 136 (Spr '07)	38.7	42.1	41.9

Table 8-5 gives an example of the ACP scores broken down by rubric category, in this case for short papers. This indicates in which aspects of an assignment students performed relatively well or relatively poorly. For short papers, the lowest scores were for forming a clear thesis and for writing mechanics; this was true for every course. There were similar results for all skills; students generally do better in some components of the rubrics than others. While the initial data from one year is not enough to prove a need for changing assignments and teaching methods, it does suggest that spending some time working with students on developing their theses and supporting good writing mechanics is probably a good idea. It also illustrates a goal of the assessment program: to work to improve student performance in areas of weakness. It will be interesting moving forward to see if there is agreement about where students are strongest and weakest when ACP scores are assigned by different faculty members.

Table 8-5. ACP Score by Rubric Components				
Short Paper	POS 136	POS 225	POS 231	POS 332
Thesis	6.4	7.0	6.9	7.6
Structure	6.9	7.4	7.4	8.1
Evidence	7.0	7.6	7.5	8.1
Analysis	7.0	7.5	7.7	8.0
Logic	7.0	7.3	7.7	8.4
Mechanics	6.2	7.0	7.0	7.5
TOTALS*	40.4	43.7	44.2	47.8
* Numbers may not add up, due to rounding				

With Access software, it's possible to run a number of queries comparing various classes, assignments, and outcomes. This provides the ability to explore potential correlations or theories about student performance, and track individual students throughout their time at Farmington. When multiple instructors are using the tool, differences in instructor perceptions can also be measured, potentially leading to interesting and useful faculty conversations on how to improve both student learning and inter-rater reliability. The tables above involve only a taste of the kind of comparisons that can be made. It is too early to reach conclusions about the meaning of the data, but these results provide a sense of the kind of information that can be generated in the future. Perhaps the most valuable part of the exercise was to communicate to students specific expectations using an agreed-upon common rubric, and then be able to talk with them in clear terms about where they need improvement.[4] It is important to follow what Alexander Astin calls "the feedback principle," which is that the goal of assessment is to facilitate the learning process (Astin 1993, 180).

LESSONS AND NEXT STEPS

After two years and some initial data, what lessons can be drawn from the Farmington experience? First, patience is a virtue. Ten years of development have led to many apparent dead ends. Yet each seeming failure, such as the skill designations or the pilot program assessment website, have improved efforts down the line. Defining goals, reaching agreements, and developing assessment tools take time. Second is the importance of institutional support. Faculty members were empowered rather than commanded, and resources were made available to assist in our efforts. The commitment of the university to take assessment and the Scholarship of Teaching and Learning into account in tenure and promotion decisions is important. Faculty members did not believe they were doing just another task that was heaped on their plates, but rather felt that their efforts were important and would be rewarded. Finally, assessment has to be seen as an ongoing process, a continually developing research project connected to the question of how to enhance student performance and learning. It is valuable to reflect on both the data and the tools used to continually critique the assessment process.

At Farmington, we believe that both the general education goals course review and the skill assessment are worthwhile and should be continued/expanded. For the former, we plan to actively gather student work to be used as examples of student performance that reflects progress in working toward general education goals. We also plan to develop assignments to address those general education goals already present in course content but not yet a part of any course assignment.

For skill assessment, the ACP score provides a promising attempt to generate a qualitative measure of student performance in a manner that can both yield quantitative data and provide an avenue of feedback to students to improve student work. In a number of courses, students are voluntarily and anonymously maintaining a time chart of their work. This was implemented on a trial basis in 2006–07, but too few students participated to make the data valuable. Starting in fall 2007, we began bi-weekly collections of the time sheets with students self-assigned an ID that allows us to track anonymously individual time on task. The goal is not only to determine how much time students are working on the courses, but what assignments and tasks take the most time.

Clearly, there are numerous difficulties to overcome if these assessment techniques are going to be continued and provide quality information. The process of assigning ACP scores was arduous to implement. However, thanks to Access software, it has become easy to use and is an excellent means for giving specific feedback to students with the goal of improving learning outcomes. As other faculty members use this tool, the question of inter-rater reliability becomes important, both for the interpretation of data between instructors and for confidence building in the measure itself (e.g., Maki 2004, 126–32). This will be a major task in the semesters ahead.

For many institutions, the path taken by Farmington may not be appealing for a variety of reasons. Some colleges and universities have not yet articulated clear general education goals. In such a case, one logical course of action would be to turn to the mission statement of the college or university. That was the starting point for the committee that drafted Farmington's goals, and most mission statements have within them an inherent sense of the general outcomes wanted for students. Another possibility would be to read what the accreditation association of the school says about general education, or investigate general education literature to develop a set of departmental general education goals. That could, in fact, spur on efforts to develop institutional goals.

Large universities might find it difficult to use either of the above as tools since many courses serving general education are taught by different instructors using different approaches, and the number of students in the classes may make this kind of feedback/rubric model too cumbersome. Also, if teaching assistants do a majority of the grading, it might be difficult to develop the kind of agreement and inter-rater reliability to which a small program can aspire. Nonetheless, large universities or programs certainly have the number of students and courses to do interesting data collection through samples and statistical analyses. For our assessment, we chose to assess all students doing particular assignments, and can track individual student development. A larger program may not want to pursue such a comprehensive approach. However, sampling a random number of students in a portion of classes at a large school would also generate quality data. Also, a larger school could hire graduate students to act as coders to generate data. While the intensive focus here is feasible at small schools, the fact that assignments can be turned into data creates a variety of opportunities for larger schools to tweak this sort of approach and make it fit their particular situation.

Some programs may not have the need to demonstrate their importance in general education if their major has prestige and success within the discipline. Similarly, colleges or universities servicing a large number of majors and relatively few non-majors may not view their general education component as important. Some may believe that simply showing a political science perspective is enough to claim to be providing a valuable contribution to general education. The trend in general education, however, is toward a coherent program rather than a dabbling of disciplines, and our experience at Farmington suggests that disciplinary insights benefit from taking general education concerns and interdisciplinarity into account. It inspires the creative thinking outside of traditional disciplinary boundaries that yields benefits in research, as well as teaching and learning.

Since general education is a campus-wide activity, the general education portion of assessment requires active engagement with relevant administrative offices—in the case of Farmington, that includes the Director of General Education and the university committees on both assessment and general education. This connects our efforts to broader institutional assessment and allows us to have a say in determining how we go about assessing our students and program. After all, political science is in large part about the study of power, and we know that in the world of university politics it cannot hurt to work on issues to which many faculty members are resistant. Moreover, assessment is here to stay, whether we like it or not. Given the way it can improve feedback to students, generate data on how well students are doing, inspire faculty communication about teaching and learning, and provide information to enhance courses and assignments, assessment is becoming much easier to appreciate. Beyond that, it provides a means for demonstrating the role of political science not just as a discipline, but as an important part of a school's general education program.

NOTES

1. These courses were POS 101, American Government; POS 121, Comparative Politics; POS 136, World Politics; POS 177, Political Theory; POS 210, The Presidency and Congress; POS 225, The European Union; POS 231, European Foreign Policy; POS 255, American Political Thought; POS 277, Islamic Politics; and POS 332, International Law and Organization.

2. For an example of a high-quality rubric with numerous "levels," see Paul Halsall's *General Evaluation Rubric for College Papers* at www.fordham.edu/halsall/med/rubric.html.

3. This includes three sections of a first-year seminar, FYS 100, Syriana; two sections of POS 125, World Politics; and one section each of POS 225, The European Union; POS 231, European Foreign Policy; and POS 332, International Law and Organization. The assignments were research papers and presentations for FYS 100; three short papers, a web-page design assignment, and a public presentation for POS 136; one short paper, one research paper, and a presentation for POS 225; three short papers, a research paper, and presentation for POS 231; and one short paper, a research paper, and a presentation for POS 332. The total was 45 web-design ACPs, 237 short papers, 85 research papers, and 137 presentations.

4. This aspect of the assessment tool was not fully realized in 2006–07. This is because in order to generate initial data to jump-start this project, ACP scores were generated in a majority of assignments in the courses using them. This is considerable work, and not as much time was spent talking with students about individual components as desired. For this reason, we have decided that, optimally, faculty members will use this tool once or twice a semester in a course, trying to cover all four skills over a semester or year.

REFERENCES

Angelo, Thomas A. 2002. "Engaging and Supporting Faculty in the Scholarship of Assessment." In *Building a Scholarship of Assessment*, ed. Trudy Banta. San Francisco: Jossey-Bass.

Astin, Alexander W. 1993. *Assessment for Excellence*. Phoenix: Oryx Press.

Atkinson, Max. 2004. *Lend Me Your Ears*. New York: Oxford University Press.

Glaser, Barney G., and Anselm L. Strauss. 1967. *The Discovery of Grounded Theory: Strategies for Qualitative Research*. Chicago: Aldine Publishing Company.

Johnson, D. Kent, James L. Ratcliff, and Jerry G. Gaff. 2004. "A Decade of Change in General Education." *New Directions for Higher Education* 125:9–28.

Maki, Peggy L. 2004. *Assessing for Learning*. Sterling, VA: American Association of Higher Education.

NEASC Commission on Institutions of Higher Education Standards of Accreditation. 2005. Bedford, Massachusetts. http://neasc.org/cihe/stancihe.htm.

Nichols, James O., and Karen W. Nichols. 2001. *General Education Assessment for Improvement of Student Academic Achievement*. New York: Agathon Press.

Singer, Mark. 2006. *Guidelines for Communication*. North Muskegon, MI: Punim Publishing.

Walvoord, Barbara E. 2004. *Assessment Clear and Simple*. San Francisco: Jossey-Bass.

White, Edward M., William D. Lutz, and Sandra Kamusikiri. 1996. *Assessment for Writing*. New York: MLA.

Examples of Classroom Assessment

Mariya Y. Omelicheva, University of Kansas[1]

Assessment *of* Learning and *for* Learning: Testing the Effectiveness and Accuracy of the Standard Scoring Instruments

The last decade has witnessed a proliferation of innovative teaching strategies. Active and collaborative learning, teaching with technologies, and other instructional methods have been designed to meet the demands for significant changes in the goals and practices of higher education. These novel teaching techniques exposed limitations of standardized tests, and urged the development of new methods of student assessment (Allen and Tanner 2006, 197; Marzano, Pickering, and McTighe 1993, 9).

Various kinds of research projects, presentations, and group assignments are now widely used for collecting evidence on students' progress in achieving higher-order learning objectives and practical skills. Other means of assessment, such as discussions and debates, have been employed to serve the summative and formative purposes of student evaluation. One challenge of applying the original assessment techniques is a degree of subjectivity and unreliability inherent in these methods of assessment. Student performance on complex educational tasks does not have the correct answer keys that typically accompany multiple choice questions (Perlman et al. 1994). To make their judgments about student performance more rigorous and sound, instructors may develop evaluation criteria or scoring guidelines that frequently appear in evaluation forms, evaluation scales, or rubrics.

Which scoring instruments are the most effective and reliable tools for evaluating student performance? The goal of this chapter is to review and examine the effectiveness and accuracy of three scoring tools—evaluation forms, evaluation scales, and evaluation rubrics, which have been employed across university curricula for evaluating a variety of student skills. The effectiveness of a scoring instrument is conceptualized as its ability to improve student performance on a task, whereas accuracy refers to the reliability of evaluation received from its application. I conducted two classroom quasi-experiments in which students applied evaluation forms, scales, or rubrics for evaluating the quality of their own and their peers' work, and compared the reliability and accuracy of students' self- and peer-assessment across experimental conditions. I relied on the experimental findings to review the conditions that make scoring instruments a valuable method of assessment and learning.

INSTRUMENTS FOR SCORING

The transformation of standards for student performance on complex educational tasks into tools for assessment and learning usually occurs through the development of various scoring instruments, such as evaluation forms, scales, or rubrics. A scoring instrument contains a set of criteria or a list of the qualities of an excellent piece of work. Its purpose is to guide students' efforts toward successful completion of an educational task as well as to provide clear benchmarks for fair and sound evaluation of student performance.

The evaluation form is the least formal tool for evaluation. It looks like a scoring sheet with a checklist of criteria accompanied by checkboxes for placing "yes" or "no" marks according to whether each criterion has been met (see Figure 9-1). Performance criteria can be formulated as broad, open-ended questions, and evaluations can be done using verbal ratings, such as "excellent," "satisfactory," or "poor"—indicating the extent to which a criterion has been met. These verbal ratings may have a numerical equivalent for converting evaluations into grades.

Another method of student assessment requires quantification of the dimensions of student performance with a rating scale. This is usually done using different types of evaluation scales. An evaluation scale also contains a checklist of criteria that is typically accompanied by a description of points to be observed in order to evaluate student performance on a given criterion (Omelicheva 2007). Evaluation is done using

Figure 9-1. Sample Evaluation Form for Assessing a Written Assignment		
Student's Name _____ Evaluate an essay using the questions provided below. For each question, place a checkmark in the "yes" or "no" column to indicate your assessment.	YES	NO
Did the student choose a topical issue of international relations?	☐	☐
Did the student choose several sources of news?	☐	☐
Did the student examine presentation of news by the news sources?	☐	☐
Did the student provide comprehensive description of the news?	☐	☐
Did the student examine the news using theoretical approaches discussed in the class?	☐	☐
Did the student prepare a well-written essay?	☐	☐

numerical weights from 1 to 5, with 1 indicating poor performance and the highest rating of 5 indicating an excellent demonstration of a skill. Figure 9-2 displays an example of a scale used for evaluating students' essays in which they were required to analyze the content and presentation of current international news by the mainstream press.

Neither evaluation forms, nor evaluation scales characterize what "poor," "satisfactory," or "excellent" levels of achievement on each of the criteria of quality mean, thus providing students with little guidance on how to improve their performance from one level to another. The latter goal is usually accomplished through the development and application of scoring rubrics. According to its original meaning, a rubric (*rubrica terra* in Latin) denoted an authoritative rule, or a set of instructions inscribed in red, which were used to guide proper performance on a task (Johnson 1996; Marzano, Pickering, and McTighe 1993, 29). Modern rubrics retain the spirit of this original Latin meaning. They are designed to direct students' preparation and performance on an educational task by listing the criteria for a piece of work, or "what counts," and explaining the gradations of quality for each criterion (Andrade 2000; Burch 1997, 55; Goodrich 1997).

Figure 9-2. Scale for Evaluating an Analysis of International News			
Evaluate the essays, including your own, on a scale of 1 to 4, with 1 = poor and 4 = excellent, using criteria provided below.	*Essay I*	*Essay II*	*Your essay*
1. *Choice of the News Topic* An essay receives the maximum point if it is concerned with a topic relevant to international relations. The topic is timely and clearly stated at the beginning of the essay.			
2. *Factual Side of News* An essay gets the maximum point if it describes the news comprehensively, without excessive amount of detail.			
3. *Analysis of News* An essay is evaluated with the maximum point if it demonstrates clear understanding of the theoretical perspectives and/or the levels of analysis and their application for the analysis of international news.			
4. *Analysis of the Presentation of News* An essay gets the maximum point if it evaluates the soundness of information presented in the selected sources and discusses whether the presentation of news is objective/subjective and complete.			
5. *Writing* An essay gets the maximum point if it flows and is organized logically. The arguments must be clear and convincing.			
Total:			

Evaluation rubrics appear in different formats. Typically, a rubric is a type of grid or matrix, in which the criteria or skills evaluated on an educational task, such as a paper or an oral presentation, are listed in the rows. The levels or gradations of performance are used as headings of the columns, and their descriptions appear in the cells of the grid (Allen and Tanner 2006, 197). Criteria and their gradations are the indicators and descriptors, which spell out for both instructors and students the requirements for different levels of success on the educational tasks. Figure 9-3 contains a fragment of the rubric for evaluating a short analytical essay, in which students had to apply a comparative method for studying democracy using examples of two democratic states.

Many instructors employing rubrics in their assessment and teaching practices have noticed a marked improvement in student learning. By defining dimensions on which student performance is rated and describing attributes of excellent work, rubrics provide students with a clear performance target. With this "vision of success," students can become

Figure 9-3. A Rubric Fragment

RUBRIC FOR EVALUATING A COMPARATIVE ANALYSIS OF TWO DEMOCRACIES

Criteria	Levels of Performance			
	1 = poor	2 = satisfactory	3 = good	4 = excellent
I. Choice of states	None of the selected states is democratic.	One of the selected states is not democratic.	Both selected states are democracies, but the explanation of what makes states democratic is lacking.	Both selected states are democracies, and there is an explanation of what makes them democratic.
II. Definition of democracy	The definition of democracy is lacking or copied from the textbook.	The definition of democracy closely resembles the one from the textbook. The vital features of democracy (popular sovereignty, rights and liberties, etc.) are omitted.	Democracy is defined in student's own words. The definition reflects some characteristics of democracy discussed in the text, but lacks others. The student does not recognize the multiplicity of definitions, and does not justify his/her choice of defining democracy in minimalist, procedural, or other terms.	Democracy is defined in student's own words. The definition contains the key characteristics of democracy. The student recognizes different ways in which the concept can be defined, and justifies his/her choice of defining democracy in minimalist, procedural, or other terms.
III. Application of the concept of democracy	No evidence from the selected states is used to demonstrate their democratic features, or the evidence is not related to the concept it is used to illustrate.	Skimpy or irrelevant examples from the selected states are used to demonstrate few of democracy's components.	Several major components of democracy are identified and substantiated with evidence from the selected states. However, some evidence is lacking or inappropriate in light of the provided definition of democracy.	All major components of democracy are identified. Sufficient and appropriate evidence from the selected states is used to demonstrate their democratic features.

better monitors and judges of the quality of their own and their peers' work (Andrade and Du 2005; Perlman et al. 1994; Stiggins 2001, 11; Tierney and Simon 2004). Researchers have found that by simply distributing and explaining rubrics they were able to improve students' scores on the written assignments (Andrade 1999). When evaluation rubrics were used in the context of self- and peer-assessment exercises, the students were better able to detect and solve problems in their own and their classmates' work (Goodrich 1997). My expectation, then, is that, compared to evaluation forms and scales, evaluation rubrics will be the most effective instrument for the assessment of student performance.

The accuracy or reliability of evaluation received from the application of the scoring instrument is yet another quality that has contributed to the popularity of evaluation rubrics. The studies of rubric-referenced grading revealed high inter-evaluator reliability (Howe 1997). The analyses of rubric-referenced peer evaluations of oral presentations showed that students' ratings correlated highly with the instructors' marks (Hafner and Hafner 2003). It can be expected that, compared to evaluation forms and scales, evaluation rubrics will be the most reliable instrument for the assessment of student performance.

RESEARCH DESIGN AND FINDINGS

OVERVIEW

To test the hypotheses about the relative effectiveness and accuracy of three scoring instruments—evaluation forms, scales, and rubrics—I carried out two quasi-experiments. Both experiments were integrated into the classroom curriculum of four undergraduate introductory-level political science courses. A total of 74 students participated in the first quasi-experiment, and 60 students took part in the second study. The data were collected during the Fall 2006 semester at Purdue University.

In the first quasi-experiment (Study I), the students were given a take-home assignment asking them to write a one-page essay. The guidelines accompanying the assignment specified that the students had to demonstrate their knowledge of relevant concepts studied in the class, as well as the skills of analysis and evaluation of the examined material. These essays were later self- and peer-evaluated during a regular class meeting. In the second quasi-experiment (Study II), the students delivered short oral presentations, which were also peer-evaluated. As in Study I, the students were provided with explicit guidelines laying out the goals and requirements of in-class presentations.

Three types of scoring instruments were used as the stimuli for the quasi-experiments. In Study I, a group of students evaluated their own and peers' papers using evaluation rubrics, another group applied evaluation scales, while students from the third group relied on evaluation forms. In Study II, one half of the participants received scoring rubrics for the assessment of classmates' presentations, while the rest of the students were provided with evaluation scales.

Within each study, all types of scoring instruments contained similar criteria aligned with the goals of the assignment and courses taught. In both studies, two criteria (e.g., "choice of states" and "definition of democracy") were used to assess the extent of students' understanding and comprehension of the material studied. The other criteria, such as "application of the concept of democracy" and "organization and clarity of arguments," measured the higher-order cognitive skills of analysis and logical reasoning (see the example provided in Figure 9-3). A four-point rating scale (1 = poor, 2 = satisfactory, 3 = good, and 4 = excellent) was used. The difference among the three scoring instruments was in the amount of detail provided to students about what constituted each level of performance on each of the items included in evaluation forms, scales, and rubrics. Evaluation forms listed broad and undefined criteria for self- and peer-evaluation. Evaluation scales described dimensions of student performance but contained no explanations of the gradations of quality (see Figure 9-2 for an example). Evaluation rubrics provided the most extensive definition of the criteria and articulated qualities characterizing poor, satisfactory, good, and excellent levels of performance on the educational task. On the day of the study, the students were asked to evaluate the performance of their peers and their own work (a written assignment or oral presentation) on a scale of 1 to 4, with 1 = poor and 4 = excellent, using the provided criteria.

MEASUREMENTS OF THE EFFECTIVENESS AND ACCURACY OF SCORING INSTRUMENTS

The *effectiveness* of a scoring instrument refers to its ability to improve student performance on a task. The participants of this study were tasked with the assessment of their own and their peers' performance. The results of the assessment were recorded on an evaluation sheet containing an evaluation form, a scale, or a rubric. Since the verbal assessments of student performance (i.e., "excellent," "poor," etc.) were accompanied by numerical equivalents (i.e., scores of 1, 2, 3, and 4), the final product of the students' evaluations was a series of numeric ratings that could be used for converting evaluations into grades. The students, however, were not asked to assign grades, and their performance on the self- and peer-assessment task was not evaluated.

Ideally, students should be able to make critical judgments about the quality of evaluated work and produce assessments devoid of bias and error. In practice, however, the students' self- and peer-evaluations are often subject to a high degree of bias and error resulting from the desire of self-enhancement, insufficient knowledge, the dearth of experience with critical evaluation of other people's work, and the lack of motivation to think critically (Kaufman, Felder, and Fuller 1999; Mabe and West 1982; Omelicheva 2005).

To measure the magnitude of bias and error in students' peer-evaluations, I calculated the deviations of students' numeric ratings from instructors' scores and averaged the deviations:[2]

$$\text{Average deviation} = \sum_{1}^{n} |\,\text{instructor's evaluation} - \text{peer evaluation}\,|$$

For the ease of interpretation of the final results, I converted the students' and instructors' scores into percentages, a practice that is commonly used for the assignment of grades. To measure the effectiveness of scoring instruments in facilitating students' self-assessment, I calculated the deviations of students' self-ratings from instructors' ratings of their work. Greater deviations of students' self- and peer-assessments from the instructors' evaluations of the same work indicate less effective scoring instruments.

Another characteristic of a scoring instrument is *accuracy*, conceptualized as the reliability of an assessment received from its application. The reliability of an assessment is commonly measured by a correlation coefficient (Pearson's r) denoting the degree of agreement between the scores assigned by two independent scorers. I calculated the correlation coefficients between students' self- and peer-evaluations and instructors' evaluations of the same works to measure the accuracy of scoring instruments. The range of the correlation coefficient is from -1 to 1. In this study, high positive correlations of students' and instructors' scores indicate greater reliability and accuracy of a scoring instrument, whereas low and negative correlation coefficients indicate inaccurate scoring.

RESULTS

Independent-samples' (students') t-tests demonstrated that the rubric-referenced peer evaluations of essays deviated from instructors' evaluations less than the ratings of those students who applied evaluation forms and scales (M = 7.99 for evaluations with rubrics; M = 10.4 for evaluations with forms and scales): t_{72} = -2.01; p = 0.024. On average, the scores of those students who applied evaluation rubrics were within an 8% range of the instructors' scores, compared to a 10.4% range for students working with evaluation forms and scales. This difference remained when the deviations of scores of those students who used forms and scales were separated into two different groups and compared, independently, with the average deviations of the rubric-referenced scores. However, the differences became less statistically significant: t_{53} = -1.58; p = 0.059 in an independent-samples' t-test of rubric-referenced evaluations against form-referenced scores, and t_{55} = -1.61; p = 0.057 in a test comparing rubric-referenced and scale-referenced ratings.

Next, I disaggregated the scores and tested whether the deviations of students' self- and peer-ratings from those of instructors on each of the dimensions of scoring instruments differed across the experimental conditions. In other words, I examined whether rubrics assisted students in providing a better evaluation of their peers' understanding, comprehension, analysis, and other skills than evaluation scales and forms. Table 9-1 reports the mean deviations of students' scores from instructors' ratings on the dimensions included in the scoring instruments.

There was little variation in student performance on those items that assessed basic understanding and comprehension skills. On average, the evaluations of students' comprehension were within a 13% range of instructors' evaluations on the same items in all experimental conditions. Those students who applied evaluation forms and scales performed somewhat better in evaluating understanding compared to the rubric-referenced evaluations of the same items (M = 11.8 for evaluations with rubrics; M = 7.6 for evaluations with forms and scales) but this difference was barely statistically significant at the 0.1 level. With regard to the assessment of higher-order cognitive skills and logical reasoning, students performed significantly better using rubrics than they did using forms and scales. On average, the rubric-referenced scores for analytical skills were within an 11% range of the instructors' scores on the same items, compared to a 20% range of difference between the students' and instructors' ratings in the forms and scales condition. This difference was highly statistically significant at the 0.001 level. Students fared better evaluating their peers' ability to think logically using rubrics than with evaluation forms and scales (M = 13.16 for evaluations with rubrics; M = 18.52 for evaluations with forms and scales). This finding was also statistically significant at the 0.001 level. The same pattern of results was found when the rubric-referenced scores on individual items were compared to the ratings produced using forms and scales separately.

Table 9-1. Itemized Differences in Student Performance					
DIMENSIONS OF THE SCORING INSTRUMENTS	Experimental Condition	N	Mean	St. Deviation	Sig. (2-tailed)
UNDERSTANDING (items assessing students' ability to select appropriate examples, sources, or topics)	Rubrics	38	11.8	8.58	0.075
	Forms and scales	36	7.6	11.33	
COMPREHENSION (items assessing students' ability to define concepts)	Rubrics	38	12.39	9.31	0.611
	Forms and scales	36	13.43	8.03	
ANALYSIS (items assessing students' ability to apply and examine concepts and theories)	Rubrics	38	11.07	8.57	0.000
	Forms and scales	35	20.23	11.66	
ORGANIZATION AND PRESENTATION OF ARGUMENTS (items assessing students' ability to think and present their arguments logically and comprehensively)	Rubrics	38	13.16	8.36	0.006
	Forms and scales	36	18.52	7.74	

Consistent with expectations, students' self-ratings deviated less from instructors' ratings of their work in a group that applied scoring rubrics (M = 6.21) than in those groups that used scales and forms (M = 9.39), and this result was statistically significant at the 0.05 level (t_{72} =

-2.03; *p* = 0.023). When broken down to individual items, the results were similar to the pattern of peer ratings. There was no difference between students' self-ratings and instructors' ratings of their work on the items assessing understanding and comprehension across all experimental conditions (M = 8.55 for evaluations of understanding with rubrics, and M = 7.64 for evaluations of understanding with forms and scales; M = 9.87 for evaluations of comprehension with rubrics, and M = 11.1 for evaluation of comprehension with forms and scales). However, students performed better assessing their analytical and reasoning skills using rubrics than they did with forms and scales. On average, the students' self-ratings of the analytical skill were within a 9.2% range of instructors' ratings, compared to a 18.1% range in the forms/scales condition. The rubric-referenced self-evaluations of students' ability to think logically were within a 11.2% range of instructors' scores, compared to a 17.4% range in the forms/scales condition. Both results were statistically significant at the 0.1 level.

When compared separately, the scores of the students using evaluation forms were within 10% of the instructors' scores, whereas the ratings of those students who relied on the rubrics fell within a 6.21% range (t_{53} = -1.94; *p* = 0.029). There was less of a difference in the deviations of rubric- and scale-referenced self-ratings. The self-evaluations of students from a group with evaluation scales were within a 8.84% range of the instructors' evaluations, compared to a 6.21% range of the rubric-referenced score (t_{55} = -1.40; *p* = 0.08). There was no statistically significant or substantial difference between the self- and peer-ratings produced with evaluation scales and those assigned using evaluation forms.

The effectiveness of scoring rubrics was further supported in Study II. The mean of the deviations of rubric-referenced peer evaluations was 9.15%, whereas the mean of the deviations of the scale-based scores was 12.86% (t_{53} = -3.21; *p* = 0.001). In a group of students with evaluation rubrics, the ratings of peers' oral presentations deviated from the instructors' scores less than the ratings from the group that used evaluation scales.

With regard to the reliability of scoring, evaluation rubrics, again, surpassed evaluation scales and forms. The application of the scoring rubrics resulted in a mean 0.44 correlation of the students' and instructors' scores for the essays compared to only a 0.04 correlation of scores from the group that used evaluation scales (t_{55} = 2.17; *p* = 0.017).

The correlation of the students' self- and peer-ratings and instructors' scores in a group with scoring rubrics was also higher than in the group with evaluation forms (M = 0.44 with rubrics; M = 0.29 with forms). This difference, however, was not statistically significant ($t_{53} = 0.80$; $p = 0.23$). There was no statistically significant difference in the reliability of students' and instructors' evaluations received from the groups applying scales and forms.

WHAT MAKES AN EFFECTIVE AND ACCURATE SCORING INSTRUMENT: DISCUSSION OF FINDINGS

The evidence collected from the undergraduate political science courses indicates that the rubric-referenced students' evaluations contain less bias and error and are more reliable than those ratings dispensed through the application of evaluation forms and scales. Compared to forms and scales, evaluation rubrics appear to be the most effective and accurate scoring instrument. They provide better guidance to students by not merely outlining the standards of performance, but also clarifying what a teacher's expectations for a high-quality piece of work are, and how those requirements can be met (Andrade and Du 2005). Not many students are familiar with the practice of self- and peer-assessment, particularly on the high-order cognitive skills dimensions of analysis and logical reasoning. A clear sense of the expectations and "direction" is particularly vital when the students are novices with respect to an educational task.

Improving students' performance was a hard test for the rubrics to pass provided that there was no student involvement in the development of scoring rubrics. No discussion of the rubrics' dimensions and gradations of quality preceded the peer-assessment task. The scoring instruments were handed out in class, prior to the peer-assessment exercises. Still, the differences in the measures of effectiveness and accuracy of rubrics compared to evaluation forms and scales were statistically significant in the majority of tests. Particularly notable is the finding suggesting that rubrics were able to improve student performance on the high-level cognitive tasks of analysis and logical reasoning. Students fared much better assessing those skills with evaluation rubrics than they did when they had to rely on evaluation forms and scales.

Substantively, however, the differences in scores across experimental conditions were moderate, at best. Armed with the rubrics, students continued to underrate or overrate their own and their peers' work. The application of scoring rubrics decreased the deviations of students' scores from those of instructors by 3% to 5%, compared to forms and scales. The only exception that surfaced in the itemized analysis was the assessment of analytical skills. The rubric-referenced assessments of higher-order cognitive skills were 9% closer to the instructors' assessments compared to assessments conferred using evaluation scales and forms.

More intensive instructional intervention is necessary to make rubrics and other scoring instruments work. The engagement of students in defining the scoring criteria can improve their understanding of the standards for excellent performance. By contributing to the development of scoring instruments, students cultivate a sense of ownership and responsibility for their work, and become more active participants of the learning process (Johnson 1996, 157). Classroom discussion of scoring rubrics can be used to illuminate what each of the rubric's criteria means. Practicing rubrics' application in instructor-monitored peer review sessions can also be used to shed light on the kinds of performance that would match the gradations of quality on the rubrics' dimensions (Goodrich 1997; Stevens and Levi 2005).

For the purpose of this study, I tried to design concise scoring rubrics that could be read by the students in full during the time allotted for the experiments. Therefore, the rubrics contained no specific examples of "poor" or "excellent" work. I also avoided further clarification of some of the descriptive terms, such as in "*clear* understanding," or "*timely* topic." However, if a scoring instrument is to teach as well as evaluate, all vague expressions must be elucidated for students. It may be problematic to pin down some commonly used adjectives or such general qualities as "poor," "satisfactory," or "excellent." A possible solution to the vagueness of language is to discuss with students all ambiguous terms. The most illustrative examples that the instructor and students will arrive at during the class talk can be incorporated into the evaluation rubric (Goodrich 1997; Johnson 1996, 157; Walvoord and Anderson 1998, 82).

I used the words "poor," "good," "satisfactory," and "excellent" to denote levels of performance on educational tasks. Some educators deprecate such value-laden terminology. Instead, they advocate adopting more positive, active descriptions of student performance, such as "beginning," "developing," "accomplished," and "exemplary." The strong language of "poor" or "unsatisfactory" performance may weaken students' ability to assess their performance objectively. The learners may try to avoid evaluating their own and others' work at the lowest levels of the scale. The use of the following labels can mitigate the problem of the negative language (Moskal 2000a; Huba and Freed 2000):

* Scale 1: Sophisticated, competent, partly competent, not yet competent
* Scale 2: Exemplary, accomplished, developing, beginning
* Scale 3: Distinguished, proficient, intermediate, novice
* Scale 4: Advanced, intermediate high, intermediate, novice

This format of the assessment scale and the accompanying descriptions of the levels of performance will provide students with more constructive feedback. The learners will be more strongly motivated to progress from the lower part of the scale described in non-negative terms (Tierney and Simon 2004).

FINAL REMARKS ON SCORING INSTRUMENTS AND THEIR APPLICATION IN THE CLASSROOM, PROGRAM, AND DEPARTMENTAL ASSESSMENT

This chapter has provided an overview and empirical assessment of the effectiveness and accuracy of the three commonly used scoring instruments—evaluation forms, evaluation scales, and evaluation rubrics. The outcomes of the quasi-experiments suggest that, compared to evaluation forms and scales, evaluation rubrics were the most effective and reliable instruments of assessment of student performance. These results are consistent with earlier analyses of assessment practices at the college and university level where evaluation rubrics have been rightfully considered one of the most successful innovations in the methodologies of student evaluation (Goodrich 1997; Luft 1997; Popham 1997). Rubrics contain qualitative descriptions of criteria for student performance and articulated gradations of quality for each criterion. These characteristics of scoring rubrics assist students in identifying strengths and weaknesses in their own and their peers' work (Andrade and Du 2005).

These features of the rubrics also calibrate expectations of instructors and teaching assistants, or several faculty members teaching the same course, thus making their grading more consistent and less time-consuming (Burch 1997, 55; Stevens and Levi 2005, 17; Walvoord and Anderson 1998, 72-73). An instructor can provide individual comments on a student's work by simply circling or underlining the descriptions of what the student should have done to achieve an "excellent" or "good" level of academic performance. This offers students "qualitative" or narrative feedback related to their learning. Instead of receiving a holistic evaluation in the form of a "B" or "C" grade, the students get a multi-dimensional matrix that weighs different aspects of their work and demystifies the calculation of their grades. The numerical ratings assigned to the levels of performance also yield quantitative results. In this way, rubrics allow for both the summative and formative and the qualitative and quantitative analyses of student performance (Allan and Tanner 2006, 203).

These qualities of the rubrics make them an important link between the classroom, program, and department levels of assessment. There is an easy way of integrating rubrics into the department's assessment program. Departments typically identify the educational goals of their academic programs, and they define learning objectives that they expect their students to achieve. Developing basic research skills, for example, can be listed as one of the goals of the department's undergraduate program, and students' ability to develop and test research hypotheses can be noted as a matching learning objective. A research paper can be used as a performance indicator measuring whether or not students developed their research skills. To assess the varying levels and dimensions of students' performance on research projects, instructors then design evaluation rubrics, whose scoring criteria correspond to the department's and program's goals. When the program's goals get translated into the items of classroom rubrics, the means of scores on different rubrics' dimensions can be used to assess whether or not the departmental objectives have been met. The extracted data on various dimensions and levels of student performance can be used for identifying what instructional or curricular changes need to be made in order to close the loop between the program's goals, teaching, and student performance (Kasimatis 2004). The systematic application of scoring rubrics can reveal the patterns of recurring problems and continuous improvement in students' work. It can also assist instructors and their departments in developing more effective instructional methods (Marzano, Pickering, and McTighe 1993, 29).

Rubrics, like many other educational strategies, can be very effective in the hands of an experienced and judicious instructor. They can also be futile and potentially harmful if used improperly. A scoring instrument will have little instructional value if it is replete with inconsistencies and vague descriptions of performance criteria across its scale levels. The performance criteria are the rubrics' most critical components that require thorough consideration. They should be clearly defined and discussed with the students. The clarity and brevity of rubrics is often achieved at the cost of surrendering the complexity and detail in accounting for how student performance is actually judged. Not only does this exclusion affect the quality of evaluation, it may also have a chilling effect on versatile student learning by restraining the development of some qualities, such as creativity or interest, which may appear to be secondary to an educational task (Broad 2003, 2; Burch 1997, 55). The greatest challenge in designing a rubric is to devise an instrument that does not stifle affective, creative, and other sides of learning, and is flexible enough to accommodate students' differing styles and strategies of working on educational tasks.

It may be a daunting and time-consuming task to design an effective evaluation rubric. One shortcut to creating the effective scoring instrument is to adapt model rubrics developed by others. A wide range of resources for a variety of projects, skills, and educational levels is available to instructors who aspire to use evaluation rubrics in their classroom. Dannelle Stevens and Antonia Levi in their *Introduction to Rubrics: An Assessment Tool to Save Grading Time, Convey Effective Feedback, and Promote Student Learning* (2005) provide a comprehensive overview of the literature on rubrics and assessment, and advice on the construction of scoring tools. An appendix to the book as well as accompanying website contains ready-to-use sample rubrics and templates for the college classroom. Moskal (2000b) has developed a web page with links to a variety of college assessment resources, including evaluation rubrics. Chicago Public Schools Rubric Bank (2007) contains hundreds of model rubrics supplemented with useful tips on choosing and using rubrics, as well as references to other assessment-related sources.

NOTES

1. The author would like to thank Heather Brown, Natasha Duncan, John Schultz, and Margarett Zetts for their assistance in carrying out the experiments used in this study.

2. It is very common in the literature on peer-assessment to compare students' self- and peer-evaluations with the marks instructors would give for the same work (Mabe and West 1982). I graded some students' assignments. Other works and presentations were evaluated by instructors. The instructors were asked to apply the same assessment criteria that were provided to students. The graders were informed that the goal of the study was to examine different scoring instruments. However, they were provided with no further details. To ensure that the evaluations are unbiased, I asked the instructors to grade a sample of assignments evaluated by me, and I performed an assessment of a sample of works evaluated by the instructors. The correlations of scores were within a 0.65–0.8 range.

REFERENCES

Allen, Deborah, and Kimberly Tanner. 2006. "Rubrics: Tools for Making Learning Goals and Evaluation Criteria Explicit for Both Teachers and Learners." *CBE Life Sciences Education* 5 (Fall): 197–203.

Andrade, Heidi. 1999. "The Role of Instructional Rubrics and Self-Assessment in Learning to Write: A Smorgasbord of Findings." Presented at the Annual Meeting of the American Educational Research Association, Montreal, Quebec, Canada, April 19–23.

———. 2000. "Using Rubrics to Promote Thinking and Learning." *Educational Leadership* 57 (February): 13–18.

Andrade, Heidi, and Ying Du. 2005. "Student Perspectives on Rubric-Referenced Assessment." *Practical Assessment, Research & Evaluation* 10 (April). PAREonline. net/getvn.asp?v=10&n=3.

Broad, Bob. 2003. *What We Really Value. Beyond Rubrics in Teaching and Assessing Writing.* Logan: Utah State University Press.

Burch, Beth C. 1997. "Creating a Two-Tiered Portfolio Rubric." *The English Journal* 86 (January): 55–58.

Chicago Public Schools Rubric Bank. 2007. intranet.cps.k12.il.us/Assessments/ Ideas_ and_Rubrics/Rubric_Bank/rubric_bank.html.

Goodrich, Heidi. 1997. "Understanding Rubrics." *Educational Leadership* 54 (January): 14–17.

Hafner, John, and Patti Hafner. 2003. "Quantitative Analysis of the Rubric as an Assessment Tool: An Empirical Study of Student Peer-Group Rating." *International Journal of Science Education* 25 (December): 1509–28.

Howe, Alice A. 1997. "Reliability Study on the Use of a Rubric in Elementary Science." Master's Thesis. Adams State College, Colorado.

Huba, Mary E., and Jann E. Freed. 2000. *Learner-Centered Assessment on College Campuses: Shifting the Focus from Teaching to Learning.* Boston: Allyn & Bacon.

Johnson, Bill. 1996. *The Performance Assessment Handbook: Designs from the Field and Guidelines for the Territory Ahead.* Larchmont, NY: Eye on Education, Inc.

Kasimatis, Margaret. 2004. "Developing and Using Scoring Rubrics as Part of a Departmental Assessment Program." Presented at the California Association for Institutional Research (CAIR) Conference, Anaheim, California.

Kaufman, Deborah B., Richard M. Felder, and Hugh Fuller. 1999. "Peer Ratings in Cooperative Learning Teams." Presented at the ASEE Annual Conference, Charlotte, NC.

Luft, J. 1997. "Design Your Own Rubric." *Science Scope* 20 (5): 25–27.

Mabe, P.A., and S.G. West. 1982. "Validity of Self-Evaluation of Ability: A Review and Meta-Analysis." *Journal of Applied Psychology* 67 (3): 280–96.

Marzano, Rober J., Debra Pickering, and Jay McTighe. 1993. *Assessing Student Outcomes: Performance Assessment Using the Dimensions of Learning Model.* Alexandria, VA: Association for Supervision and Curriculum Development.

Moskal, Barbara M. 2000a. "Scoring Rubrics: What, When and How?" *Practical Assessment, Research & Evaluation* 7 (3). PAREonline.net/ getvn.asp?v=7&n=3.

———. 2000b. *Assessment Resource Page.* www.mines.edu/Academic/assess/Resource.htm.

Omelicheva, Mariya. 2005. "Self- and Peer-Evaluation in Undergraduate Education: Structuring Conditions That Maximize Its Promises and Minimize the Perils." *Journal of Political Science Education* 1 (May): 191–206.

———. 2007. "Resolved: Academic Debate Should Be a Part of Political Science Curricula." *Journal of Political Science Education* 3 (May): 1–15.

Perlman, Carole, Arne Duncan, Barbara J. Eason-Watkins, and Philip J. Hansen. 1994. *Ideas and Rubrics.* Board of Education of the City of Chicago. intranet.cps. k12.il.us/Assessments/Ideas_and_Rubrics/ideas_and_rubrics.html.

Popham, W.J. 1997. "What's Wrong–and What's Right–with Rubrics." *Educational Leadership* 55 (October): 72–5.

Stevens, Dannelle D., and Antonia Levi. 2005. *Introduction to Rubrics: An Assessment Tool to Save Grading Time, Convey Effective Feedback, and Promote Student Learning.* Sterling, VA: Stylus. styluspub.com/resources/introductiontorubrics.aspx.

Stiggins, R.J. 2001. *Student-Involved Classroom Assessment.* 3rd ed. Upper Saddle River, NJ: Merrill/Prentice-Hall.

Tierney, Robin, and Marielle Simon. 2004. "What's Still Wrong with Rubrics: Focusing on the Consistency of Performance Criteria across Scale Levels." *Practical Assessment, Research & Evaluation* 9 (January). PAREonline.net/getvn.asp?v=9&n=2.

Walvoord, Barbara E., and Virginia J. Anderson. 1998. *Effective Grading: A Tool for Learning and Assessment.* San Francisco: Jossey-Bass.

Juan Carlos Huerta, Texas A&M University–
Corpus Christi

10

Classroom Assessment of Learning Communities for Political Scientists

Learning communities (LCs) provide an environment for promoting student learning that is particularly useful for political scientists, as demonstrated by the growing body of literature examining the use of learning communities in political science (Huerta 2004; Sanders 2000; Thies 2005). Learning communities are most commonly used with core curriculum/general education courses, although they also are used in upper-division courses and graduate school. Learning communities are well established in a wide variety of institutions including community colleges, research universities, regional institutions, and liberal arts colleges (Taylor et al. 2003).

LCs are defined as "[a]ny one of a variety of curricular structures that link together several existing courses—or actually restructure the curricular material entirely—so that students have opportunities for deeper understanding and integration of the material they are learning, and more interaction with one another and their teachers as fellow participants in the learning enterprise" (Gabelnick et al. 1990). Research and assessment of LCs has demonstrated that they are effective in promoting student learning, achievement, promoting intellectual development, and helping students feel more connected to their institutions (Smith et al. 2004; Taylor et al. 2003).

While LCs can take on a variety of formats, there is a general consensus on the essential qualities of LCs. LCs enroll a common cohort of students in two or more courses that are intentionally linked. Typically, the LC is organized around an interdisciplinary theme (Smith et al. 2004).

There is a well-developed literature on learning community classroom assessment (Laufgraben 2005; Smith et al. 2004; Taylor et al. 2003). Hence, this chapter will not introduce new techniques for classroom assessment; rather, it will introduce and familiarize political scientists with the well-developed learning community classroom assessment (LCCA) literature.

The chapter will begin with a brief overview of the reasons to distinguish between LCCA and typical classroom assessment, LCs, and the LC learning model. Also, the chapter will introduce established strategies for LCCA and provide examples. The chapter will conclude with suggestions on how to convert the assessment into publishable scholarship of teaching and learning (SOTL) research. The chapter will not address LC program assessment as such but rather present examples and suggestions of classroom assessment of LCs.

WHY CLASSROOM ASSESSMENT OF LEARNING COMMUNITIES?

LCs are by design collaborative; hence, it is important to assess the collaborative goals—whether they are learning or pedagogy (process) goals. An additional reason to assess LCs is to examine if they provide a benefit over traditional teaching models. Assessing why LCs have an impact on student learning is another reason to assess. Finally, assessing POLS classes in LCs can provide a foundation for transforming the assessment into publishable, peer-reviewed SOTL research.

UNDERSTANDING LEARNING COMMUNITIES

Political scientists may be unaware of the well-developed literature about learning communities. An essential resource for understanding, designing, and assessing LCs is *Learning Communities: Reforming Undergraduate Education* by Barbara Leigh Smith, Jean MacGregor, Roberta S. Matthews, and Faith Gabelnick (2004), which is frequently referred to. A list of additional LC resources is listed in Appendix 10-1.

Because there is variation among LCs, the focus is not on the structure of the LCs; rather, it is on what happens in an LC. Typically,

LCs have the following intentions:
* Aim to foster a sense of community among students and teachers
* Attempt to create curricular coherence and connections
* Teach skills in a meaningful context
* Encourage academic and social connections for students
* Offer a more intensified learning environment
* Provide learning communities for teachers (Smith et al. 2004)

Leading LC scholars have recommended that LCs contain the following, interrelated, core practices:
* Community
* Diversity
* Integration
* Active Learning
* Reflection and Assessment (Smith et al. 2004)

There is a wide range of goals for LCs; nonetheless, there is a general agreement on student goals, including:
* Academic maturity
* Increased intellectual development
* Demonstration of learning outcomes
* Achievement (grades, GPA)
* Increased interaction with other students, faculty, and student affairs professionals
* Higher levels of satisfaction (Smith et al. 2004)

This is not an exhaustive list, nor is it limiting. LC teams can create their own goals.

Another factor to consider when preparing to perform LCCA is the learning model. The model should be familiar to political scientists because it is essentially the input–output model political scientists use when studying the policy process (inputs, government, outputs). For LC, it is inputs, environment, and outcomes. Just as the policy formation model includes feedback, so does the learning community model. Smith et al (2004) refer to the LC learning model as a "Learning Community Assessment Framework." The inputs include LC program goals, student characteristics, teaching team composition, and program resources. The environment includes curricular, co-curricular, and pedagogical elements. Then there are the outcomes—for students, teaching teams, curriculum, and institution. Like the policy model, the LC model includes feedback. The model is useful for assessment because it provides a causal order that one can use when creating an assessment design.

LEARNING COMMUNITY CLASSROOM ASSESSMENT MODEL

Smith, MacGregor, Mathews, and Gabelnick provide an indispensable framework for assessing LCs (2004). Their "Assessment Cycle" framework includes the following steps:

1. Goal formation

2. Design and planning

3. Implementation

4. Data collection, analysis, and synthesis

5. Interpretation, reflection, and judgments

6. Using results for decisions and revisions

These steps represent a cycle, so Step 6 cycles back into goal formation (Step 1). Step 6 can also lead directly to Step 2 (design and planning) and Step 3 (implementation). This framework provides a useful guide for planning LCCA that is based on experience.

STEP 1

The critical first step for LCCA is to establish the goals of the LC. The goals may be goals developed by the particular learning community team, or they may be goals for the LC program that all LCs are expected to meet. It can be a daunting task to assess all the goals, thus it may be a good idea to focus on certain goals one year, and then assesses different goals the following year. These goals can be considered the outcomes of the LC.

STEP 2

In this step, the LC team develops means to assess the LC goals. The most straightforward method to assess the LC goals is to design an integrative assignment for the LC that requires students to demonstrate their mastery of the LC goal. For example, if the goal of the LC is for the students to recognize that political science is connected to other academic disciplines, then the assignment needs to be designed so students demonstrate the connections. The assignments are designed collaboratively by the LC teaching team.

Perhaps an assignment is not an appropriate method. The LC team could consider designing a simple student survey. A pre-test/post-test could also be used to measure gains. One thing to do is an inventory of available data. If new data needs to be collected, then the LC team can consider how it will be collected and what kind of data is needed to assess the goals. Finally, it is important to establish the criteria for successfully achieving the LC goal.

There are sources for identifying appropriate, and innovative, classroom assessment techniques (Angelo and Cross 1993). Angelo and Cross's book is highly regarded and contains numerous techniques for classroom assessment that can also be used in LCs. Furthermore, these techniques do not require any special training to administer.

STEP 3

Once the design and planning decisions have been made, it is then time to implement the assessment during the semester. A master LC calendar can be useful for noting the dates when the various assessments will be administered.

STEP 4

After the techniques for assessing the goals have been selected and implemented, it is time to collect the data. Following the collection of the data is the analysis and subsequent synthesis.

STEP 5

This step is the interpretation, reflection, and judgment phase. What do the findings mean? Recall that criteria for success are established in Step 2. Does a 70% satisfaction rate signify a setback if the expectation was 80%? What does it mean if 95% of the students display the ability to learn collaboratively, instead of the expected 80%? Perhaps there are some other factors to take into consideration. Also, what does this mean for the expectations that were set? The teaching strategies selected? The goal formation? These are all issues for reflection and judgment for the LC team.

Step 6

In this step, the results are used for revision and decision-making. Suppose 98% of the students on a written assignment display mastery of connecting the course material in the learning community. Based on these results, the LC team may decide to assess a different goal. Alternatively, if they found a low percentage, then that could lead to a redesign of a part of the course.

Assessing the Learning Community Classroom

The collaborative nature of LCs is what distinguishes LC classroom assessment from regular classroom assessment. Useful tools for goal formation in learning communities are available (Malnarich and Lardner 2003; Smith et al. 2004). It is advisable to use one of the heuristics. The Malnarich and Lardner heuristic has been developed over several years, and is based on their work helping institutions develop learning communities. These heuristics are appealing because they are practical guides that encourage learning community teams to develop learning community goals—not simply goals for individual classes. The advantages of these heuristics are that they develop LC goals and build the assessment into the development of the LC itself.

A key early step is for the LC team to set aside time for curriculum planning, and to meet to develop the important learning goals for the LC. Teams are encouraged not to think only in terms of "their" class, but rather to focus on LC goals. Participants are asked to list their goals on sticky notes, and then the team gets together and compares these notes. From this comparison, and ensuing discussion, the LC develops common goals for itself. Individual professors can have their own goals for their classes. Nonetheless, a successful LC needs to have overarching goals that bind the LC.

The LC team then works at developing the assignments that can assess if their goals are being met. For example, if there is a process goal of having students learn collaboratively, then the LC team needs to develop an assignment or assignments to assess whether collaborative learning is occurring. Also, the LC team needs to agree on how it will be assessed—through a regular assignment, through an informal class activity, or perhaps through both.

Consistent with the LC Assessment Framework, the LC team needs to agree on the assessment methods, and then also work together to implement the assessment. Likewise, they need to agree on how to collect, analyze, and interpret the findings. Finally, it is advisable that they also meet to reflect and use the findings for improving the LC.

It is not necessary to assess all the LC goals at the same time. In fact, it is advised that, when beginning classroom assessment, troublesome goals should be avoided, and instead goals that the team believes it is reaching should be assessed (Angelo and Cross 1993; Malnarich and Lardner 2003; Smith et al. 2004).

Since there are likely to be multiple goals, one criterion for determining which goals to focus on is to determine what kind of assessment is needed—an assessment of process, outcomes, or both? The LC Assessment Framework focuses on goals, or outcomes. However, the LC team might be more interested in assessing a process goal. An assessment of process examines whether or not the teaching strategies in an LC are occurring. Are the students engaged in active or collaborative learning? Is there engagement with material from other disciplines? The process assessment then examines whether the teaching techniques adopted by the community are actually occurring.

Suppose a goal of a learning community is to use collaborative learning techniques. This is an example of assessment of process. There are several means to assess whether or not collaborative learning is occurring in an LC. First, determine the criteria for success. Perhaps the LC is successful if 80% of the students report they experienced collaborative learning. This could be measured by asking some survey questions. If a control group of non-LC students is desired, the survey could also be taken in a class that is not part of an LC. Alternatively, it could be measured by having students write reflective essays about their learning experiences. The professor could then read the essays and note in what percentage of essays students reported evidence of collaborative learning.

What about outcome assessment? A goal of the LC could be that students are able to understand how they can have an impact in improving their communities. This could be measured with survey questions, with a pre-set threshold as the marker of success. For example, 80% of the students in the LC will report that they understand how they can have an impact in improving their communities. Perhaps a survey could be administered the first day of class, and then again at the end of the semester to measure changes in attitudes.

Assignments could also be used to measure the "improving their community" goal. Students could be given a written assignment, and part of the assignment (or the entire assignment) could be about demonstrating how they can improve their communities. A success criterion will need to be established—perhaps 80% of the students will earn a "B" or better on the assignment.

Another outcome to assess is achievement. Students in the LC may be expected to earn higher grades, or to do better on a post-test. Additionally, retention could be considered an outcome. In this case, a comparison to students in a non-LC class is advisable.

ASSESSMENT EXAMPLES

In this section, specific examples of LCCA from Texas A&M University–Corpus Christi (A&M–Corpus Christi) are provided. The First-Year Learning Communities Program (FYLCP) at A&M–Corpus Christi was established in fall 1994—the semester when the university admitted its initial cohort of first-year students. Prior to fall 1994, the university was an upper division and graduate program university. The LCs are the linked class model, and are comprised of large lecture courses with 150 (up to 275) students divided into First-Year Seminars of 25 students (six seminars for 150 students with more seminars if the lecture class is bigger). The seminars are discussion sections that integrate the material in the LC. Most of the seminars are also linked to First-Year Composition (English Composition). LCs with one large lecture class are known as Triads. Some LCs have two large lecture courses (Tetrads), and beginning in fall 2007, math courses will be linked to the Biology and Chemistry LC (Pentad). All full-time, first-year students register in a learning community in each regular semester of their first year. Two of the learning communities have political science courses—U.S. Government and Politics and State and Local Government.

A common feature of the LCs at A&M–Corpus Christi is that they use portfolios for composition and seminar, which can be used by the LC team for assessment purposes. The political science professors typically are not involved with the actual grading of the portfolios. Rather, what they do is help set the LC goals and then integrate them into the grading rubric of the portfolio. The portfolios are graded by the composition instructors and seminar leaders.

At A&M–Corpus Christi, a typical goal in many LCs is for students to develop multiple perspectives. Often, there are questions the LC is centered on that help the students develop multiple perspectives. In political science, a common question guiding the LC asks students, "How do diverse experiences shape our interpretations and perspectives?" The LC team has chosen to assess the goal of "develop multiple perspectives" with a section of the portfolio the students submit to their composition instructors and seminar leaders. A portion of their portfolio grade is based on how well the students develop multiple perspectives. Successfully achieving this goal is defined as 80% of the students earning a grade of "B" or better on the perspectives section of their portfolio. Hence, if the perspective section is worth 10 points of the portfolio, then the goal is successfully met if the students, on average, earn at least 8 points. If an assignment is developed with the aim of assessing LC goals, one does not need to create additional assessment instruments.

In another semester, the goal was that the students would experience significant learning (Fink 2003). To assess this, a rubric was developed to grade an assignment, with a portion of the assignment used to assess significant learning. The rubric defined significant learning and provided a scale for grading it. An example of the assignment and rubric is included in Appendix 10-2.

The criterion for success was that 80% of the students would earn a grade of 85% or better on the portion of the assignment measuring significant learning. The assignment was worth 100 total points with 40 of those points counting toward significant learning. Thus, the student needed to earn 34 points on the significant learning section to demonstrate mastery. The assessment revealed that over 80% of the students met the criteria, indicating that the criteria for success was met. The reflection on that assessment was that the goal was successfully achieved. No changes were planned on the basis of the assessment, and the assessment rubric will be used again.

Another example of assessment is to compare the learning outcomes or achievement from LC to non-LC classes. In this example, the LC goal was that the political science LC students would perform better on political science exams compared to political science classes not in an LC. Additionally, the LC student-satisfaction responses would be more positive than those from the non-LC classes. This assessment confirmed that students earned higher exam grades and were more satisfied with an introductory American Government class that was part of an LC in comparison to one that was not part of an LC (Huerta 2004). This assessment confirmed the value and benefit of LCs, and settled questions about whether LCs were worth the effort and resources. This type of assessment can make a strong argument for the expansion, or adoption, of LCs.

CONVERTING CLASSROOM ASSESSMENT INTO PUBLISHABLE RESEARCH

The Scholarship of Teaching and Learning (SOTL) offers an opportunity for political scientists to make academic inquiries into the nature of student learning (Hutchings 2000). To take the assessments to a new level and engage in SOTL, assessment data can be used, and perhaps new data collected, to generate publishable research. For example, one could examine the factors that lead to, or hinder, success in learning communities. This could be done either qualitatively or quantitatively. It is important to obtain Institutional Review Board approval prior to collecting data for SOTL research.

An analysis comparing students in an LC and students not in an LC could yield findings about the impact of collaborative learning on achieving LC goals. Likewise, if data can be obtained on student background characteristics (standardized test scores, class rank, first generation college, race/ethnicity, and sex), then one could examine potential impacts the LC has for different types of students.

SOTL research is grounded in the academic disciplines. Thus, to engage in this research, political scientists can use the research methods they use in their regular research, whether quantitative or qualitative, and use them to examine the LC. The LC goals become the dependent variable and the inputs and environment are the independent variables.

There are venues for publishing political science SOTL research, including *PS: Political Science & Politics* and the *Journal of Political Science*

Education. In addition, there is the relatively new *Journal of Learning Communities Research* that also provides an outlet for political science LC research.

CONCLUSIONS

Learning community classroom assessment is distinct from regular classroom assessment because the assessment centers on common LC goals. Ideally, the LC team will meet prior to the beginning of the semester, and collaboratively develop goals, design the assessment assignments, implement them, and then complete the assessment cycle. Naturally, the ideal and reality are not the same thing. Just as political scientists need to search for data to conduct research, there are times when the same happens with LCCA. Professors may find themselves looking for assessment data at the end of the semester. While that is not the ideal, the reality is that assessment can still occur if appropriate measures can be identified. Moreover, the political scientist interested in LCCA can draw on a well-developed literature on LCs and on LCCA.

LCs represent a powerful method of helping students learn and they offer a great deal of potential for political scientists. Research has shown that students are not interested in politics (Bennett and Bennett 2001). LCs offer political scientists an opportunity to help students understand political science by connecting it to different disciplines and issues. LCs then offer a chance to help students become more engaged with political science, and hence more likely to appreciate it and learn about it.

Appendix 10-1. Learning Community Resources

- *Washington Center for Improving the Quality of Undergraduate Education. Learning Communities National Resource Center:* learningcommons.evergreen.edu/.
- *Learning Communities: Reforming Undergraduate Education*, by Smith, B. L., MacGregor, J., Matthews, R. S., and Gabelnick, F. (2004). San Francisco: Jossey-Bass.
- *Classroom Assessment Techniques* (2nd ed.), Angelo, T. A., and Cross, K. P. (1993). San Francisco: Jossey-Bass Publishers.
- *Designing Integrated Learning For Students: A Heuristic for Teaching, Assessment and Curriculum Design*, by Malnarich, G., and Lardner, E. D. (2003). (Occasional Paper No. 1.) Olympia, WA: Washington Center for Improving the Quality of Undergraduate Education, The Evergreen State College. www.evergreen.edu/washcenter/resources/upload/Winter2003-Number1.doc.

Appendix 10-2. Portfolio Two Focus[1]

SIGNIFICANT LEARNING

Definition: For learning to occur, there has to be some kind of change in the learner. No change, no learning. And significant learning requires that there be some kind of lasting change that is important in terms of the learner's life (Fink 30).

For your second portfolio, you will be asked to compile evidence of learning that relates to the focus of significant learning (consider learning experiences that evoke change in your thinking, change in the way you look at the world, etc.). We will do some activities in Seminar to expose you to the Significant Learning Taxonomy (see below), but it will be up to you to select the evidence that best relates to this focus.

Don't forget the political science addition!!!

FINK'S TAXONOMY OF SIGNIFICANT LEARNING

This is organized from higher to lower:

- Learning How to Learn ——————————————————
  - Becoming a better student
  - Inquiring about a subject
  - Self-directing learners
    - Ask yourself: *What learning experience(s) have caused me to want to inquire more about a subject on my own because I want to, not because I have to? — OR — What learning experience(s) have caused me to change as a student in regard to learning?*

- Caring ——————————————————————
  - ○ Developing new
    - » Feelings
    - » Interests
    - » Values
      - › Ask yourself: *What learning experience(s) have caused me to care enough to develop new feelings, interests, and/or values?— OR— What new learning experience(s) have become a part of my life?*
- Human Dimension ——————————————————
  - ○ Learning about
    - » Oneself
    - » Others
      - › Ask yourself: *What learning experience(s) have caused me to look at the human significance of what I have learned/am learning?*
- Integration ——————————————————————
  - ○ Connecting
    - » Ideas
    - » People
    - » Realms of Life
      - › Ask yourself: *What learning experience(s) caused me to make new connections?*
- Application ——————————————————————
  - ○ Skills
  - ○ Thinking
    - » Critical, creative, and practical thinking
  - ○ Managing Projects
      - › Ask yourself: *What learning experience(s) have allowed me to use what I have learned?*
- Foundational Knowledge ——————————————————
  - ○ Understanding and Remembering
    - » Information
    - » Ideas
      - › Ask yourself: *What learning experience(s) have provided me with basic understanding that is necessary for other kinds of learning?*

(Fink, L. Dee. 2003. *Creating Significant Learning Experiences: An Integrated Approach to Designing College Courses.* San Francisco: Jossey-Bass.)

(continued, next page)

PUTTING TOGETHER YOUR PORTFOLIO

- Your first step will be to gather evidence. The easiest way to gather evidence is to consider your significant learning experiences in your triad courses (as well as other courses/life experiences). Then choose evidence that represents your most valuable learning experiences. Your evidence will come primarily from seminar, political science, and/or your other courses; however, you can include evidence from life outside the classroom (school events, work, community activities, current events, etc.). You will then organize that evidence in a folder.

- Your next step will be to write a Reflective Overview (RO) that will guide the reader through the material you have chosen. Each piece of evidence will translate into a paragraph of your reflective overview, in which you will provide the reader with the "background" on your evidence—what it is, why you added it, how it represents your learning, and how it is related to the focus of significant learning (be sure to use the language from the six areas of the Significant Learning Taxonomy—Learning How to Learn, Caring, Human Dimension, Integration, Application, and/or Foundational Knowledge).

NUTS AND BOLTS TO HELP YOU WITH YOUR PORTFOLIO AND RO

- Does my RO have an introduction, conclusion, and transition for each piece of evidence?
- Did I discuss each piece of evidence in my portfolio?
- Did I provide more than a superficial reflection of the evidence?
- Did I write a complete paragraph for each piece of evidence?
- This requires more than just saying, "I chose this piece of evidence because I learned ... from it."
- Did I address the idea of significant learning when describing each piece of evidence?
- Did I state the change/learning that the experience caused in me?
- Did I accurately use the language of significant learning when describing each piece of evidence?
- Did I discuss the level of significant learning chosen for each piece of evidence? (More than just saying, "This piece of evidence is an example of foundational knowledge.")
- Does my RO include a portion that discusses what grade I think I deserve on this portfolio and why?

Rubric Used for Grading Purposes

Portfolio Rubric

_____Reflective Overview (50 points possible)
In the reflective overview did you...

* guide the reader through your portfolio?
* describe what is in your portfolio?
* include why you added each item and how it demonstrates learning?
* address the portfolio focus?
* explain to the reader what grade you think you deserve?
* make sure that it is free of major problems with grammar and/or spelling?

_____ Evidence (45 points possible)
Is the evidence...

* representative of a variety of learning experiences? (5 pieces recommended)
* related to the portfolio focus?
* included in the portfolio?
* a result of careful thought?
* include material from political science?

Presentation (5 points possible)

* if online (wiki), is an effort made to make the portfolio easy to navigate?
* if in a folder, is the portfolio put together in a professional manner?

NOTE

1. The portfolio assignment was created by Chloe Yowell, seminar leader coordinator, A&M–Corpus Christi, and Rita Sperry, seminar leader, A&M–Corpus Christi, in consultation with the author. The assessment of Significant Learning came from bullets 2, 3, and 4 in the Reflective Overview from the rubric. Yowell and Sperry determined that bullets 2, 3, and 4 were worth 40 total points. Thus, 85% of 40 points (34 points) was the criterion established to indicate mastery of significant learning.

REFERENCES

Angelo, Thomas A., and K. Patricia Cross. 1993. *Classroom Assessment Techniques.* 2nd ed. San Francisco: Jossey-Bass.

Bennett, Stephen Earl, and Linda L. M. Bennett. 2001. "What Political Scientists Should Know about the Survey of First-Year Students in 2000." *PS: Political Science & Politics* 34 (June): 295–99.

Fink, L. Dee. 2003. *Creating Significant Learning Experiences: An Integrated Approach to Designing College Courses.* San Francisco: Jossey-Bass.

Gabelnick, Faith, Jean MacGregor, Roberta S. Matthews, and Barbara Leigh Smith. 1990. *Learning Communities: Creating Connections Among Students, Faculty, and Disciplines.* Vol. 41. *New Directions for Teaching and Learning.* San Francisco: Jossey-Bass.

Huerta, Juan Carlos. 2004. "Do Learning Communities Make a Difference?" *PS: Political Science & Politics* 37 (April): 291–96.

Hutchings, Pat, ed. 2000. *Opening Lines: Approaches to the Scholarship of Teaching and Learning.* Menlo Park, CA: Carnegie Foundation for the Advancement of Teaching.

Laufgraben, Jodi Levine. 2005. "Learning Communities." In *Challenging and Supporting the First-Year Student: A Handbook for Improving the First Year of College.* M. L. Upcraft, J. N. Gardner, and B. O. Barefoot, ed. San Francisco: Jossey-Bass, 371–87.

Malnarich, Gillies, and Emily Decker Lardner. 2003. "Designing Integrated Learning for Students: A Heuristic for Teaching, Assessment and Curriculum Design." Olympia, WA: Washington Center for Improving the Quality of Undergraduate Education, The Evergreen State College.

Sanders, Arthur. 2000. "Teaching Introductory American Politics as Part of a Learning Community." *PS: Political Science & Politics* 33 (June): 207–12.

Smith, Barbara Leigh, Jean MacGregor, Roberta S. Matthews, and Faith Gabelnick. 2004. *Learning Communities: Reforming Undergraduate Education.* San Francisco: Jossey-Bass.

Taylor, Kathe, William S. Moore, Jean MacGregor, and Jerri Lindblad. 2003. *Learning Community Research and Assessment: What We Know Now, National Learning Communities Project Monograph Series.* Olympia, WA: Washington Center for Improving the Quality of Undergraduate Education, The Evergreen State College, in cooperation with the American Association for Higher Education.

Thies, Cameron. 2005. "A Crash Course in Learning Communities for the Political Scientist." *Journal of Political Science Education* 1 (February): 129–42.

PHILIP H. POLLOCK, UNIVERSITY OF CENTRAL FLORIDA
KERSTIN HAMANN, UNIVERSITY OF CENTRAL FLORIDA
BRUCE M. WILSON, UNIVERSITY OF CENTRAL FLORIDA/CMI, BERGEN, NORWAY

11

ASSESSMENT IN THE ONLINE ENVIRONMENT

The way professors are instructing college students is undergoing a process of change. Two decades ago, lectures and seminars constituted the dominant form of college teaching, while now many professors are experimenting with new teaching strategies emphasizing active learning (including strategies such as interactive learning, simulations, and case-based learning) to make learning more student-centered and increase student engagement. Professors have also defined new learner objectives to include skill-building in an effort to equip students to be life-long learners. Finally, professors have embraced new teaching tools, especially electronic delivery of course materials, including the use of the Internet. Online teaching has embraced tools such as online course management software (e.g., WebCT or Blackboard), pod-casting, wikis, and the use of virtual worlds. This shift in teaching strategies has been facilitated by the development of popularly accessible technology and is rapidly taking hold in colleges and universities across the United States.

In addition, online teaching is of particular interest to college administrators since it tends to appeal to non-traditional students, who are not able to attend classes during the day due to work or family obligations or because they cannot easily relocate to a place in the vicinity of a college. It can also help alleviate the pressure for classroom space in universities with an expanding student population. Students enrolling in online classes often state that they like the flexibility of working on their own time and not having to attend classes at times that are often inconvenient for their schedules (Garson 1998, 587; Moskal et al. 2006, 28). Many universities understand online education as a way "to better serve the needs of their students," to respond to student demand to have courses available online, and to meet their strategic institutional goals (Moskal et al. 2006, 26).

It is thus unsurprising that an increasing number of college courses are delivered over the Internet and that the number of students signing up for online courses has been rising. As early as 1997–1998, almost 1,680 institutions offered 54,000 college courses in the online format, enrolling approximately 1.6 million students (Eaton 2001, 4, based on data provided by the U.S. Department of Education). In 2002, over one-third of all accredited institutions (1,979 out of 5,655) offered some type of distance learning courses or programs (CHEA 2002, 5). More recently, almost half of the 287,000 students in Florida's state university system took at least one online class in 2005–2006, and while Florida is aiming at taking an even stronger leadership role in the development of online college education, other states, including Illinois and Georgia, have already built prominent online degree programs based on courses developed at their respective state universities (Zaragoza 2007). Overall, nearly 3.5 million students (or close to 20%) enrolled in one or more online courses during the fall 2006 term, signifying almost a 10% rise over the year before, and the 1.5% growth rate in enrollment in the higher education student population overall pales in comparison to the 9.7% growth rate in online enrollments (Allen and Seaman 2007,1). These numbers underscore that online teaching can no longer be ignored as a vital component of higher education.

Critics of online teaching, on the other hand, argue that online education tends to be sub-standard, and that students miss out on the interactive aspects of instruction and instead are isolated from other students when completing their work. For instance, over 800 faculty members of the University of Washington protested the partial replacement of face-to-face college instruction with online classes in an open letter, and argued that education should not be reduced to "the downloading of information, much less to the passive and solitary activity of staring at a screen" (Cleary 2001). Sometimes, online classes are viewed as "glorified correspondence courses" (Cleary 2001). Similarly, politicians are sometimes skeptical of the merits of online education. Rep. Nick Smith (R–MI), for example, declared that "students who take courses online don't interact as much as their peers in traditional courses, and that they may walk away with knowledge but not with an understanding of how to think for themselves"

(Carnevale 2000). In addition, online students sometimes miss interaction with other students and feel isolated (Yang and Cornelius 2004).

These discussions highlight the need for assessment of online courses. We know that changing the medium of instruction necessitates change in the way we deliver courses. However, we understand little about what and how students actually learn in online classes. Furthermore, little is known about how online courses can contribute to a department's objectives and how they can feed into departmental assessment. In this chapter, we therefore briefly introduce how online classes can "fit" into a departmental assessment plan. We then outline several ways in which online classes themselves can be assessed, first by looking at learner outcomes, and second by analyzing learning behavior. We illustrate these examples with a brief discussion of and evidence from our own work assessing online courses in political science.

ONLINE CLASSES AND DEPARTMENTAL ASSESSMENT

As several chapters in this volume point out, the objectives stated in departmental or program assessment are multiple and can vary from learner outcomes relating to objective knowledge ("Which facts did the students learn?") to skills such as critical thinking, communication, or research skills, and learning behavior (e.g., engaging students in the learning process), among many others. In some places, departments have to assess multiple objectives, including knowledge, skills, and communication.[1] Departments employ a host of instruments to assess these objectives, including exit interviews, national norm-referenced tests, and existing student work that was produced for a particular course (see Chapter 4 by John Ishiyama, this volume).[2] Online courses as part of degree programs must comply with accreditation standards set for departments and universities much like any other class offered at a university (CHEA 2002), and as such contribute to departments', programs', and universities' accreditation processes. Since all student work is written and can easily be archived and restored, online classes provide a wealth of data that can usefully be analyzed for assessment. In some cases, analytical tools built into online course management software facilitate the collection of useful assessment data. Thus, distance-learning courses provide some unique advantages for assessment since all coursework is written and stored and can thus easily serve a range of assessment objectives, including objective knowledge, communication skills, and active learning and student engagement, as we will illustrate below.

OBJECTIVE KNOWLEDGE

If departments are interested in finding out how much students learn over the course of a semester, online classes can conveniently provide data. Most online course management software is equipped with a quiz function, which allows students to take multiple-choice or short-answer tests. The software (such as WebCT) analyzes how many students answered each question correctly and which answers were chosen. It is thus easy to group questions according to content or other criteria and evaluate the results. It is also straightforward to deliver tests at the beginning and end of the semester to monitor students' progress in a pre- and post-test design, or to deliver the same test to the same students over multiple semesters to see how students develop their knowledge base throughout their college career. Similarly, discussions, essays, and term papers provide material for content analysis to monitor students' grasp of critical concepts.

COMMUNICATION SKILLS

Online courses provide a valuable environment to assess students' written communication skills. They also provide a relatively convenient medium to analyze student writing on many dimensions–from grammar to clarity of argument or any other attribute professors and departments might deem important. Furthermore, different types of writing can be compared, gauging students' capability to adjust their written communication to specific contexts, such as formal papers or essays and less formal online discussions. Writing rubrics can be employed to ensure consistency of assessing student work even when the rubrics are not used for grading, and can also include discipline-specific knowledge such as the correct use of political science terminology and concepts (for a simple rubric, see Appendix 11-1).[3]

ACTIVE LEARNING AND STUDENT ENGAGEMENT

While it might be assumed that online learning is primarily passive (staring at a computer screen and reading lecture notes posted online or watching streaming videos of taped classroom lectures), many online courses are designed around active learning principles. These include, but are not limited to, group assignments, asynchronous online discussions, synchronous discussions via "chat," online simulations, and writing assignments. Again, online course software facilitates a simple analysis of student activity and engagement, for instance by counting the number of times students opened their peers' discussion postings, or by providing search functions that count how many times a student has posted a discussion contribution. It is also possible to search for specific discussion postings by topic or date, so progress can be monitored over the course of a semester. In-depth analysis of the quality of these contributions can be obtained through content analysis and can serve as an indicator of the students' cognitive engagement (see Richardson and Newby 2006).

In sum, online classes can be usefully employed to contribute to departmental assessment goals as well as for classroom assessment. Online course management software can be employed to facilitate some aspects of data collection and analysis. The following sections provide some examples of various aspects of classroom assessment in courses taught partially or fully online in the Political Science Department at the University of Central Florida over the past ten years. The assessment goals for these courses could easily be adapted to serve departmental assessment objectives as well.

Assessing Online Classes: Learner Outcomes

Much of the scholarship on learner outcomes in online political science courses has centered on the effectiveness of instruction via the Internet compared with traditional, face-to-face classroom instruction. Two general areas, objective knowledge and citizenship skills, have served as criteria of assessment. For example, Garson (1998) compares two sections of an American government class, one taught online and one in lecture format, and concludes that "in terms of the amount learned, it is not clear that web-based instruction is significantly better or significantly worse than traditional instruction" (Garson 1998, 587). Botsch and Botsch (2001, 141) also compare an online section of an American government class with one delivered in a traditional lecture/discussion format and conclude that

> "…web classes in American government are at least as effective as traditional lecture/discussion classes in nurturing a healthier, more active, and knowledgeable citizenry. Web classes may even be more effective in improving the general factual knowledge of lower-GPA students because such classes inevitably place more responsibility on students who are likely to be passive in more traditional classes".

Our own research on online instruction has focused on objective knowledge, skill-building, and the development of civic orientations. Our work analyzes data from students in two different settings—a face-to-face American national government course and a web-enhanced version of the same course.[4] Both courses were taught by the same instructor, used the same book, shared the same substantive emphases, and had the same midterm and final. The key difference was that the web-enhanced section employed Internet-based learning modules, tasks requiring students to read and process information, and then discuss it with their peers in small online discussion groups. These online activities replaced half of the class-time, a teaching modality often referred to as the "reduced seat-time model" or "blended learning." A pre-and-post questionnaire gauging student perceptions and attitudes toward civic engagement and computer competency, and a separate pre-and-post 18-item instrument measuring basic knowledge of American institutions and processes (later revised to 16 items), were our main vehicles of comparative assessment.[5] The study included a pilot phase and a final phase.

Several findings from the pilot data, which we have described elsewhere (Pollock and Wilson 2002), suggested that the web-enhanced format was in some ways superior to the lecture setting. For example, although both formats showed statistically significant gains in substantive knowledge, students in the web-enhanced section posted larger gains than students in the traditional section. We found this comparison to be especially noteworthy given initial selection differences between formats. The pre-course questionnaire revealed that, compared with their lecture-format counterparts, students in the web section had less academic experience, less prior exposure to computer-based courses, and lower levels of motivation to learn about American politics.

Our findings from the final-phase data set are more in line with studies concluding that, in the worst-case scenario, partial online teaching is as effective as teaching in the traditional classroom. Table 11-1 reports several key comparisons. There are few emergent differences between formats on these assessment-relevant attributes. Students in both settings made significant increases on the political knowledge index, but the inter-format comparison yields little difference. To be sure, students in the reduced seat-time format distributed themselves more widely across the index, with proportionately more students in the upper and lower ends of the distribution, but again the similarities between the two distributions are more prominent than their differences. Thus, programs and departments concerned with accreditation issues regarding their online or mixed-mode courses can use classroom assessment results on objective knowledge to demonstrate that blended (in-class and online) instruction is at least as effective in producing positive student learner outcomes as is teaching in the traditional classroom, and that online or mixed-mode courses can make a valuable contribution to the curriculum.[6]

Table 11-1: Traditional Lecture and Reduced Seat-Time Compared: Pre–Post Changes in Political Knowledge, Attentiveness, Efficacy, and Trust

	FORMAT	
PRE–POST CHANGE IN:	**TRADITIONAL LECTURE**	**REDUCED SEAT-TIME**
Political knowledge		
None	20.7%	27.3%
1–3 points	56.5%	45.3%
4 or more points	22.8%	27.4%
Mean interval change	2.28[b]	2.15[b]
High political attentiveness, percentage-point change	+7.6	+12.8[b]
High political efficacy, percentage-point change[a]	+5.4	-13.7[b]
High political trust, percentage-point change	-8.7	-9.4
Self-assessed "A" in computer competency, percentage-point change	-2.1	+8.6[b]
Number of cases	92	117

[a] On political efficacy, difference between formats is significant (p<.05).
  None of the other format differences are statistically significant.
[b] Pre–post change is statistically significant (p<=.05).

Our results on a second commonly assessed outcome, civic orientations, were less clear-cut. We tracked changes in three sorts of attitudes: political attentiveness, political efficacy, and political trust. Large percentages of students in both settings professed high levels of attentiveness to public affairs, in both the pre- and post-questionnaires. Even so, students' attentiveness increased between the start and finish. The percentage of those saying they follow politics "most" or "some" of the time rose by about 8 points in the lecture section and by nearly 13 points in the web-enhanced venue. Though statistically modest, at least in the lecture format, these numbers signal a heightened cognitive engagement among students in the introductory course. The patterns for efficacy and trust were inconsistent and rather less encouraging. Students in both settings posted nominal declines in political trust—about a 9-point drop in the percentages saying that the government in Washington can be trusted "always" or "most of the time." On efficacy, lecture-format students remained statistically unchanged. Their web-format peers, on the other hand, reported a large and significant drop on this measure. Thus, although format-dependent asymmetries in the use of computer skills returned expected differences—reduced seat-time students were more likely to report enhanced computer competency—our findings on political competencies are decidedly mixed. As assessed outcomes, our research has not shown a consistent, positive relationship between civic orientations and enrollment in introductory American government courses.

ASSESSING ONLINE CLASSES: LEARNING BEHAVIOR

Departments and professors might not only be interested in how much students learn (either on an objective knowledge test, civic orientations, or skills), but also in *how* they learn and, more specifically, how engaged they are in their learning processes. It is difficult to systematically gauge student engagement in the traditional classroom since recording, transcribing, and analyzing student participation in the classroom is time consuming and technologically demanding, particularly in large classes. Student surveys such as NSSE (National Survey of Student Engagement) are expensive, and even when universities administer campus-wide NSSE surveys, it is often difficult or impossible to obtain data broken down to the level of the department. Yet, understanding student engagement is potentially important as knowledge of student learning behavior helps professors design classroom environments and teaching strategies that encourage many, or all, students to be actively involved in their learning experience. Online courses can provide partial remedy for the lack of available data on student engagement because some aspects of learning behavior are already recorded and easily available. Discussion participation in online classes is one way in which one aspect of student engagement can be measured. We focus here on discussions as a primary active learning strategy given the importance the literature has ascribed to the role of discussions as a way to engage students in higher-order thinking both in the traditional and the online classroom (e.g., Bender 2003; Bligh 2000; Du, Harvard, and Lee 2005; Picciano 2002; Schrire 2006). For example, which students tend to participate in online discussions, and how do they participate? Is there a way in which the design of an online discussion can maximize student discussion and interaction?

We chose to assess two specific aspects in our online courses. First, one of our objectives is to foster student-to-student interaction as part of an active learning process. We deem interaction particularly important in the online environment, where students have to overcome the physical isolation from other students. Existing literature has identified that gender inequalities are commonplace in traditional college classrooms and found that women tend to be less involved in active learning through discussion than men (Wolfe 1999; 2000). Accordingly, we assessed the effects of gender on student participation and, more specifically, on student interaction in online discussion groups. Second, and more generally, we wanted to determine whether a teaching strategy based on active learning through discussion has positive effects on student learner outcomes.

INTERACTIVE BEHAVIOR IN ONLINE CLASSES

Early research on gender differences in online behavior sent a mixed message. Some pioneering studies (Herring 1993; Selfe and Meyer 1991) were pessimistic about the democratizing, gender-neutralizing potential of online communication. An apposite literature (Dubrovsky et al. 1991; Sproull and Kielser 1991) suggested otherwise. Yet a third perspective (Bhappu et al. 1997; Postmes and Spears 2002; Yates 1997) indicated that discussion behavior is heavily conditioned by group composition, with gender-balanced contexts producing greater leveling of differential attention and influence. Our own work supports this third view. Adapting a protocol developed by Henri (1992), we coded the rhetorical content of students' online discussion statements (Pollock, Hamann, and Wilson 2005; see Appendix 11-2 for coding protocol). Of particular interest as indicators of interactive behavior were the determinants of dependent statements, those that signaled a response to (and interaction with) other group participants, as opposed to independent statements, contributions made without reference or response to others. In our online classes, students are grouped together in small discussion groups of about 8–10 students each, thus overcoming the problems of discussion often present in large classes. Furthermore, we did not require students to engage in a dialogue with each other for their structured discussions, meaning that the discussion behavior patterns we observed were not driven by student concern for grades.

Gender composition of the discussion groups had intriguing effects on the incidence of dependent statements in online discussions (see Table 11-2). For men, gender composition had little effect. Dependent statements comprised about half (51%) of the average male-initiated message. For women, however, the group's composition mattered a great deal. While all-female groups produced little interaction (the average message was 26% dependent), gender-balanced groups occasioned much female-initiated interchange (the average female message was 47% dependent). Our findings lend clear support to instructors' efforts to create gender-balanced online discussion environments. Our more recent work suggests that the number of discussion postings read—an assessment measure easily obtained from online course management software—is a reliable indicator of student engagement in online discussions (Wilson, Pollock, and Hamann 2007). Our findings also guide professors to "close the feedback loop," the last step in an assessment process, and of practical importance for those attempting to foster student-to-student interaction: If it is possible to create gender-balanced discussion groups, then instructors should do so to maximize online dialogue.

Table 11-2. Mean Percentage of Independent and Dependent Statements, by Gender and Gender Composition				
PERCENT FEMALE	**GENDER**	**PERCENT INDEPENDENT**	**PERCENT DEPENDENT**	**N**
<50%	Males	44	52	241
	Females	44	51	125
50%	Males	43	51	89
	Females	46	47	104
51-70%	Males	50	47	194
	Females	59	37	367
71-90%	Males	43	54	129
	Females	55	42	516
100%	Females	71	26	143
TOTAL	Males	46	51	653
	Females	56	40	1255
	Total	52	44	1908

ACTIVE LEARNING AND LEARNER OUTCOMES

Vibrant student interchange may serve as an assessment goal in itself. Alternatively, instructors may view discussion as a process through which students develop academically relevant resources, such as engagement and knowledge of the material, which in turn shape learning outcomes such as course performance and grades. Indeed, interaction plays a crucial role in the learning process in general and in the online environment in particular (Bryant 2005; Garrison and Anderson 2003; Spiceland and Hawkins 2002; Webb et al. 2004; Weinberger and Fischer 2005). How strong is the link between online discussion and student course performance? In an analysis of a large number of upper division undergraduates (N = 279), we examined the effect of a measure of discussion behavior (number of postings read) on course grade (on a 100-point scale), controlling for previous-term grade point average (GPA) (see Hamann, Pollock, and Wilson 2009). Table 11-3 reports mean course grade for students reading below the median number of postings ("low readers") and for students reading above the median number of postings ("high readers"), at each GPA quintile. Not surprisingly, regardless of reading behavior, GPA is strongly related to course grade. Mean grade increases by 18 points for low readers and by 14 points for high readers. Yet, regardless of GPA, high readers perform better than do low readers. Remarkably, this effect is greater for students who have lower GPAs at the outset—a "reading effect" of over 15 points for students in the lowest GPA group, compared with an effect of about 11 points for students in the highest GPA group. This effect persisted when we regressed course grade on reading behavior and an array of demographic and background controls (senior standing, female, white, Hispanic), a dummy control for instructor, as well as a control for previous-term GPA. Our results point to a robust and independent effect of discussion engagement, as measured by postings read. Again, the "reading effect" is strongest for students who entered the course with the lowest GPAs and declines in potency as GPA increases.

Table 11-3. Average Course Grade, by GPA and Reading Behavior[a]			
GPA QUINTILE[b]	MEAN GRADE, LOW READERS (N)	MEAN GRADE, HIGH READERS (N)	TOTAL (N)
Lowest	62.6	78.1	68.1
	36	20	56
2	63.8	85.6	70.8
	38	18	56
3	69.3	85.3	78.1
	25	31	56
4	80.6	91.3	87.1
	22	34	56
Highest	80.6	91.8	87.9
	19	36	55
TOTAL	69.4	87.4	78.4
	140	139	279

[a] Table entries are mean course grades by GPA quintiles for students reading below the median number of postings ("low readers") and for students reading above the median number of postings ("high readers"). Median is equal to 160.

[b] Quintile midpoints (ranges): lowest quintile, 2.32 (1.84–2.52); quintile 2, 2.78 (2.53–2.89); quintile 3, 2.99 (2.90–3.18); quintile 4, 3.30 (3.19–3.49); highest quintile, 3.69 (3.50–4.00). Mean GPA for all students, 3.01.

Online courses can thus be useful sources of data to assess student engagement. In our study, students were not required to read a specific number of postings, meaning that the data we collected from our online course management program reflects, to some extent, students' self-motivation and engagement. Online courses can also nudge students to become more engaged by requiring them to participate in interactive behavior in online discussion boards. Finally, our findings map out strategies instructors of online classes can use to increase student learning.

Conclusion

In conclusion, online courses lend themselves to student assessment and can consequently provide a useful building block for departmental and program assessment. Online course software facilitates the assessment of political science courses delivered over the Internet because most of these software packages have built-in tools for analysis, and all student contributions are recorded. For example, auto-graded quizzes provide evaluations for each question, thus making it easy for instructors to assess which concepts students have successfully mastered. All discussions are available in writing, which allows the professor to take samples of discussions that could be analyzed for writing skills, mastery of the substantive material, and correct referencing skills. The same is true for essays or papers delivered online. In other words, online courses allow for the assessment of student learner outcomes, but they also facilitate the assessment of student learning behavior, such as student engagement. Progress can be monitored throughout the semester or over several semesters.

Clearly, not all classes delivered over the Internet are designed the same way. Our examples refer to online courses that put heavy emphasis on written interaction, that encourage students to "talk" to each other, and that put emphasis on active learning rather than posting long lecture notes or streaming videos of taped lectures. If online classes are structured to emphasize student engagement with the material posted on the web as opposed to peer-to-peer learning, other assessment objectives might need to be defined to track student learning behavior. In other words, much like a large lecture class might not fit easily into a department's objective to foster oral communication skills, online classes can be defined in a number of ways to match course or departmental objectives. Overall, though, online instruction can meet departmental and programmatic objectives and can also be an effective teaching tool in political science.

APPENDICES

Appendix 11.1 Simple Rubric for Writing Assignments				
CRITERIA	**PROFICIENT** 4	**VERY GOOD** 3	**SATISFACTORY** 2	**UNSATISFACTORY** 1
Organization and structure				
Use of appropriate terminology and concepts				
Appropriateness of topic				
References and bibliography				
Length				
Grammar and sentence structure				
Spelling				

Note: The criteria and their relative weight can easily be adjusted; cells can be filled in with detailed description of expectation for each criterion (see Chapter 9 by Mariya Omelicheva, this volume).

Appendix 11.2 Coding Protocol for Online Discussions				
STATEMENTS	**CODE**	**DEFINITION**	**EXAMPLES/ INDICATORS**	
Social statement	7	Statement or part of statement not related to formal subject content	"I'm feeling good today"; self-introduction; verbal support	
Meta-cognitive knowledge	8	Comparing oneself to another; Being aware of self as agent	"As a black male, I ..."	
Meta-cognitive skill	9	Verification or evaluation of one's own skills or learning	"I learned a lot about parliamentary systems from the chapter"	
Interactive statements:				
Direct, 1 Indirect, 2 Independent, 3	Cognitive, 1		Surface, 1	Proposing solutions or opinions without explanation or evidence
			In-depth, 2	Suggesting hypotheses; Linking facts with ideas, explanation, or evidence
	Evaluative, 2		Surface, 1	Stating that one dis/ agrees without explanation
			In-depth, 2	Justifying dis/ agreement, proposing solutions, using metaphors
Note: These coding guidelines are based on Henri (1992).				

NOTES

1. The Board of Governors in Florida, for example, requires all BA programs in public universities in the state to assess the following three areas: discipline-specific knowledge, skills, attitudes, and behaviors; communication; and critical thinking. See www.oeas.ucf.edu/alc/academic_learning_compacts.htm for more details concerning these Academic Learning Compacts.

2. Many universities provide excellent assessment support online. For instance, the University of Central Florida provides online guides and handbooks that departments and programs can use to design their own assessment plans, such as the Program Assessment Handbook at www.oeas.ucf.edu/doc/acad_assess_handbook.pdf.

3. On the use of rubrics, see also Chapter 9 by Mariya Omelicheva in this volume. Many web sites provide help with building customized rubrics to serve specific assessment purposes as well as with scoring, such as the free rubric builder available at www.rcampus.com/rubricshellc.cfm?mode=gallery&sms=home&srcgoogle&gclid=CNDKzIGMyZECFQsYgQodeHuwxQ; a rubric template that can easily be adjusted to serve different objectives is available at http://edweb.sdsu.edu/triton/july/rubrics/Rubric_Template.html.

4. The study was funded by a grant to redesign and evaluate the new course design from the Pew Learning and Technology Program, Center for Academic Transformation, Pew Grant Program in Course Redesign. For further discussion of the study and learner outcomes regarding gender differences, see Wilson, Pollock, and Hamann (2006).

5. The questionnaires are available from the authors upon request.

6. To be clear, we do not argue that all online courses are necessarily superior to all face-to-face courses, or suit all students better than traditional instruction methods. Instead, our point is that our research on the effectiveness of online teaching has yielded encouraging results in that it facilitates student learning and that online courses can make valuable contributions to a department's course offerings.

REFERENCES

Allen, I. Elaine, and Jeff Seaman. 2007. *Online Nation: Five Years of Growth in Online Learning.* Needham: The Sloan Foundation. Needham, MA: The Sloan Consortium. www.sloan-c.org/publications/survey/pdf/online_nation.pdf.

Bender, Tisha. 2003. *Discussion-Based Online Teaching to Enhance Student-Learning.* Sterling, VA: Stylus.

Bligh, Donald A. 2000. *What's the Use of Lectures?* San Francisco: Jossey-Bass.

Bhappu, Anita D., Terri L. Griffith, and Gregory B. Northcraft. 1997. "Media Effects and Communication Bias in Diverse Groups." *Organizational Behavior and Human Decision Processes* 70 (3): 199–205.

Botsch, Carol S., and Robert E. Botsch. 2001. "Audiences and Outcomes in Online and Traditional American Government Classes." *PS: Political Science & Politics* 34 (March): 135–41.

Bryant, Brenda K. "Electronic Discussion Sections: A Useful Tool in Teaching Large University Classes." *Teaching of Psychology* 32 (4): 271–75.

Carnevale, Dan. 2000. "U.S. Lawmaker Questions Quality of the Online Learning Experience." *Chronicle of Higher Education* 46, May 26: A51.

CHEA (Council for Higher Education Accreditation). 2002. *Accreditation and Assuring Quality in Distance Learning.* CHEA Monograph Series 2002, No. 1. Washington, DC: CHEA. www.chea.org/pdf/mono_1_accred_distance_02.pdf.

Cleary, Sharon. 2001. "The Classroom—The Downside: Why Some Critics Give Web-based Education Less than Stellar Grades." *Wall Street Journal*, March 12: R32.

Du, Jianxia, Byron Havard, and Heng Li. 2005. "Dynamic Online Discussion: Task-oriented Interaction for Deep Learning." *Educational Media International* 42 (3): 207–18.

Dubrovsky, Vitaly J., Sara Kiesler, and Beheruz N. Sethna. 1991. "The Equalization Phenomenon: Status Effects in Computer-Mediated and Face-to-Face Decision-Making Groups." *Human-Computer Interaction* 6 (2): 119–46.

Eaton, Judith S. 2001. *Distance Learning: Academic and Political Challenges for Higher Education Accreditation.* Council for Higher Education Accreditation, CHEA Monograph Series 2001, No. 1. www.chea.org/pdf/mono_1_dist_learning_2001.pdf.

Garrison, D.R, and Terry Anderson. 2003. *E-learning in the 21st Century: A Framework for Research and Practice.* London & New York: RoutledgeFalmer.

Garson, G. David. 1998. "Evaluating Implementation of Web-Based Teaching in Political Science." *PS: Political Science & Politics* 31 (September): 585–90.

Hamann, Kerstin, Philip H. Pollock, and Bruce M. Wilson. Forthcoming 2009. "Learning from 'Listening' to Peers in Online Political Science Classes." *Journal of Political Science Education* 5(1).

Henri, F. 1992. "Computer Conferencing and Content Analysis." In *Collaborative Learning Through Computer Conferencing: The Najaden Papers*, ed. A. R. Kaye. Berlin: Springer, 117–36.

Herring, Susan. 1993. "Gender and Democracy in Computer-Mediated Communication." *Electronic Journal of Communication* 3(2).

Moskal, Patsy, Charles Dziuban, Randall Upchurch, Joel Hartman, and Barbara Truman. 2006. "Assessing Online Learning: What One University Learned about Student Success, Persistence, and Satisfaction." *Peer Review* 8 (Fall): 26–29.

Picciano, Anthony. 2002. "Beyond Student Perceptions: Issues of Interaction, Presence, and Performance in an Online Course." *Journal of Asynchronous Learning Networks* 6 (July): 21–40.

Pollock, Philip H., Kerstin Hamann, and Bruce M. Wilson. 2005. "Teaching and Learning Online: Assessing the Effects of Gender Context on Active Learning." *Journal of Political Science Education* 1 (1): 1–16.

Pollock, Philip H., and Bruce M. Wilson. 2002. "Evaluating the Impact of Internet Teaching: Preliminary Evidence from American National Government Classes." *PS: Political Science & Politics* 35 (September): 561–66.

Postmes, Tom, and Russell Spears. 2002. "Behavior Online: Does Anonymous Computer Communication Reduce Gender Inequality?" *Personality and Social Psychology Bulletin* 28 (August): 1073–83.

Richardson, Jennifer C., and Tim Newby. 2006. "The Role of Students' Cognitive Engagement in Online Learning." *The American Journal of Distance Education* 20 (1): 23–37.

Schrire, Sarah. 2006. "Knowledge Building in Asynchronous Discussion Groups: Going Beyond Quantitative Analysis." *Computers & Education* 46 (January): 49–70.

Selfe, Cynthia L., and Paul R. Meyer. 1991. "Testing Claims for On-Line Conferences." *Written Communication* 8 (2): 163–92.

Spiceland, J. David, and Charlene P. Hawkins. 2002. "The Impact on Learning of an Asynchronous Active Learning Course Format." *Journal of Asynchronous Learning Networks* 6 (July): 68–75.

Sproull, Lee, and Sara Kiesler. 1991. *Connections: New Ways of Working in the Networked Organization.* Cambridge, MA: MIT Press.

Webb, Eileen, Alan Jones, Philip Barker, and Paul van Schaik. 2004. "Using E-learning Dialogues in Higher Education." *Innovations in Education and Teaching International* 41 (1): 93–103.

Weinberger, Armin, and Frank Fischer. 2006. "A Framework to Analyze Argumentative Knowledge Construction in Computer-Supported Collaborative Learning." *Computers & Education* 46 (January): 71–95.

Wilson, Bruce M., Philip H. Pollock, and Kerstin Hamann. 2006. "Partial Online Instruction and Gender-Based Differences in Learning: A Quasi-Experimental Study of American Government." *PS: Political Science & Politics* 39 (April): 335–39.

———. 2007. "Does Active Learning Enhance Learner Outcomes? Evidence from Discussion Participation in Online Classes." *Journal of Political Science Education* 3 (2): 131–42.

Wolfe, Joanna L. 1999. "Why Do Women Feel Ignored? Gender Differences in Computer-Mediated Classroom Interactions." *Computers and Composition* 16 (1): 153–66.

———. 2000. "Gender, Ethnicity, and Classroom Discourse." *Written Communication* 17 (October): 491–519.

Yang, Yi, and Linda F. Cornelius. 2004. "Students' Perceptions towards the Quality of Online Education: A Qualitative Approach." Presented at the Association for Educational Communications and Technology, Chicago, IL, October 19–23.

Yates, S. J. 1997. "Gender, Identity, and CMC." *Journal of Computer Assisted Learning* 13:281–90.

Zaragoza, Luis. 2007. "Florida's Students are Opting More and More for the Convenience of Online Courses." *Orlando Sentinel*, July 23. www.orlandosentinel.com/orl-lid2307jul23,0,3823485.story.

VERONICA DONAHUE, GEORGETOWN UNIVERSITY
JOHN ISHIYAMA, UNIVERSITY OF NORTH TEXAS

12

THE CRITICAL PORTFOLIO:
FACILITATING THE REFLECTIVE POLITICAL SCIENCE
STUDENT IN THE EXPERIENTIAL ENVIRONMENT

Although there have been several recent studies that have examined the role of portfolios in program assessment in political science and general education as well as in the classroom (e.g., Long 2007; Banda 2004; 2003; Young 1996; Thompson 1991; Hutchings 1990), relatively little work has been done on using the portfolio to directly assess *experiential* learning, particularly a student's experience in a structured internship. In this chapter, we focus on the development of a "critical portfolio," or a portfolio assignment that promotes student reflection on his/her experiential learning. Deriving techniques suggested by the American Association of Higher Education's Portfolio Clearinghouse, we propose several guidelines as to how to construct such a critical portfolio assignment. Further, we argue that the critical portfolio assignment is a more effective technique than are the more often used journal assignment techniques, because the critical portfolio: 1) better improves student reflection regarding the experience, 2) better integrates the experience with the undergraduate political science curriculum, and, perhaps most importantly, 3) better facilitates assessment of student learning as a result of the experience.

Today, colleges and universities are pioneering new educational practices as a way to teach students how to make sense of complexity, how to find and use evidence, and how to apply their knowledge to new problems and unscripted questions. Now, more than ever, faculties are looking for new classroom approaches to best prepare graduates for a rapidly changing work environment at a time when shifts in the marketplace occur at an unprecedented pace. For example, over their lifetimes, graduates in the class of 2008 will have not one career but most likely several. In fact, 30% of current college students may eventually work in jobs that do not yet exist (Fong 2004, 9). To cope with this kind of change, everyone involved in higher education needs a working familiarity with a vast and growing body of knowledge that has lasting value.

Increasingly, internships have become one way to prepare students for such a dynamic post-graduate environment. Over the past several decades, internships have become a fairly common option for almost all post-secondary students, particularly in disciplines that are traditionally without a field component, such as political science (Pederson and Provizer 1995, 232). As a result, the internship's popularity in many institutions has led to a unique model of liberal arts education in general and political science in particular that acknowledges both the classroom and work world as laboratories of learning.

In fact, those institutions that include currents of experiential education opportunities and classroom experiences promote complementary patterns of growth and development in their students (Linn and Jako 1992). This complementary pattern is possible because traditional classroom work, replete with knowledge, places the focus on listening. The design of the internship, on the other hand, is to expressly enhance what scholars note as the "artistry" of professional practice—that is, where "the knowing is in the action" (Linn and Jako 1992, 93).

Although simple in its approach, it is important to recognize that there is an inherent complexity when students are asked to learn from action at the internship site. Donald Schön notes this intricacy. In his deeply influential works about processes and development, Schön makes "reflection" central to the practitioner's understanding of what happens in the field (Johnston and Usher 1997). Schön (1995; 1991; 1967) focuses his efforts in this area on the notions of reflection-in-action and reflection-on-action. The former is sometimes described as "thinking on our feet" and involves the need to look at experiences and attend to theories in use to connect with practice.

While it is the intention of reflection-in-action to narrow the gap between theory and practice, reflection-on-action, much more exploratory by nature, also assists in the process of experience-based learning. In order to learn from activity, students must start to uncover meanings about why those at the work site acted in a certain way. This form of reflection helps the practitioner—or, in the case of experiential education at the undergraduate level, the political science intern—to develop questions and ideas about occurrences and then make sense of the experience.

This inherent complexity in experiential learning presents special challenges in assessing student learning. There have, of course, been efforts advocated to assess the impact of experiential learning. For instance, political science faculty frequently relies on the popular journal assignment as one way to facilitate both forms of reflection and as a means to assess student learning. When properly undertaken, the assignment requires that the students spend time writing at regular intervals about internship experiences. This written exercise encourages students to think about work site experiences, to learn from them, and then to achieve the ultimate understanding that each one has some meaning. Succinctly put, the journal, as an element of reflective practice, helps the students understand what they learned from a particular experience and how they learned it. The faculty member in turn is able to assess substantive learning at the field site.

But there are two problems with the journal. The first is that, over time, faculties at numerous institutions have questioned whether such assignments truly mirrored reflective practice (Verkler et al. 2001). The problem occurs when students treat reflective assignments, like the journal, as a product or artifact, rather than as one element in a process. This product approach was made vividly clear by one senior political science university faculty member when he noted the candid nature of some students in his program's internship courses. Several times, students reported that they would stay up all night and recreate various experiences the day before the journal was due in their internship course at the end of the semester. In order to successfully accomplish this devious task, the students further revealed that they would utilize different pens for different entries. With varied ink colors, they would keep their "all-nighters" to finish a semester's worth of journal entries a secret from their unsuspecting internship professors. Their youthful end-of-the-semester rush to meet a submission deadline is not uncommon among students and is not limited to political science majors (Verkler et al. 2001). But, for all involved in experiential education, this product approach runs contrary to the very rationale behind the journal assignment: it negates the process of reflective learning. Without reflection, students fail to make connections between their academic knowledge about political activity and the actual action at the internship site (Hedlund 1973, 21).

Even worse, this lack of reflective practice signals the start of an overall downward spiral for rest of the internship's academic components. When journals consist mostly of summary detail, they tend to facilitate very little analysis. As a result, students miss numerous opportunities to integrate new knowledge with their already acquired political science curriculum. This lack of integration, in turn, significantly impacts the practicum classes that accompany the internship. Class discussion can remain adrift as discussions center on more personal problems at the internship site that should or could be addressed individually.

Finally, even though the goal of the academic component is to provide a framework in which to structure experiential learning, this goal remains elusive because assignments like the journal do not uniformly require or supply evidence of learning. This brings faculty to the second problem: assessing the learning experience. As a credit-bearing exercise, then, assessment of the internship becomes a difficult task for the faculty member that supervises internships. The validity of the learning experience remains questionable despite the growth and popularity of the internship in political science departments nationwide (Pederson and Provizer 1995, 232). Clearly, for those committed to experiential education as one element in the political science curriculum, there is a need for a pedagogy that is not only more active and engaged but one that also explores the relationship between internships and assessing learning in the undergraduate political science curriculum.

To accomplish this mission, the academic requirements of students in a semester-long university-based experiential learning program became the focus of a series of both formal and informal workshops convened over the course of three years from 2002–2005 for full-time and part-time faculty. As discussions progressed, it became increasingly clear that simply re-working the journal assignment was not an acceptable alternative. Small changes—such as the establishment of weekly deadlines so that students produced more journal entries at regular intervals—still had the potential to miss the heart of reflective learning and assessment: to process and integrate newly acquired knowledge with previous learning and show evidence of substantive learning.

As a result of this focus, discussions moved from the use of a single reflective task for accompanying internship courses to an assignment-driven piece of work whereby faculty could assess evidence of learning at regular intervals. To this end, a portfolio approach to learning emerged as the organizing tool for the internship coursework.

Like any portfolio, the success of this new project would depend on whether or not it would have clearly stated goals (Huber 1998). As the workshops progressed, three fundamental goals emerged: First, to include assignments that facilitate reflective practice; second, greater integration of the internship with the student's previously acquired political science curriculum; and, finally, the development of greater assessment tools for the faculty.[1]

A NEW ASSIGNMENT: THE CRITICAL PORTFOLIO

With three goals in hand, and after an extensive review of secondary sources, the next point in the internship portfolio's formation became a content analysis of portfolios already in use. To borrow from Schön (1995; 1991; 1967) again, the effort here is to offer an approach to an epistemology of practice with an examination of what a small number of different practitioners actually do. To this end, the Portfolio Clearinghouse, a database hosted by the American Association of Higher Education that list schools engaged in various portfolio projects, formed the basis of the content analysis for workshop discussions. The Portfolio Clearinghouse is a collection of portfolio projects from around the world and the database serves as a tool for institutions to research portfolio programs in use at institutions of higher education (AAHE 2005). Their work lays the foundation for elements and ideas that would enable achievement of the three goals of stimulating reflective practice, greater curriculum integration, and improved assessment tools. What emerged from the workshop were elements for a new internship portfolio, the critical portfolio.[2]

Finally, it is important to note that the portfolio provided here is not exhaustive but represents possible features and instances of real people engaged in actual practice.[3] With this in mind, the quest here is a new approach that will help political science students demonstrate experienced-based learning and provide more rigorous assessment tools for faculty. The goal of this study then is to broaden the discussion as well as the instruments of pedagogy and learning and create a more inclusive course of study for political science students engaged in experiential education. This paper is only a means to stimulate important and necessary discussion amongst practitioners in today's learning environment, rather than a way to test specific examples of assessment and learning.

BUILDING THE CRITICAL PORTFOLIO

There are many types of portfolios, including student, faculty, electronic, and paper—to name a few. Like teaching portfolios, which allow for reflective practice in pre-service teachers, numerous universities across the country are implementing portfolios as a way to begin the development of reflective practice in students (Hutchings 1998). The portfolio's attraction as a pedagogical tool is that it inherently involves learning development. For example, Lee Shulman, noted for his epistemology scholarship, describes the learning process that portfolio development fosters and he details its all-encompassing nature. He defines the portfolio as "a structured documentary history of a set of coached or mentored accomplishments substantiated by samples of work" (Verkler et al. 2001, 27). For Shulman (1998a; 1998b), the importance is to convey the idea to both faculty and students that it is necessary to avoid the building approach to the portfolio development as a scrapbook of materials. The problem with this approach is that a scrapbook is only an accumulation of information. What turns the data into evidence is reflection about the meaning of selected materials (Dede 2000).

Workshop participants recognized the need for students to build the portfolio over the course of the semester (like so many in the AAHE database) and in this way avoid the scrapbook of materials approach that Shulman found so problematic. But how to build the portfolio became the center of much deliberation. Eventually, the idea to center the entire work on a single political or policy issue selected by the student and central to the internship site emerged as the organizing principal for the entire project. This single-issue approach, it was argued, would bring both continuity and critical thinking exercises to the portfolio assignments detailed below in Figure 12-1.

Figure 12-1. Contents of the Critical Portfolio
SECTION ONE: INTRODUCTION
Title Page
Table of Contents
Introductory Essay
Issue Selection
Literature Review
Previous Applicable Political Science Coursework
SECTION TWO: PROFESSIONAL DEVELOPMENT
Internship Contract
Resume
Cover Letter
Letters of Reference
Business Contacts
SECTION THREE: ACADEMIC INQUIRY
Short Essay: Introduction to Organization
Internal Organizational Chart
Short Essay: Introduction to the Policy Community
External Organization Chart
List of Issues
Substantive Issue
Bibliography
Interview Summary
SECTION FOUR: CONCLUSION
Concluding Essay
Faculty Narrative

The assignments also provide a platform for faculty and students to conductb unfettered investigation of social institutions, power relationships, and value commitments. As the portfolio develops, it provides a conceptual map as well as points of discussion throughout the semester of the relationships among the parts—between previous coursework, the internship class, and field experience. Faculty, in turn, can assess learning at junctures they find critical to the course and the students' overall political science learning.

BUILDING THE PORTFOLIO:
ACHIEVING STUDENT REFLECTION

A series of reflective essays for inclusion in the portfolio, one to two pages in length, became one way to accomplish the first goal of an overall increase in reflective activity to help build critical thinking skills. Exercises and assignments rooted in reflective practice in general tend to help students identify possible explanations for the instances at the internship that surprise them (Beckman 2002). Whereas the journal tends to scour every aspect of the internship, the reflective essay, on the other hand, requires students to write down and develop several ideas about specific learning events at the work site.

For example, students may fulfill the reflective essay requirements by attending a function held at or sponsored by the organization where they are placed, or even at one of its peer institutions. Students provide a description of the event, which increases both observation and perception skills, and then continue the essay with a discussion of their assumptions held prior to the event. In many cases, earlier assumptions are rooted in previous classroom learning. This is true for many students that submit reflective essays on their first experience at a Congressional Hearing on Capital Hill. The students end the essay with a discussion of the difference between previous expectations and actual learning. Such narrative practice can help the students address the central themes and issues throughout the semester and provide opportunities to wed theory and practice (Young 1996).

Those engaged in reflective practice maintain that it is important to assign reflective essays at the start of the semester when the element of surprise is still fresh in the students' learning. However, the second reflective element, a critique of the critical portfolio, engages students in reflective practice at the end of the semester. In general, when students share their experiences with their peers, they are encouraged to convert information into knowledge (Dede 2000). Students have the opportunity to do so when they present their portfolios at the end of the internship through class presentation. The professor structures the dialogue and facilitates the same with various prompts for the students to look for certain components, and notes the importance of paying particular attention in the presentations to how each student utilized previous knowledge.

Achieving the First Goal: Overcoming Problems with Reflective Exercises

Although it is argued that any systematic process of contemplative analysis constitutes reflective practice, in general, students do not automatically understand the great value of reflection (Verkler et al.). To further their understanding, a "hook" that ties reflection to things they already value by and large helps. For many students in the experiential learning environment, the "hook" often centers on the use of their portfolios for future employment or graduate work.

To address this concern, elements of one portfolio prototype, the professional portfolio, were included as a way to stimulate and increase student engagement in reflective practice. Faculty included the following elements in a separate section entitled Professional Development, section two in the critical portfolio: A supervisor's internship contract that lists the intern-specific tasks and duties, an updated resume, letters of recommendation, a business cover letter that details the internship experience and their approach to the same, writing samples of professional work such as letters to clients or constituents, and, finally, a list of possible future professional contacts. These assignments, dispersed and completed throughout the semester, help students cultivate professional skills, materials, and contacts for post-graduate endeavors.

The Second Goal: Integration with the Undergraduate Political Science Curriculum

To accomplish integration, the next portfolio section, entitled Academic Inquiry, was designed to help move the internship from the technique and process focus found in the Professional Development section to one of content and substance. Even though the assignments make the relationships between theory and practice explicit, the use of selected questions, however, became an important way to deepen each student's voyage into the learning environment. Experience shows that a well-crafted question acts like a wedge because it broadens the student's understanding of how events and ideas interconnect between particular facts and general issues (McClymer and Ziegler 1991). One additional benefit is that specific questions sharpen the student's academic inquiry during the internship because they concentrate on a manageable unit of analysis rather than on the entire internship experience.

To reach these objectives, the Academic Inquiry section contains assignments that require students to examine the organization in two ways: first, with a look at its internal community and functions and, second, with an investigation into the organization's relationship to the larger or outside public, referred to as the "external community." For example, students answer questions like: What is the organization's mission statement? How do the staff personnel's roles and responsibilities help accomplish this mission? What is the organization's structure? Is the power relationship among staff hierarchal? To answer these questions, students begin their path of inquiry by developing an organizational chart that lists the internal design of the organization. That design, in turn, must also address how the structure fulfills, or does not fulfill, the organizational mission.

After students complete the internal community exercises, and as the internship progresses, they become better equipped to evaluate the external community, also known as the organization's clientele. For example, students begin this investigation by answering some of the following questions: Who are the organization's clients? How does the organization serve client interests? What role does the organization play in the policymaking arena in relation to similar organizations? What other organizations have the same mission? What are the tools that the organization utilizes to address the same? How do they get their message out? (Do they use public hearings, free and paid media, etc.?) Students conclude the examination with an organizational chart that shows the group's relationship to the larger public.

Once the examination of both the organization's internal and external communities is completed, the next assignment in the Academic Inquiry section asks the students to provide a comprehensive list of the issues central to the organization. The student then selects a substantive issue that is both a priority for the organization and is of interest to them. One way to facilitate this selection is to pose two questions: What are the distinctive issues that the organization may bring to bear on the policy process? How does the organization address one issue in particular that is of interest to you in both its internal and external communities?

Another way to fully engage the student in the issue arena is to have them conduct interviews with two individuals from other organizations that work on the same issue or in the same issue area but hold different perspectives from their internship site. All perspectives are then combined in a written summary for inclusion in the critical portfolio in the Academic Inquiry section. The interviews and subsequent written work prompts the students to use their critical thinking and news-gathering skills as they pursue original research in the policy arena. Then, to further research skills at the secondary source level, the Academic Inquiry section asks the students to choose a single aspect of, or time period related to their issue, and discuss how two or more scholars and/or analysts are covering the same. The students answer questions such as: Do their perspectives converge or diverge? What are the relative merits of the viewpoints they hold?

Alternatively, another way to further secondary source research skills is to have the students produce an annotated bibliography that surveys relevant journal articles and/or book chapters on the topic. For each selection in the bibliography, students write a compact summary (six or seven sentences) of the author's main arguments, themes, or findings.

Once all the assignments are completed, the critical portfolio becomes a collection of work brought together with an introduction and conclusion. The portfolio introduction requires the student to identify and describe previous learning that helped them with the internship experience. Students should include in their answers courses on the same subject, participation in other internships, work experience, and even travel abroad.

While the introduction talks about possible learning, the concluding essay brings all learning elements together by answering the following: Did the internship help you develop any of the skills you learned in previous courses? Did the experience change how you will go about approaching the learning process in the rest of your academic career? Or, did it challenge you to face any ethical dilemmas? These questions inherently contain a normative quality, which is so important in a concluding essay.

Although there is a normative quality to the concluding essay in particular, there is also a normative quality to the critical portfolio in general. Many workshop participants found that students continue their internship class work by using the elements in the critical portfolio to complete more extensive independent research projects in both their academic and professional pursuits. Questions that successfully prompt students into thinking about using their critical portfolio in the future are: If you were going to turn this research into a thesis, how would you continue the work? From where would you gather information on this topic?

Finally, in terms of the integration component, the critical portfolio fosters systematic, focused discussion of significant issues in the internship practicum because activities take place at key points during a study, rather than just at the completion of the internship. These assignments start a path of inquiry that invokes insight and gives rise to revisions and refinements critical to improving knowledge in a student-driven learning environment, elements so important to the successful development of a portfolio (Starnes 1999).

THE THIRD GOAL: IMPROVING ASSESSMENT

Like so much of the movement toward portfolios today, the desire arises not only from external pressures for documentation but also pressure for internal accountability regarding teaching and learning as well (Black 2000). To some degree, today's call for portfolio use in the classroom rests on its ability to provide a means of assessment. The critical portfolio answers this call in two ways. First, because it provides a clear measurement of results, and second because it details newly acquired knowledge and skills over the course of the semester.

Indeed, portfolios have inherent advantages over other means of assessing a student's experience in internships (such as via survey questionnaires, journals, or exit interviews). In addition to promoting student self-evaluation, reflection, and critical thinking (better than journal assignments can accomplish), the critical portfolio assignment allows for the measurement of multiple dimensions of student progress by including different types of data and materials. Qualitative assessment of student assignments allows for more in-depth analysis of student learning, far more than student self assessments in surveys or responses as the result of obtrusive face-to-face exit interviews. In addition, the assignment itself includes the student in the assessment process by giving students the opportunity to have extensive input into the learning process and to provide evidence on their own learning. In the end, the portfolio provides political science faculty and departments that sponsor interns with an informative evaluation of both the internship and the student's entire credit-bearing experience, both practical and academic.

There is also a very practical benefit derived from the critical portfolio assignment. Faculty members already overwhelmed by the time and investment it takes to properly supervise students engaged in internships tend to shudder at the thought of more information to digest and process (Cambridge 1998). The critical portfolio, however, as a course component, can overcome the already over-scheduled undergraduate faculty's sense of being besieged because, as a pedagogical tool, the critical portfolio and all its concomitant assignments provide a high degree of flexibility in terms of both the number of assignments and length of each assignment. Each assignment provides a means by which the faculty member can assess student learning at the internship site as well as in reflective practices. It is also important to note that the assignments, as advocated here, focus the faculty's minds as well as the those of the students by making clear decisions in advance about what content students must start to familiarize themselves with, as well as what skills are necessary for successful completion of the internship and the internship class.

What techniques are available to assess critical portfolios? Although it is beyond the scope of this chapter to provide an exhaustive list of techniques, three commonly used techniques warrant mentioning here: checklists, rubrics, and rating/scoring scales (which are not mutually exclusive techniques and can be used in combination with each other). Checklists are simple measures involving checking off whether certain documents or parts are included in the portfolio. This might include using the features in Figure 12-1 (above) and checking to see if the portfolio includes the listed elements.

A second, more sophisticated, technique is the use of the rubric. Rubrics measure a body of work based on varying degrees of multiple factors. A rubric is a scoring guide or a set of expectations used to judge student performance. Generally, it is used to measure a stated objective, using a range to rate performance. Characteristics are arranged in levels, indicating the degree to which a standard has been met, and multiple coders are often used to assess the level of proficiency demonstrated. Rubrics are especially useful for assessing complex assignments in a relatively easy and accessible way. Also, if the criteria are spelled out in each cell (i.e., how different levels of proficiency become operational), and this is distributed to the students before completing the portfolio, this includes the students in the assessment process, by compelling them to critically assess their own work before including it in the portfolio. Below, in Figure 12-2, we show an example of a rubric based upon section 3 of the critical portfolio, above.

Figure 12-2. Example Rubric

SECTION THREE: ACADEMIC INQUIRY

Dimensions	LEVELS				Score
	Proficient 4	Very good 3	Acceptable 2	Not yet 1	
Short Essay: Introduction to Organization					
Internal Organizational Chart					
Short Essay: Introduction to the Policy Community					
External Organization Chart					
List of Issues					
Substantive Issue					
Bibliography					
Interview Summary					

Third, there is the rating scale, which is generally used to measure a body of work. The use of a rating scale gives students and faculty an opportunity to assess the portfolio as a whole or in parts. It can be used in conjunction with rubrics and, like rubrics, it often involves the use of multiple coders. Figure 12-3, below, illustrates an example of a rating scale that could be used to assess the process of building the critical portfolio (but, of course, skills exhibited in the portfolio could also be assessed using rating scales).

Figure 12-3. Examples of Rating Scales

1) The required items are present in the portfolio.	1 Low	2	3	4	5 High
2) The works presented are a good representation of the student's work.	1 Low	2	3	4	5 High
3) The works selected give an accurate picture of the strengths of the student.	1 Low	2	3	4	5 High
4) The student summary essay shows serious reflection on the part of the student.	1 Low	2	3	4	5 High

Conclusion:
Experiential Education and the Undergraduate Political Science Major

In the end, faculty involved in experiential education must help students independently manage their own learning. In fact, in the experiential environment, survey research finds that the most important role of faculty is an instructional one—that is, to assist students as they learn from their field experience and then connect with academic study (Whitaker 1989). The critical portfolio detailed here does this because it maintains a channel of open communication between the faculty member and student, with the ability to compliment the process with immediate feedback and in the end serves as a "connecting activity." This connecting activity, in turn, reminds faculty that in order to help young people actively learn from their experience, encouragement remains the foundation for students developing new skills.

But perhaps the most important reason for the political science professor to consider the use of the portfolio is that it helps students take responsibility for their learning during the internship. The journal assignment brought to light the notion that there is a delicate balance between ceding all responsibility to a student and encouraging each one to take a reasonable amount of responsibility to shape their experiences (Light 2001). The critical portfolio provides the personal investment in the acquisition of knowledge and skills that is so necessary in the experiential education. Without this personal investment, the opportunity for a valuable internship is greatly reduced (Cassidy and Ryan 1996). In the end, portfolios, like the critical portfolio, can begin to provide an important assessment tool for political science faculty.

NOTES

1. The authors are deeply indebted to Dr. John Calebrese of American University for his contributions to the workshop and to the portfolio elements.

2. The Portfolio Clearinghouse is available at: http://ctl.du.edu/portfolioclearinghouse/search_portfolios.cfm.

3. With some modification, some of the suggestions contained on the following pages could be adapted for a variety of experiential learning activities (such as service learning). Although we do not specifically focus on service learning in this chapter, the techniques mentioned could be fruitfully adapted to assess such experiences as well. Nonetheless, although assessment of service learning has been a longstanding point of interest among scholars (see Krain and Nurse 2004; Hunter and Brisbin 2000; Eyler and Giles 1999), the use of portfolios has not been widespread in service learning.

REFERENCES

American Association of Higher Education. The Portfolio Clearinghouse. http://ctl.du.edu/portfolioclearinghouse/search_portfolios.cfm.

Aloi, Susan L., William S. Gardner, and Anna L. Lusher. 2003. "A Framework for Assessing General Education Outcomes Within the Majors." *The Journal of General Education* 52 (4): 237–52.

Banda, Trudy W., ed. 2003. *Portfolio Assessment: Uses, Cases, Scoring and Impact.* San Francisco: Jossey-Bass.

———. 2004. *Hallmarks of Effective Outcomes Assessment.* San Francisco: Jossey-Bass.

Beckman, Mary. 2002. "The Midnight Run: From Surprise to Critical Thinking." *Journal on Excellence in College Teaching* 13 (1): 83–94.

Black, Laurel, J. 2000. "Fear and Desire in Course and Student Portfolios." *Journal on Excellence in College Teaching* 11 (1): 43–55.

Cambridge, Barbara, L. 2001. "Electronic Portfolios as Knowledge Builders." In *Emerging Practices for Students, Faculty and Institutions*, ed. Barbara L. Cambridge. Washington, D.C.: AAHE, 1–11.

Cassidy, John R., and Mary Ryan. 1996. "Internships and Excellence." *Liberal Education* 82 (3): 16–23.

Dede, Christopher, J. 2000. "Rethinking How to Invest in Technology." In *The Jossey-Bass Reader on Technology and Learning.* San Francisco: Jossey-Bass, 184–91.

Eyler, Janet., and Dwight E. Giles, Jr. 1999. *Where's the Service in Service Learning?* San Francisco: Jossey-Bass.

Fong, Bobby. 2004. "Looking Forward: Liberal Education in the 21st Century." *Liberal Education* 90 (1): 8–12.

Hartman, Virginia F. 1995. "The Annotated Portfolio: An Experiential, Proactive Learning Strategy." *Virginia Community College Association Journal* 9 (Summer): 35–38.

Hedlund, Ronald, D. 1973. "Reflections on Political Internships." *PS: Political Science & Politics* 6 (Winter): 19–25.

Huber, Mary T. 1998. "Why Now? Course Portfolios in Context." In *The Course Portfolio: How Faculty Can Examine Their Teaching to Advance Practice and Improve Student Learning. The Teaching Initiatives*, ed. Pat Hutchings. Washington, D.C.: American Association for Higher Education, 29–34.

Hunter, Susan, and Richard A. Brisbin. 2000. "The Impact of Service Learning on Democratic and Civic Values." *PS: Political Science & Politics* 33 (September): 623–26.

Hutchings, Pat. 1990. "Learning Over Time: Portfolio Assessment." *American Association for Higher Education Bulletin* 44 (April): 5–8.

———. 1998. "A Course Portfolio for a Creative Writing Course." In *The Course Portfolio: How Faculty Can Examine Their Teaching to Advance Practice and Student Learning*, ed. Pat Hutchings. Washington, D.C.: American Association for Higher Education, 85–90.

Johnston, Rennie, and Robin Usher. 1997. "Rethinking Experience: Adult Learning in Contemporary Social Practices." *Studies in the Education of Adults* 29 (2): 137–53.

Krain, Matthew and Anne M. Nurse. 2004. "Teaching Human Rights Through Service Learning." *Human Rights Quarterly* 26 (February): 189–207.

Light, Robert J. 2001. *Making the Most of College: Students Speak their Minds.* Cambridge: Harvard University Press.

Linn, Patricia L., and Katherine L. Jako. 1992. "Alternating Currents: Integrating study and work in the undergraduate curriculum." *Journal on Excellence in College Teaching* 3:93–100.

Long, Dianne. 2007. "Portfolio Assessment for Political Science." Presented at the American Political Science Association Teaching and Learning Conference, February 9–11, Charlotte, NC.

McClymer, John F., and Paul R. Ziegler. 1991. "The Assignment-Driven Course: A Task-specific Approach to Teaching." *Journal on Excellence in College Teaching* 2:25–33.

Pederson, William D., and Norman W. Provizer. 1995. "A Comparison of Washington Semesters at Public Colleges and Universities: Who Gets What, When and How." *PS: Political Science & Politics* 38 (June): 232–35.

Schön D. A. 1967. *Invention and the Evolution of Ideas.* London: Tavistock.

———. 1991. *The Reflective Turn: Case Studies in and on Educational Practice.* New York: Teachers Press, Columbia University.

———. 1995. "Knowing-in-Action: The New Scholarship Requires a New Epistemology." *Change* 27 (6): 27–34.

Sennett, F. 2004. *400 Quotable Quotes from the World's Leading Educators.* Thousand Oaks, CA: Corwin Press.

Shulman, Lee. 1998a. "Teacher Portfolios: A Theoretical Activity." In *With Portfolio in Hand*, ed. N. Lyons. Columbia, NY: Teachers College Press, 23–27.

———. 1998b. "Course Anatomy: The Dissection and Analysis of Knowledge through Teaching." In *The Course Portfolio: How Faculty Can Examine Their Teaching to Advance Practice and Student*, ed. Pat Hutchings. Washington, D.C.: American Association for Higher Education, 5–12.

Stanton, Timothy K. 1990. "Liberal Arts, Experiential Learning and Public Service: Necessary Ingredients for Socially Responsible Undergraduate Education." In *Combining Service and Learning: A Resource Book for Community and Public Service: Vol. 1.*, ed. J. C. Kendall. Raleigh, NC: National Society for Internships and Experiential Education, 175–98.

Starnes, Bobby Ann. 1999. "The Foxfire Approach to Teaching and Learning: John Dewey, Experiential Learning, and the Core Practices." Charleston, WV: ERIC Information Analysis Products.

Thompson, Joan H. December. 1991. "Outcomes Assessment: One Department's Experience with Portfolios and Outside Evaluators." *PS: Political Science & Politics* 24 (December): 715–18.

Verkler, Karen W., Gregory A. Wiens, J. Susan Lynch, David W. Gurney, Patricia E. Higginbotham, Barry W. Siebert, and W. Scott Wise. 2001. "What Our Students Have to Say: Students' Reflections on the Professional Portfolio." *Journal on Excellence in College Teaching* 12 (1): 23–45.

Young, Candace C. 1996. "Triangulated Assessment of the Major." In *Assessment in Practice: Putting Principles to Work on College Campuses*, eds. Trudy W. Banta, Jon P. Lund, Karen E. Black, and Frances W. Oblander. San Francisco: Jossey-Bass, 101–04.

Young, Rosalie R. 1996. "Brief Field Experiences: An Instructional Tool for Undergraduate Political Science Classes." *PS: Political Science & Politics* 29 (December): 695–96.

Whitaker, Urban G. 1989. *Assessing Learning: Standards, Principles & Procedures.* Philadelphia: Council for Adult and Experiential Learning.

EDITORS
AND
CONTRIBUTORS

EDITORS

MICHELLE D. DEARDORFF (Ph.D. Miami University, Ohio) is Associate Professor of Political Science at Jackson State University (Mississippi). Previously, as chair of the Political Science department at Millikin University (Illinois), she directed departmental assessment; the *Journal of Political Science Education* and *PS: Politics & Political Science* has published her research on classroom and program assessment. As a founding faculty member of the Fannie Lou Hamer National Institute on Citizenship and Democracy, she and her colleagues were named 2005 Mississippi Humanities Educators of the Year. Her research on the constitutional and statutory protections surrounding gender, race, and religion has been published in disciplinary and interdisciplinary journals, as well as in edited collections. She currently serves as chair of the Political Science Education Section of the American Political Science Association and as editor of the *Political Science Educator*, the section's newsletter.

KERSTIN HAMANN (Ph.D. Washington University, St. Louis) is Professor of Political Science at the University of Central Florida. Her research on classroom assessment in online classes and the Scholarship of Teaching and Learning has been published in journals such as the *Journal of Political Science Education*, *PS: Politics & Political Science*, *Politics & Policy*, and *Academic Exchange Quarterly*. She has won a university-wide Scholarship of Teaching and Learning Award as well as numerous teaching awards including the UCF Excellence in Undergraduate Teaching Award. Her publications include *Democracy and Institutional Development: Spain in Comparative Theoretical Perspective* (co-edited with Bonnie N. Field; Palgrave, 2008) and book chapters and articles on Spanish politics and Western European political economy in journals such as *Comparative Political Studies, British Journal of Industrial Relations, European Journal of Industrial Relations, Publius, Industrial and Labor Relations Review*, and *South European Society and Politics*, among others.

JOHN ISHIYAMA (Ph.D. Michigan State University) is Professor of Political Science at the University of North Texas. Previously, he was Professor of Political Science and Director of the Ronald E. McNair Program at Truman State University. He was the 2004 CASE/Carnegie Foundation Professor of the Year from Missouri, a 2003 National Carnegie Scholar, and winner of the Missouri Governor's Award for Teaching Excellence in 2003. He has published three books and 84 journal articles on democratization, political parties, and post communist politics in Russia, East-Central Europe, and Africa, as well as the Scholarship of Teaching and Learning (SOTL) His work on SOTL and assessment has been published in *PS: Politics & Political Science, International Studies Perspectives, Politics and Policy, Social Science Journal, Journal of College Student Development, College Student Journal, Journal of College Student Retention*, and the *Illinois Political Science Review*. He is currently the Editor-in-Chief of the *Journal of Political Science Education.*

CONTRIBUTORS

VERONICA DONAHUE (Ph.D. Johns Hopkins University) is the Associate Dean, for Summer and Special Programs at Georgetown University. Her published interests include the politics of education reform as well as curriculum issues at the undergraduate level. Her most recent publication "Experiential Education: Is it Time to Re-Examine the Liberal Arts in the New Academy?" appeared in the *Journal of General Education.*

SCOTT D. ERB (Ph.D. University of Minnesota) is Professor of Political Science at the University of Maine at Farmington. He earned his MA from Johns Hopkins School of Advanced International Studies. He is the author of *German Foreign Policy: Navigating a New Era*, and teaches courses on International Relations, Foreign Policy, and European Politics. Erb won university teaching awards in 2002 and 2005, and is involved in a number of team-taught interdisciplinary courses.

PAUL J. FOLGER is Director of the Instructional Development Center and Instructional Assessment at Heartland Community College in Normal, Illinois. He was formerly the Coordinator of Institutional Research and Assessment and Instructor of Political Science at Millikin University in Decatur, Illinois. He has given several presentations at local, regional and national assessment and assessment related conferences covering such topics as Student Learning Outcomes, General Education Assessment, and Department Based Assessment.

JEFFREY S. HILL (Ph.D. University of Rochester) is Associate Professor and former chair of the Department of Political Science at Northeastern Illinois University in Chicago. His research on assessment has been published in the *Journal of Political Science Education* and has been presented at the Illinois Board of Higher Education Workshop on Assessing Student Learning, at the 107th Annual Meeting of the North Central Association, and at the Midwest Political Science Association Meetings. He has also published research on American Politics that has appeared in the *American Journal of Political Science*, the *Journal of Politics*, as well as in other places.

JUAN CARLOS HUERTA (Ph.D. University of Houston) is Professor of Political Science and Co-Director of the University Core Curriculum Programs at Texas A&M University-Corpus Christi. Dr. Huerta has been an active participant in the university's recognized First Year Learning Communities Program, and as Co-Director is responsible for learning community assessment. He has also served as a Resource Faculty member at the National Summer Institute on Learning Communities at The Evergreen State College. Huerta's research on learning communities has been published ("Do Learning Communities Make a Difference?" *PS: Political Science and Politics*, 2004), and presented at conferences. His current learning community research focuses on promoting active learning in large lecture courses and examining the impact of learning communities for Latino students. In political science, his published and current research examines Latino political representation.

E. FLETCHER MCCLELLAN (Ph.D. University of Tennessee-Knoxville) is Professor and Chair of the Department of Political Science at Elizabethtown College in Lancaster County, Pennsylvania. As department chair, Associate Dean of Faculty and Interim Provost, he has led the College's assessment efforts at the program and institutional levels. He has presented papers and workshops on assessment at national conferences in political science and higher education administration. In addition to his work in teaching and learning, his research focuses on the American presidency, the politics of administration, and U.S. government policy toward Native Americans.

MARIYA OMELICHEVA (Ph.D. Purdue University) is an Assistant Professor of Political Science at the University of Kansas. She also holds a law degree in international law and a certification for teaching human rights law and government from Russia. Dr. Omelicheva has taught courses in international relations and politics of post-Communist states. In her scholarship of teaching, she focuses on the issues of students' assessment and application of various research techniques to the analysis of learning outcomes. Her teaching articles have been published in the *Journal of Political Science Education* and *International Studies Perspectives*. During her graduate studies, she had been a recipient of several teaching awards. Mariya Omelicheva's research focuses on Eurasian security, particularly, post-Communist states' domestic and international responses to terrorism.

CHARLES R. PASTORS (Ph.D. University of Chicago) is Professor Emeritus of Political Science, former Chair of the Department of Political Science, and former Acting Dean of the College of Arts and Sciences at Northeastern Illinois University. Currently vice president of Education Development Growth Enterprises, Inc., he has presented workshops at regional and national conferences and published papers on Learning Communities, Assessment, and Academic Leadership Development.

PHILIP H. POLLOCK III (Ph.D. University of Minnesota) is Professor of Political Science at the University of Central Florida, where he teaches courses in American public opinion, voting behavior, interest groups, and quantitative methods. His collaborative pedagogical research, which has appeared in the *Journal of Political Science Education* and *PS: Political Science & Politics*, investigates the effects of online instruction on gender equity and learning outcomes. Other recent publications include a methods textbook, *The Essentials of Political Analysis*, and two instructional workbooks, *An SPSS Companion to Political Analysis* and *A Stata Companion to Political Analysis*.

CHRISTOPHER J. VOPARIL (Ph.D. New School for Social Research) teaches political theory in the interdisciplinary doctoral program at Union Institute & University in Cincinnati, OH. He was Assistant Professor and Chair of the Department of Humanities at Lynn University, where he chaired the Committee on Teaching Excellence. He is the author of *Richard Rorty: Politics and Vision* (Rowman & Littlefield, 2006), and articles in *Education and Culture, Contemporary Pragmatism,* and *Philosophy and Social Criticism.*

BRUCE M. WILSON (Ph.D. Washington University) is an Associate Professor of Political Science at the University of Central Florida and an Adjunct Researcher at the Chr. Michelsen Institute, Bergen, Norway. His research on the scholarship of teaching and learning has been published in journals including *PS: Political Science & Politics* and the *Journal of Political Science Education* and has been recognized with international, national and university-wide awards. His research on Latin American politics has been published in journals including the *Journal of Latin American Studies, Comparative Political Studies,* and *Comparative Politics.* He was the editor of *The Latin Americanist,* a multidisciplinary peer-reviewed journal, for six years and was a founding editor of the *UCF Undergraduate Research Journal.*

CANDACE YOUNG (Ph.D. University of Missouri) is a Professor of Political Science at Truman State University. She has research, teaching, and professional interests in American politics and policy and public administration. At Truman, she has had the opportunity to be extensively involved in the transformation of a university from a comprehensive regional university into the state's liberal arts and sciences university, serving high ability students. It was in the context of this transformation that she began to focus on how closely assessment in higher education mirrored policy and public administration literature on program evaluation, implementation, and knowledge utilization. She also is responsible for the university's Missouri government internship program and has been researching the impact of term limits on state politics and policy.